Lecture Notes in Computer Science 554
Edited by G. Goos and J. Hartmanis

G. Grahne

The Problem of Incomplete Information in Relational Databases

Springer-Verlag
Berlin Heidelberg New York
London Paris Tokyo
Hong Kong Barcelona
Budapest

Series Editors

Gerhard Goos
Universität Karlsruhe
Postfach 69 80
Vincenz-Priessnitz-Straße 1
W-7500 Karlsruhe, FRG

Juris Hartmanis
Department of Computer Science
Cornell University
5148 Upson Hall
Ithaca, NY 14853, USA

Author

Gösta Grahne
University of Helsinki, Department of Computer Science
Teollisuuskatu 23, SF-00510 Helsinki, Finland

CR Subject Classification (1991): H.2.1-2, F.2.2, I.2.3-4

ISBN 3-540-54919-6 Springer-Verlag Berlin Heidelberg New York
ISBN 0-387-54919-6 Springer-Verlag New York Berlin Heidelberg

Printed in Germany

Typesetting: Camera ready by author
Printing and binding: Druckhaus Beltz, Hemsbach/Bergstr.
45/3140-543210 - Printed on acid-free paper

Preface

In practice it is often the case that the available information is incomplete with respect to the information that is supposed to be recorded in a database. This monograph considers the problems raised by information incompleteness in the context of the relational model.

The basic semantic assumption is that an incomplete database represents a set of complete databases (relations). We show that there are two natural lattice structures on the set of all sets of relations. These lattices enable us to give precise meanings to operations performed on incomplete databases. The operations are querying, dependency enforcement and updates.

There are several candidate tools for storing and manipulating databases with incomplete information. We focus on generalizations of relations. These generalizations, called *tables*, allow variables representing unknown values as entries, as well as entries constraining the variables. We define four increasingly (syntactically) strict classes of tables and we study their abilities to serve as a basis for implementing incomplete databases and the operations on them. It turns out that the new class of *Horn tables* is the most significant from a practical point of view. In this class of tables we are able to efficiently evaluate positive existential queries and in some cases least fixpoint (recursive) queries. In Horn tables we can also efficiently incorporate the information contained in one join dependency and a set of equality generating dependencies, as well as hold the result of a subclass of the update operations.

An earlier version of the present work was submitted as the author' s Ph. D. dissertation in 1989 to the Department of Computer Science at the University of Helsinki. With respect to the process of writing the thesis, I want to make the following acknowledgements.

The best way to learn a craft is to work under the guidance of a skilled professional. Professor Kari-Jouko Räihä kindly initiated me in this way into computer science. He has given me invaluable support through his constructive advice and through his balance and wisdom. I am proud of being his student.

I was very fortunate in coming into contact with Professor Esko Ukkonen. His deep insight and sharp technical advice, as well as his warm-hearted encouragement, have been a great source of inspiration for me. May the sun always shine for him.

I would like to express my appreciation of Professor Martti Tienari, who has created an excellent research milieu, with fine facilities and a high standard for the staff to live up to. It has been both a pleasure and a challenge to work at his department.

The research community has many distinguished members, some of whom I would like to mention in addition, since they have willingly shared their time and thoughts with me. They are Serge Abiteboul, Paris Kanellakis, the late Witold Lipski, Pekka Orponen, Michalis Spyratos, and Nicolas Spyratos. I am especially grateful to Serge and Paris, who granted me the privilege of collaborating with them.

Finally, I would like to thank all my friends and colleagues at the Department of Computer Science for creating a stimulating atmosphere to work in. The financial support of the Academy of Finland and the Ministry of Education is also gratefully acknowledged. In addition, thanks are also due to the referees of Springer-Verlag, whose reports I have used in trying to improve the presentation of the material, and to the Department of Computer Science at the University of Toronto, who provided the necessary logistics for the present work.

Toronto G. Grahne
September 1991

Contents

1. Introduction 1

2. Relational databases 6

2.1 The relational model and query languages 6

2.2 Data dependencies 15

2.3 Updates to databases 25

2.4 Computational complexity 30

3. Semantic aspects of incomplete information 33

3.1 Incomplete databases and queries 33

3.2 Dependencies and incomplete information 44

3.3 Updating incomplete databases 46

4. Syntactic and algorithmic aspects of incomplete information . . 55

4.1 Tables as representations of incomplete information 55

4.2 Querying tables 61

4.3 Dependencies and tables 77

4.4 Updates and tables 92

5. Computational complexity aspects of incomplete information . 104

5.1 The complexity of query evaluation 104

5.2 The complexity of dependency enforcement 122

5.3 The complexity of updates 130

6. Some conclusive aspects 132

6.1 Relation to other work 132

6.2 A conclusion 140

References 143

Index of notation 150

Appendix. Problems used in reduction proofs 154
A1. 3CNF Satisfiability 154
A2. 3DNF Tautology 155
A3. HC Satisfiability 156
A4. Bipartite graph matching 156

1. Introduction

The reader is invited to imagine him- or herself filling out a form, for instance for an application of a visa or a grant. Many things are asked, and the applicant obediently provides the information to the best of his or her knowledge. But sometimes the best of one's knowledge is not enough. Some things one simply does not know. For instance, the space for "the maiden name of the applicant's mother-in-law" receives a question mark. Some other things asked do not make sense. For instance, if the applicant is unmarried or male, then a dash is put in the space for "applicant's maiden name".

After the form is filled out, it is left to a clerk who enters the data into a database. The database management system is of the latest fashion, but yet it probably does not have a mechanism for treating the question marks and dashes. If this is the case, the clerk will encode them in his own way, for instance by blanks, zeros etc. When the data is then processed, the treatment of the blanks and zeros can be arbitrary. Probably they are processed according to their bit codes, which then is taken as the encoding of "the maiden name of the applicant's mother-in-law".

If a database management system is truly to fulfil its purpose it must thus know how to treat incomplete information. Codd [Cod82] requires that "a fully relational system" has this feature. Before such a database management system can be designed, there are however theoretical problems that have to be solved: what does incomplete information mean, how can it be processed, and how incomplete can the information be and still be processed efficiently. This thesis aims at deepening the understanding of these problems, and it offers at least a partial solution to them. As we saw in our example, there are two major types of incomplete information: the question marks, corresponding to values *unknown*, and the dashes, corresponding to values *not applicable* in the particular context. In this thesis we shall consider incomplete information of the first type, i.e. missing information. Our work is based on the *relational model*, introduced by Codd in the early 1970's [Cod70, Cod72a]. The relational model has been subject to intensive research since then, perhaps because it is "an elegant, well motivated, and appropriately restricted model" [Kan86]. It is also nowadays the basis of most commercially available database management systems.

The relational model assumes that the data is stored as relations. A relation can be thought of as a table, with rows corresponding to entities or associations between entities. The values of the columns correspond to the characteristics of the entity or the association. The rows are called the *tuples* of the relation. The relational model assumes that all values of the tuples are specified, i.e. that there is no incomplete information. A missing value would correspond to a missing value of some column.

From a formal point of view, a relation is a *structure* containing the facts for which the relationship holds. A *query* is a first order formula that is to be evaluated on the relation. The major feature of the relational model is that all (first order) queries correspond to expressions of simple algebraic operators on relations. These algebraic expressions are the procedural counterparts of the queries, and they can be used as the basis for a "bottom up" evaluation of the queries.

A relation is defined on a scheme, corresponding to the columns of the table. Not all relations on a scheme are of interest in some particular application. Therefore the designer of the database usually gives a set of *integrity constraints*, restricting the set of relations that is considered to be meaningful in the application. The integrity constraints form a language for specifying the semantics of the relation. In the relational model this language consists of the *data dependencies*. A data dependency is a first order sentence that has to be true in the structure defined by the relation.

When the "universe of discourse" modeled by the database changes, the database has to be *updated*. Updating is one of the least investigated areas of database theory. In practice, the relations are updated by adding, deleting, and modifying rows in the tables.

Queries, verification of integrity constraints and updates are the main *operations* on relations. We aim to extend the relational model to include missing information. We shall provide a formal interpretation of the missing values (semantics), and extend the operations to take these missing values into account in a coherent way. We shall also consider a "language" for storing relations with missing values (syntax), and provide algorithms that implement the extended operations. Finally, we are going to analyze the complexity of the algorithms, in order to isolate the structures that can be efficiently implemented.

Before we proceed, we shall take a brief exclusive look at what has been done in the area to date. (A more thorough, although not completely up-to-date survey of the area can be found in [Grh84a].)

Codd himself considers the problem of missing values, or null values as we are going to call them from now on, in [Cod75] and in [Cod79]. An occurrence of a null value in a tuple is denoted by ω. Data is extracted from tuples and relations with ω according to a three-valued logic. The truth value of an atomic sentence p(t) is "unknown" if a tuple containing one or more occurrences of the null value ω is in the relation that is the interpretation of the predicate p, and the following conditions hold:

(i) Each occurrence of ω can be replaced by a nonnull value, yielding the value "true" for the sentence, and

(ii) Each occurrence of ω can be replaced by a nonnull value, yielding the value "false" for the sentence.

The truth values of more complicated sentences are determined by truth tables for the three-valued logic, e.g. "true" or "unknown" is "true", and "unknown" or "unknown" is "unknown". The answer to a query is the set of tuples for which the sentence is "true" (we shall call it the "certain" answer), and the set of tuples for which the truth value of the sentence is "unknown" (here called the "possible" answer). Codd then redefines the relational operators in accordance with his three-valued logic. No extra computational complexity is added by the redefinition.

There is an anomaly in the approach that is noted in [Cod79], and further criticized in [Grt77]. Suppose that we have an employee named Jones, whose age is unknown. Then we query the database for all employees aged less than or equal to 50, or employees over 50. According to the three-valued logic, Jones will not be included in the certain answer to the query, though intuitively he should be. The problem is that the query is tautological with respect to the age, and that the three-valued logic does not preserve tautologies.

Still, the work of Codd benefits from the (implicit) semantic interpretation of a relation containing null values. Since each occurrence of a null value can be substituted by a nonnull value, the relation containing nulls can be seen as a shorthand for a set of relations, each obtained by different substitutions. This will also be the basic semantic assumption in this thesis: an incomplete relation represents a set of (complete) relations.

The deficiencies of Codd's attempts are remedied by Vassiliou in [Vas80b] (see also [Vas79, Vas80a]), and by Biskup in a series of papers [Bis81a, Bis81b, Bis83]. The work of Vassiliou conquers the tautology problem, and it also considers dependencies. The main drawback of the work is that it only treats selection queries, i.e. only a fragment of all queries. The work on dependencies in [Vas80a, Vas80b] suffers from a somewhat syntactic approach. On the other hand, Vassiliou discovered an important notion, called the weak instance, to which we shall return towards the end of this thesis.

Biskup redefines all relational operators in an intuitively appealing and formally rigid way. No extra computational complexity is added. His approach however has some shortcomings when we move from algebraic operators to algebraic expressions, as noted by Imielinski and Lipski [IL84]. Any nontrivial query is essentially an algebraic expression. In such an expression the arguments are not necessarily independent from each other. For instance, in the query "list all pairs of suppliers and projects, such that the supplier sells a tool used by the project", the tool referred to in both parts is the same unique tool. If the information is stored in one relation (no dependencies), the query would be implemented as the join of two projections. Thus any nulls for the tool in the two parts of the query cannot be independently replaced, i.e. the basic operators in the query cannot be independently evaluated.

The work of Imielinski and Lipski [IL84] (also reported in [IL81]) is perhaps the first fully satisfactory solution to the problem of querying relations with nulls. The nulls are assumed to be marked, and nulls with the same mark represent the same unknown value. A complete relation represented in this way is obtained by substituting the nulls by proper values, committing the substitutions to the restrictions imposed by the marks. The answer to a query is then the set of tuples that would be in the answer for the same query posed to any of the complete relations represented by the relation with marked nulls. Thus one is not concerned with facts that "maybe" hold, as in [Bis83] and [Cod79] (i.e. the possible answer). The major and significant result of [IL84] is then that under suitable restrictions (no negations allowed), the queries can be evaluated as if there were no nulls at all, i.e. the nulls are treated as ordinary constants. Thus no extra computational complexity is introduced.

The work of this thesis is built on the foundation laid down in [IL84]. These results will be extended in several ways. We also consider the possible answer to queries, as well as dependencies and updates. We are going to use more complicated representatives of incomplete databases, namely relations with marked nulls along with further restrictions on the nulls.

To conclude this brief review, short mention will be made of another approach to the null value problem. The relational model is essentially an algebraic counterpart of a subset of first order logic. In particular, a relation is regarded as a structure. If the information is incomplete, then our knowledge consists of a set of structures. One can then reverse the process, and regard a relation as a set of sentences on a predicate corresponding to the structures (the title of Reiter's paper [Rei84] is "Towards a logical reconstruction of relational database theory"). A tuple t in a relation r corresponds to a sentence p(t), where p is the predicate corresponding to the relation r. A null value in a tuple is then modeled by an existentially quantified variable in the corresponding sentence. A database is a theory, and the models for the theory are the set of complete relations that the theory represents. A tuple is in the answer to a query if it can be proved to be so from the theory (hence the name "proof theoretic approach"). The work of Reiter [Rei86] then looks for algorithms that are essentially algebraic ways to implement query evaluation. The results he arrives at are very close to those of [IL84]. We shall briefly return to the "proof theoretic" or "logical databases" approach in Section 6.1.

The outline of the thesis is the following. Chapter 2 reviews the relational model and the operations in a uniform fashion. We shall impose a lattice structure on the set of all relations (defined by the set inclusion of relations). Then several concepts, such as dependency satisfaction and updates can be defined in terms of operations on the lattice.

The basic intuitive assumption is that an incomplete relation represents a set of relations. Chapter 3 is a generalization of Chapter 2 to the incomplete case, i.e. to sets of sets of relations. We shall show that there are two lattice structures on sets of sets of relations. The operations introduced in Chapter 2 are generalized elementwise to sets of relations, according to the basic intuitive assumption. (An operation on a set of relations yields a set obtained by applying the operation on each element in the set.) We show that the elementwise generalization can in most cases be given a declarative characterization in terms of one of the lattices. We shall also consider operations that are defined in terms of the other lattice.

Chapter 4 treats the implementation of sets of relations as so called tables. A table is a relation with null values and restrictions on the null values as entries. We will define four increasingly stricter classes of tables. We then study the abilities of the four table classes to serve as a basis for evaluating the results of the operations, and we will give algorithms that implement the operations on the different table classes. The algorithms will essentially be algebraic in nature, in that they generalize the algebraic "bottom up" evaluation method. "While" and "For Each" constructs will also be needed in some cases.

In Chapter 5 we will then analyze the computational complexity of the algorithms introduced, in the pursuit of finding a table class and a set of operations that can be efficiently implemented. The notions of Horn clauses and monotone expressions will play a crucial role in discovering the borders of efficiency.

Chapter 6 is the conclusion of the thesis. In it we will briefly compare our results to other work in the area, and we summarize the significant implications of the previous chapters.

2. Relational databases

In this chapter we review relational databases, in order to give a uniform framework for the sequel. We introduce the notions as they pertain to complete databases. First we define the relational model and the relational algebra. Then we show how the set inclusion of relations gives a complete lattice on the set of all relations (over the same scheme). Using the lattice structure we can then define least fixpoint queries (recursive queries). We also consider data dependencies, both as first order logical formulas and as algebraic equations. The lattice structure enables us to define the completion of a relation, i.e. a minimal extension that satisfies the dependencies. Finally, we treat updates as operations on the lattice.

Chapter 3 will be a generalization of Chapter 2 for incomplete information databases (sets of relations).

2.1. The relational model and query languages

Schemes and relations

The first construct we need for a relational database is a countably infinite set U of *attributes*. Attributes will be denoted by by capital letters from the beginning of the alphabet, while capital letters from the end of the alphabet will stand for finite sets of attributes. Indexed names will also be used (e.g. A_i). Following standard convention in the field, the union of two attribute sets is sometimes denoted by concatenation. Thus $X \cup Y$ is written XY. Set brackets are also omitted wherever there is no risk of confusion. In some "real-world" examples we also use names like SUPPLIER, PART and PROJECT for attributes.

Each attribute A is associated with a set, called the *domain* of A, and denoted by *Dom*(A). Examples of domains occurring in practice are integers and character strings. We assume *Dom*(A) to be countably infinite, for all $A \in U$. For a subset V of U, *Dom*(V) stands for $\bigcup_{A \in V} Dom(A)$.

The elements of the domains will sometimes be called *constants*, and they are denoted by (possibly indexed) small letters from the beginning of the alphabet. It is assumed that differently named constants stand for different domain elements.

A *relational scheme* is a finite subset R of U. The *arity* of a scheme is the number of attributes in it. Let $R = A_1A_2...A_k$. Then a *tuple* t on R is a mapping from $A_1A_2 ... A_k$ to $Dom(A_1) \cup Dom(A_2) \cup ... \cup Dom(A_k)$, such that $t(A_i) \in Dom(A_i)$, for $1 \leq i \leq k$. For a subset X of R, t(X) is the restriction of t to X. When we want to explicitly give the values of a tuple t we write (a, b, c, ...). In this notation a is the value of $t(A_1)$, b of $t(A_2)$ etc. The restriction of any tuple t to the empty set Ø, i.e. t(Ø), is denoted by ε, and it stands for the *empty* fact.

A *relation* r on R is a (possibly infinite) set of tuples on R. An *empty* relation (a relation with no tuples) is denoted by ø. The infinite relation (on a scheme R) containing all possible tuples is denoted by r_∞. The set of all relations on a scheme R is denoted by *Rel*(R). Given a relation r, we mean by its *type* the scheme on which r is defined. The type of r is denoted by $\alpha(r)$. The type $\alpha(t)$ of a tuple t is also the scheme on which it is defined.

When we want to give examples of relations we shall use either *set* or *tabular* forms. Let r be a relation on AB, consisting of tuples (a,b) and (c,d). Then the set form of r is {(a,b), (c,d)}. In the tabular form r is written as

r =

A	B
a	b
c	d

A database consists of several relations. We define a *multischeme* **R** to be a sequence $<R_1, ..., R_n>$, where each R_i is a scheme. A *multirelation* **r** is then an element of $Rel(R_1) \times ... \times Re(R_n)$, i.e. a multirelation **r** is a sequence $<r_1, ..., r_n>$, where each r_i is a relation on R_i, $1 \leq i \leq n$. The *type*, $\alpha(\mathbf{r})$, of **r** is **R**. The set $Rel(R_1) \times ... \times Rel(R_n)$ is denoted by *Rel*(**R**). The empty multirelation in *Rel*(**R**) is **ø** = <ø, ..., ø>, and the "largest" multirelation is $\mathbf{r}_\infty = <r_{1\infty}, ..., r_{n\infty}>$. A multirelation is finite, if all its component relations are finite.

The relational algebra

When a user extracts information from the database he uses a *query language*. The relational model is equipped with two such languages: the *relational algebra* and the *relational calculus*. The relational calculus is a variant of the first order predicate calculus. A fundamental result in relational theory, known as the Codd completeness theorem, is that the two languages have the same expressive power [Cod72b] (see also [Ull82]). The theorem means that the two languages can express the same queries. In this thesis we shall use the algebraic language.

In the relational algebra queries are expressed by applying specialized operators on a multirelation. The *answer* to the query is the result of these operators, and it is a relation. (A query in the relational algebra can thus be seen as a mapping from multirelations to relations.) We note that if the multirelation on which the operators are applied is finite, then the resulting relation is also finite.

The relational algebra consists of the following seven basic operators.

Projection. Let r be a relation on R, and X a subset of R. Then the projection of r on X is

$$\pi_X(r) = \{t(X) : t \in r\}.$$

Although it is implicit in the definition, we note that

$$\pi_{\emptyset}(r) = \begin{cases} \varepsilon & \text{if } r \neq \emptyset \\ \emptyset & \text{if } r = \emptyset. \end{cases}$$

(This projection on the empty set is needed to express calculus queries without free variables, i.e. "yes-no" queries).

Selection. Let E be a formula of atoms of the form A=a, A=B, **true** and **false**, and combined by negation ($\neg$), conjunction ($\wedge$) and disjunction ($\vee$), and properly parenthesized. In the atom A=a, A is an attribute in R and a is a constant from *Dom*(A). In the atom A=B, A and B are attributes in R, such that *Dom*(A) = *Dom*(B). Now a selection with E on r is defined as

$$\sigma_E(r) = \{t : t \in r, \text{ and } E(t) = \textbf{true}\}.$$

By E(t) we mean E with all attribute names A in E substituted with t(A). An atomic formula A=a or A=B is **true** in E(t), if t(A)=a or t(A)=t(B). Then E(t) is evaluated using the standard semantics for the boolean connectives. A selection will be called *positive* if its formula does not contain negation. For negations we shall frequently use the notation $x \neq y$ instead of $\neg(x=y)$.

Union. Let r and s be relations on R. Then

$$r \cup s = \{t : t \in r, \text{ or } t \in s\}.$$

Join. Let r be a relation on R, and s a relation on S. Then the join of r and s is

$$r * s = \{t : \alpha(t) = R \cup S, \text{ and } t(R) \in r \text{ and } t(S) \in s\}.$$

We note that if R = S, then the join becomes the usual set theoretic *intersection.* In this case we shall sometimes use the notation $r \cap s$. On the other hand, if $R \cap S = \emptyset$, then the join behaves as the set theoretic *Cartesian product.*

Renaming. An attribute A can be seen as the name of a "column" in a relation. The column name can be changed by a renaming operation. The values of the tuples remain the same. To put it formally, let r be a relation on R, A an attribute in R and B an attribute in *U*-R, such that *Dom*(A) = *Dom*(B). Then r with A renamed to B is

$$\theta_B^A(r) \quad = \quad \{\theta_B^A(t) : t \in r\}, \text{ where}$$

$$(\theta_B^A(t))(C) \; = \; \begin{cases} t(C) \text{ if } C \in R-A \\ t(A) \text{ if } C = B. \end{cases}$$

and $\alpha(\theta_B^A(r)) = (R-\{A\}) \cup \{B\}$.

Difference. Let r and s be relations on R. Then

$$r\text{-}s \; = \; \{t : t \in r \text{ and } t \notin s\}.$$

The purpose of the previous definitions is to fix the formalism, and not to teach the sophisticated reader the basics of the relational model. Thus we omit examples at this point. We note however that the Cartesian product is not an operator in this version of the relational algebra. We saw earlier that if two relations are defined over disjoint schemes, then the join of the two relations is in effect the Cartesian product. In the case where the schemes overlap we can simulate the Cartesian product by making the schemes disjoint through renaming. (A similar construction can be done for the intersection.) We shall introduce the following shorthand.

Cartesian product. Let r be a relation on R and s a relation on $S = A_1 \ldots A_n$, and let $B_1 \ldots B_n$ be attributes in U -RS, with $Dom(B_i) = Dom(A_i)$, for $1 \leq i \leq n$. Then

$$r \times s = r * (\theta_{B_1}^{A_1}(\ldots(\theta_{B_n}^{A_n}(s))\ldots)),$$

and $\alpha(r \times s) = R \cup \{B_1 \ldots B_n\}$.

Note that the result of $r \times s$ is unique up the the choice of the attribute names B_i.

Relational expressions and equations

In order to express queries we need to use several operators from the algebra, in building expressions of operators. For the purpose of defining relational expressions we associate *relational variables* R with each scheme R, i.e. R ranges over *Rel*(R). The type of the variable, $\alpha(R)$, is R. A *multirelational variable* $\boldsymbol{R}$ ranges over the set of multirelations *Rel*(**R**). That is, if $\mathbf{R} = <R_1, \ldots, R_n>$, then $\boldsymbol{R} = <R_1, \ldots, R_n>$, and $\alpha(\boldsymbol{R}) = \mathbf{R}$. (Schemes and variables are concatenated in the following way: if $\mathbf{R} = <R_1, \ldots, R_n>$ and $\mathbf{S} = <S_1, \ldots, S_m>$, then $<\mathbf{R}, \mathbf{S}>$ means $<R_1, \ldots, R_n, S_1, \ldots, S_m>$.)

A *relational expression* f($\boldsymbol{R}$) is obtained by a finite number of applications of the following rules:

(i) Let R be a relational variable. Then $f(R) =_{def.} R$ is a relational expression (the identity). The *argument type*, $\alpha(f)$, of f is $\alpha(R)$, and the *result type*, $\beta(f)$, of f is $\alpha(R)$. The *result* of applying the expression f(R) to a relation r in *Rel*(R), denoted by f(r), is r.

Let f($\boldsymbol{R}$) and g($\boldsymbol{S}$) be relational expressions.

(ii) If $Y \subseteq \beta(f)$, then $h(\boldsymbol{R}) =_{def.} \pi_Y(f(\boldsymbol{R}))$ is a relational expression. Here $\alpha(h) = \alpha(f)$, $\beta(h) = Y$, and for any $\mathbf{r}$ in $Rel(\alpha(h))$, $h(\mathbf{r}) = \pi_Y(f(\mathbf{r}))$.

(iii) If E is a selection formula that mentions only attributes in $\beta(f)$, then $h(\boldsymbol{R}) =_{def.} \sigma_E(f(\boldsymbol{R}))$ is a relational expression. Here $\alpha(h) = \alpha(f)$, $\beta(h) = \beta(f)$, and for any $\mathbf{r}$ in $Rel(\alpha(h))$, $h(\mathbf{r}) = \sigma_E(f(\mathbf{r}))$.

(iv) If $\beta(f) = \beta(g)$, then $h(<\boldsymbol{R}, \boldsymbol{S}>) =_{def.} f(\boldsymbol{R}) \cup g(\boldsymbol{S})$ is a relational expression. Now $\alpha(h) = <\alpha(f), \alpha(g)>$, and $\beta(h) = \beta(f)$. For any $<\mathbf{r}, \mathbf{s}>$ in $Rel(\alpha(h))$, $h(<\mathbf{r}, \mathbf{s}>) = f(\mathbf{r}) \cup g(\mathbf{s})$.

(v) $h(<\boldsymbol{R}, \boldsymbol{S}>) =_{def.} f(\boldsymbol{R}) * g(\boldsymbol{S})$ is a relational expression. Now $\alpha(h) = <\alpha(f), \alpha(g)>$, and $\beta(h) = \beta(f) \cup \beta(g)$. For any $<\mathbf{r}, \mathbf{s}>$ in $Rel(\alpha(h))$, $h(\mathbf{r}) = f(\mathbf{r}) * g(\mathbf{s})$.

(vi) If A is an attribute in $\beta(f)$, and B is an attribute in U- $\beta(f)$, then $h(\boldsymbol{R}) =_{def.} \theta_B^A(f(\boldsymbol{R}))$ is a relational expression with $\alpha(h) = \alpha(f)$, $\beta(h) = (\beta(f)\text{-}A) \cup B$. For any $\mathbf{r}$ in $Rel(\alpha(h))$, $h(\mathbf{r}) = \theta_B^A(f(\mathbf{r}))$

(vii) If $\beta(f) = \beta(g)$, then $h(<\boldsymbol{R}, \boldsymbol{S}>) =_{def.} f(\boldsymbol{R}) - g(\boldsymbol{S})$ is a relational expression with $\alpha(h) = <\alpha(f), \alpha(g)>$, and $\beta(h) = \beta(f)$. For any $<\mathbf{r}, \mathbf{s}>$ in $Rel(\alpha(h))$, $h(<\mathbf{r}, \mathbf{s}>) = f(\mathbf{r}) - g(\mathbf{s})$.

We shall use the abbreviations P, S, S^+, U, J, R, D as generic names for the operation classes projection, selection, positive selection, union, join, renaming and difference, respectively. Let Ω stand for a subset of these operations.

By an *Ω-expression* we mean a relational expression obtained by only using the inductive rules for the operators in Ω. For example, $\pi_A(R)\text{-}S$ is a PD-expression (it is of course also an Ω-expression for any $\Omega \supseteq \{P, D\}$).

Obviously an Ω-expression f($\boldsymbol{R}$) defines a *mapping* $f : Rel(\alpha(f)) \rightarrow Rel(\beta(f))$. In some cases we shall work with *restricted* mappings. It will be convenient to "curry" these mappings. Let $\alpha(\boldsymbol{R}) = \mathbf{R} = <R_1, \ldots, R_n>$, $n \geq 2$. Then let $\mathbf{S} = <R_1,\ldots,R_k>$, and $\mathbf{P} = <R_{k+1},\ldots,R_n>$, where $1 \leq k \leq n\text{-}1$. Suppose that **s** is a multirelation in *Rel*(**S**) and that $\alpha(\boldsymbol{P}) = \mathbf{P}$. Then $f_{\mathbf{s}}(\boldsymbol{P})$ defines a mapping from *Rel*(**P**) to *Rel*(β(f)), by putting $f_{\mathbf{s}}(\mathbf{p}) = f(<\mathbf{s},\mathbf{p}>)$, for all **p** in *Rel*(**P**). We shall take $\mathbf{R} = <S, R>$ as a clarifying example. If s is a relation on S, *S* and *R* are relational variables for S and R, and $f(<S, R>) = S * R$, then $f_s(R)$ defines a mapping from *Rel*(R) to *Rel*(S∪R), given by $f_s(R) = s * R$.

In the above Ω stands for a subset of {P, S, S^+, U, J, R, D}. When there is no risk of confusion, we shall sometimes use Ω for the the set of all Ω-expressions.

Expressions can also be used to specify various constraints through equations. An *equation* φ is a statement of the form $f(\boldsymbol{R}) = g(\boldsymbol{R})$ or $f(\boldsymbol{R}) \subseteq g(\boldsymbol{R})$, where $\beta(f) = \beta(g)$. Implicitly we also have $\alpha(f) = \alpha(g)$. The *type* of the equation is $\alpha(\phi) = \alpha(f)$. A *solution* to such an equation is a multirelation **r**, $\alpha(\mathbf{r}) = \alpha(\phi)$, such that $f(\mathbf{r}) = g(\mathbf{r})$, or $f(\mathbf{r}) \subseteq g(\mathbf{r})$. Let φ be an equation. Then *Sat*(φ) is the subset of those multirelations in *Rel*(α(φ)) that are solutions to φ. A solution to a *set of equations* Φ is a multirelation which is a solution to all $\phi \in \Phi$. It is assumed that all equations in a set are homogeneous, i.e. they have the same argument types. The notion α(Φ) and the set *Sat*(Φ) are defined in the obvious way.

We call an equation φ *trivial*, if *Sat*(φ) = *Rel*(α(φ)). The equation φ is *contradictory*, if *Sat*(φ) = Ø. An equation which is neither trivial, nor contradictory, is called *proper*. The same notions apply, mutatis mutandis, to sets of equations.

The relational calculus and the Codd completeness theorem

A query in the relational calculus is an expression of the form x.φ(x), where φ is a formula in the relational language for the database scheme. (This relational language is the standard first order, function-free language with one predicate symbol p corresponding to each relation scheme R, plus the equality predicate =. In addition there are some syntactic restrictions on the formulas, see [Ull82]). In the query x.φ(x), x is a vector consisting of the free variables of φ. The answer to the query in a database **r**, denoted by $\|\varphi\|_{\mathbf{r}}$, is $\{t : \mathbf{r} \models \varphi(t)\}$, i.e. a set of tuples, constructed from the domain values of the attributes for the free variables, such that when these values are substituted for the variables, the formula φ is true in **r**, where **r** is regarded as an interpretation of the formula.

A query expressed in the relational calculus is thus declarative. The completeness theorem [Cod72b] states that for each calculus query φ there is a relational expression f_φ (and vice versa), such that for all databases **r**, $\|\varphi\|_{\mathbf{r}} = f_\varphi(\mathbf{r})$. The relational algebra is a procedural version of the declarative queries.

Lattices and least fixpoint queries

The relational algebra has been criticized for not having enough expressive power [AU79]. For instance, the *transitive closure* of a binary relation is not expressible in the relational algebra. One way to enhance the language is to introduce a *least fixpoint operator*. For this purpose we review some notions from lattice theory [Grä71, Sto77].

Let $<Q, \leq>$ stand for a set Q with a partial order $\leq$ (a binary relation $\leq$ is a partial order if it is reflexive, antisymmetric and transitive). An element $q \in Q$ is the upper bound of a subset P of Q, if $p \leq q$, for all $p \in P$. Likewise, q is a lower bound of P, if $q \leq p$, for all $p \in P$. If q is an upper bound of P, and if for all upper bounds q' of P, we have $q \leq q'$, then q is the *least upper bound* of P. Similarly, the *greatest lower bound* of P is a lower bound q of P, such that for all lower bounds q' of P, $q' \leq q$ holds. The last two bounds are denoted by *lub*(P) and *glb*(P), respectively. If these bounds exist they are unique by definition.

A couple $<Q, \leq>$ is a *lattice* if *lub*(P) and *glb*(P) exist for every finite subset P of Q. The couple $<Q, \leq>$ is a *complete lattice* if *lub*(P) and *glb*(P) exist for every subset P of Q. In a complete lattice the *top element* is *lub*(Q), and the *bottom element* is *glb*(Q).

Let $T : Q \rightarrow Q$ be a mapping, where $<Q, \leq>$ is a complete lattice. The mapping T is called *monotonous* if $T(q) \leq T(p)$, whenever $q \leq p$. A *fixpoint* for a mapping T is an element $p \in Q$, such that $p = T(p)$.

The *least fixpoint* of T is a fixpoint p of T, such that for all fixpoints p' of T, it is true that $p \leq p'$. A fundamental result in lattice theory is that the least fixpoint exists and is unique if T is monotonous. The least fixpoint of a mapping T is denoted by *lfp*(T). Alternatively, *lfp*(T) can be regarded as the smallest (w.r.t. $\leq$) solution to the equation $x = T(x)$. (Here x is a variable ranging over Q.) The following lemma will be needed later on.

Lemma 2.1. Let S and T be monotonous mappings on a complete lattice $<Q, \leq>$, such that $p \leq S(p)$ and $p \leq T(p)$, for all $p \in Q$. Then $lfp(T \circ S) = lfp(S \circ T)$. (The symbol $\circ$ denotes the composition of the mappings, i.e. $(T \circ S)(p) = T(S(p))$.)

Proof. As $T \circ S$ is monotonous, it has a fixpoint, say q. Then $q = T(S(q))$. By our assumptions $q \leq S(q) \leq T(S(q))$. Hence $q = S(q) = T(S(q))$, and consequently $q = T(q)$. Thus $S(q) = S(T(q))$. We now have $q = S(T(q))$, i.e. q is a fixpoint of $S \circ T$.

We have shown that every fixpoint of $T \circ S$ is a fixpoint of $S \circ T$. By symmetry, every fixpoint of $S \circ T$ is a fixpoint of $T \circ S$. Hence $T \circ S$ and $S \circ T$ have the same fixpoints. In particular, they have he same least fixpoint. *Q.E.D.*

Let us now return to the relational model. A set *Rel*(R) is obviously partially ordered by the set inclusion $\subseteq$ of relations. The least upper bound of a set of relations is their union, the greatest lower bound their intersection. The bottom element is ø, and the top element is r_∞. Thus <*Rel*(R), ⊆> is a complete lattice. The set *Rel*(Ø) needs special attention. It contains two elements, ø and ε, the empty relation and a relation with the empty tuple, respectively. These two elements are ordered by ø ⊆ ε.

Now a set *Rel*(**R**) = *Rel*(R_1) × ... × *Rel*(R_n) defines a *Cartesian* lattice. Let **r** = <r_1,...,r_n> and **s** = <s_1,...,s_n>. Then **r** ⊆ **s** if $r_i \subseteq s_i$, for $1 \leq i \leq n$. The inclusion ⊆ of multirelations defines a partial order. The greatest lower bound of a set of multirelations is their componentwise intersection, e.g. in the binary case **r**∩**s** = <$r_1 \cap s_1$, ..., $r_n \cap s_n$>. Similarly, the least upper bound of a set of multirelations is their union (taken componentwise, as the intersection). The bottom element *glb*(*Rel*(**R**)) is **ø** = <ø, ..., ø>. The top element *lub*(*Rel*(**R**)) is $\mathbf{r}_\infty$ = <r_{1_∞}, ..., r_{n_∞}>. Thus the couple <*Rel*(**R**), ⊆> is a complete lattice.

Assuming that β(f(*S*)) = α(*S*) = S, an expression f(*S*) can be seen as a mapping on the lattice <*Rel*(S), ⊆>. Monotonicity of a mapping f : *Rel*(S)→*Rel*(S) means in this context that for any r and s in *Rel*(S), r ⊆ s implies that f(r) ⊆ f(s). It is known that a sufficient condition for a relational expression to be monotonous is that it does not contain the difference operator [AU79]. Thus any PSUJR-expression is monotonous.

We are now able to add an operator to the relational algebra.

Least fixpoint. Let f(*S*) be a PSUJR-expression with α(f) = β(f). Then ψ(f(*S*)) = *lfp*(f(*S*)). Furthermore, α(ψ) = α(f) and β(ψ) = β(f).

Let [*Rel*(R)→*Rel*(R)] denote the set of all PSUJR-expressions f, with α(f) = β(f) = R. Then ψ as an operation is a mapping from [*Rel*(R)→*Rel*(R)] to *Rel*(R). The abbreviation Y will be used as a generic name for the class of fixpoints operators, when f is a PSUJR-expression. The abbreviation Y^+ is used when f is a PS^+UJR-expression.

The least fixpoint can be computed in the following way. Let $f^n(S)$ stand for the n-fold composition of f with itself, e.g. $f^3(S)$ means f(f(f(*S*))). (For any f, f^0 is the identity mapping.) Then it can be shown [AU79] that for any monotonous f there is a k, such that ψ(f(*S*)) = f^k(ø). We note that the least fixpoint is always finite. This is because the relational mappings do not introduce any new values, and because $f^n(ø) \subseteq f^{n+1}(ø)$, for any n. Thus a folding sequence must converge after a finite number of applications of the mapping.

As an example of the least fixpoint operator we look at the *transitive closure* of a binary relation r on AB. We abbreviate by *R*∘*S* the expression

$$\pi_{AB}(\sigma_{B_1=A_1}(\theta^{B}_{B_1}(R) * \theta^{A}_{A_1}(S))).$$

Here $\alpha(R) = \alpha(S) = AB$. The operator $\circ$ joins R and S over B in R and A in S, and keeps in the result A from R and B from S. This operator is well known as the *composition* of two binary relations. The transitive closure of a relation r on AB is now the least fixpoint of the mapping

$$f_r(R) = R \circ r \cup r.$$

An example follows.

r =

A	B
a	b
b	c

$f_r(\emptyset)$ =

A	B
a	b
b	c
c	d

$f_r(f_r(\emptyset))$ =

A	B
a	b
b	c
c	d
a	c
b	d

$\psi(f_r(R)) = f_r(f_r(f_r(\emptyset)))$ =

A	B
a	b
b	c
c	d
a	c
b	d
a	d

Note in the example that the "input" relation r has to be part of the definition of the mapping f_r. It might be difficult to design a practical query language on this basis. Aho and Ullman [AU79] suggest an alternative way of expressing the least fixpoint operator. We give a set Φ of equations, consisting of a basis rule and an inductive rule. For example, Φ could be given as equation (1) below.

$$(1) \quad \begin{cases} g(\mathbf{r}) \subseteq R \\ h(R) \subseteq R. \end{cases}$$

In (1), $g(\mathbf{r}) \subseteq R$ is the basis rule, and $h(R) \subseteq R$ is the inductive rule. We are now interested in the smallest (w.r.t. $\subseteq$) relation $s \in Sat(\Phi)$. This relation can be obtained by the following algorithm:

$s \leftarrow g(\mathbf{r})$
repeat
  $s' \leftarrow s$
  $s \leftarrow s \cup h(s)$
until $s' = s$

It is shown in [AU79] that the relation s, computed by the above algorithm, is equal to $\psi(f_{g(r)}(R))$, where $f_{g(r)}(R) = g(r) \cup h(R) \cup R$. Conversely, any least fixpoint operator $\psi(f(R))$ can be expressed as the smallest solution to the equation set

$$(2) \quad \begin{cases} \emptyset \subseteq R \\ f(R) \subseteq R. \end{cases}$$

The transitive closure of a relation r on AB is in this framework the smallest solution to the equation set (3) below. ($\alpha(R) = \alpha(r) = AB$.)

$$(3) \quad \begin{cases} r \subseteq R \\ R \circ r \subseteq R. \end{cases}$$

One can in this context note that the relational algebra augmented with a least fixpoint operator is equivalent in expressive power to function-free Horn clause programs (also known as *Datalog queries*, and in particular as *recursive queries*) [CH85]. (Note that the equations (1) - (3) are clearly recursive). The computation of the least fixpoint through the folding sequence is nowadays also called "naive evaluation" [BR86].

2.2. Data dependencies

A database is not merely characterized by the relational multischeme. In addition, the designer usually gives a set of *integrity constraints*. These constraints express properties that any database extension must possess, in order to be regarded as a legal state. The data dependencies can also be seen as a language for assigning semantics to the database (cf. [FV86]). The choice of constraints is a task for the database designer. The role of database theory in this context is to study the properties of the constraints, in order to come up with methods for incorporating them in a database system.

In relational databases the integrity constraints are expressed as *dependencies*. The theory of dependencies was first established in 1972 when Codd defined the *functional dependencies* [Cod72a]. It was soon realized that functional dependencies were not strong enough to express all desired constraints. Several authors invented new, more powerful dependencies, until it was agreed that sufficient expressibility had been achieved. There are several classes of dependencies that have this sufficient expressive power: Embedded implicational dependencies [Fag82], tuple and equality generating dependencies [BV84], and algebraic dependencies ([YP82] and [Abi83]). The difference between these classes lies more (though not entirely) on the level of formalism than in the expressive power. For a survey of dependencies the reader can turn to [Abi85], [FV86] or [Var85].

Here we shall study dependencies defined on unirelational schemes. Thus we will cover all dependencies, except the so called inclusion dependencies [CFP84]. A further restriction is that we consider only typed and total dependencies. Typing and totality will be explained below. We are going to use the formalism of algebraic dependencies as it appears in [YP82], which can only express typed dependencies. The restriction to total dependencies is made in order to guarantee that the algorithms that we shall propose terminate. Thus when the term dependency is used in the sequel it will mean a typed and a total one.

Dependencies as first order formulas

A general formalism to express dependencies is by a closed formula of the form

$$\text{(4)} \qquad \forall\, x_1, \ldots, x_s((p_1 \wedge \ldots \wedge p_m) \Rightarrow q),$$

in the relational language for the database scheme. (Recall that the relational language is the standard first order function-free language with one predicate p corresponding to each relation scheme R, plus the equality predicate =). Formula (4) is a Horn clause (see [Fag82]). In the formula each p_i is of the form $p(z_1, \ldots, z_n)$, and q is of the form z=w or of the same form as the p_i:s. In the first case we call the dependency *equality generating*, and in the second case it is called *tuple generating*. Note that the formula is universally closed, i.e. the variables in the p_i:s and in q are exactly $x_1, \ldots, x_s$. Note also that the formula has only one predicate, i.e. all p_i:s stand for the same p.

The *totality* of the dependency means that if a variable appears in q, then it appears in some p_i. *Typing*, on the other hand, means that the variables can be partitioned into n different sets (n is the arity of p), and that a variable from the i:th set can only appear in position i in p. These variables are said to be of type i. Also, z and w have to be of the same type in any equality generating dependency.

Intuitively, a dependency states that if the relation contains some tuples with a certain pattern, then, in the case of equality generation, some values must be equal, and in the case of tuple generation, the relation must contain a tuple which is a combination of values matching the pattern. The totality prevents the implied tuple from containing any new values. (In a non-total, i.e. in an *embedded* dependency, q would contain some existentially quantified variables.) The typing restriction is more of a syntactic nature. From a practical viewpoint it means that for instance the requirement for a relation to be transitively closed is not expressible as a typed dependency.

The well known *functional dependency* is an example of an equality generating dependency. Consider a scheme on attributes ABC. The relational language will have a ternary predicate, say p, corresponding to this scheme. The functional dependency $A \rightarrow B$ on ABC can be expressed by the formula

$$(5) \quad \forall\, x, y, z, y_1, z_1\ (p(xyz) \wedge p(xy_1z_1) \Rightarrow y = y_1).$$

The also well known *multivalued dependency* $A \rightarrow\rightarrow B$ on ABC is written in the form

$$(6) \quad \forall\, x, y, z, y_1, z_1\ (p(xy_1z) \wedge p(xyz_1) \Rightarrow p(xyz)).$$

Dependencies will be denoted by δ. The scheme on which a dependency is defined (i.e. the scheme R corresponding to the predicate p occurring in δ) is called the *type* of the dependency and it is denoted by $\alpha(\delta)$. A finite set of dependencies of the same type is denoted by Σ. The type of Σ is $\alpha(\Sigma)$. A relation r *satisfies* a dependency δ, where $\alpha(r) = \alpha(\delta)$, if r is a model of the formula δ (in the sense of mathematical logic). A relation r satisfies a set Σ of dependencies if it satisfies all δ in Σ. We denote by *Sat*(Σ) the set of all relations in *Rel*($\alpha(\Sigma)$) that satisfy Σ.

Dependencies as algebraic equations

The above formalism is declarative, and does not indicate any constructive method for checking satisfaction. A major result in the theory of dependencies is that the dependency formulas can be expressed as algebraic equations [YP82], [Abi83] (the result is an analogue to the Codd Completeness Theorem). We will here adopt the formalism of Yannakakis and Papadimitriou [YP82], where a dependency is expressed by the equation

$$(7) \quad f(\uparrow^n(R)) \subseteq g(\uparrow^n(R)), \quad n \geq 0.$$

The equation (7) is called an *algebraic dependency*. Here f and g are PJ-expressions. The symbol $\uparrow$ denotes the *duplicate* operator, $\uparrow^n$ stands for an n-fold duplication. The duplicate of a relation r is $\uparrow(r) = \{\uparrow(t) : t \in r\}$. If $t = (a, b, c, \ldots)$, then $\uparrow(t) = (a, b, c, \ldots, a, b, c, \ldots)$. Let $\alpha(r) = ABC$. Then $\beta(\uparrow) = ABCA_1B_1C_1$. The attributes stemming from further duplications will be indexed by 2, 3, ... The duplicate operator is in fact a shorthand, since it is expressible as a S^+JR-expression. Suppose that r is a relation on ABC. Then

$$\uparrow(r) = \sigma_{A=A_1 \wedge B=B_1 \wedge C=C_1}(r * (\theta^{A}_{A_1}(\theta^{B}_{B_1}(\theta^{C}_{C_1}(r))))).$$

A relation r on R satisfies an algebraic dependency $f(\uparrow^n(R)) \subseteq g(\uparrow^n(R))$ if $f(\uparrow^n(r)) \subseteq g(\uparrow^n(r))$, i.e. if r is a solution to the equation. We can now cite the following important result:

Theorem 2.1 [YP82]. For any dependency δ there exists an algebraic dependency ρ, such that $Sat(\delta) = Sat(\rho)$, and vice versa.

We shall illustrate the theorem by our two dependencies. The algebraic version of the multivalued dependency (6) is the equation

(8) $\pi_{ABC}(\pi_{AB_1C}(\uparrow(R)) * \pi_{ABC_1}(\uparrow(R))) \subseteq \pi_{ABC}(\uparrow(R)).$

Since $\pi_{ABC}(\uparrow(r))$ obviously is equal to r, for any r on ABC, we can write equation (8) as $f(\uparrow(R)) \subseteq R$, where $f(\uparrow(R))$ is the left-hand side of (8).

The functional dependency (5) can be written as

(9) $\pi_{BB_1}(\pi_{ABC}(\uparrow(R)) * \pi_{AB_1C_1}(\uparrow(R))) \subseteq \pi_{BB_1}(\uparrow(R)).$

The proof of Theorem 2.1 can be found in [YP82]. Here we will only show how the algebraic version of a given dependency is constructed. We shall see that the general form of the equations can be simplified as a consequence of our restriction to total dependencies.

Suppose $R = \{A_1, ..., A_n\}$. Let the dependency δ be

(10) $\forall x_1, ..., x_s ((p_1 \wedge ... \wedge p_m) \Rightarrow q).$

The algebraic version ρ of δ is the equation

(11) $\pi_W(\pi_{Z_1}(\uparrow^k(R)) * ... * \pi_{Z_m}(\uparrow^k(R))) \subseteq \pi_W(\uparrow^k(R)).$

Here k is one less than the maximum number of distinct variables of the same <u>type</u> in formula (10). As usual, $\uparrow^k(R)$ stands for the k-fold composition of the duplicate operator. We associate each variable of type i in (10) with a duplicate A'_i of attribute A_i in $\uparrow^k(R)$, or with A_i itself. Each Z_i corresponds to p_i in δ. Remember that p_i is of the form $p(z_1...z_n)$. Now Z_i is $A'_1...A'_n$ where A'_j is the duplicate of A_j associated with the variable z_j in p_i.

For W there are two cases:

(i) **q is of the form $p(z_1 \ldots z_n)$.**

In this case δ is a tuple generating dependency. W is now $A'_1 \ldots A'_n$, where A'_j is the duplicate of A_j associated with the variable in the j:th position in q. (W is constructed exactly as the Z_i:s in this case.) It should be clear that we can choose A_j itself as A'_j. Thus the right-hand side of equation (11) can be written as $\pi_{A_1 \ldots A_n}(\uparrow^k(R))$, which we obviously can replace by R.

An example could be illustrative at this point. Let us recall the multivalued dependency (6):

$$\forall\, x, y, z, y_1, z_1\ (p(xy_1z) \wedge p(xyz_1) \Rightarrow p(xyz)).$$

The set of variables of type 1 is $\{x\}$, of type 2 $\{y, y_1\}$, and of type 3 $\{z, z_1\}$. Hence k=1. We associate x with A, y with B, y_1 with B_1, z with C, and z_1 with C_1. Following the rules given above the algebraic dependency now becomes

$$\pi_{ABC}(\pi_{AB_1C}(\uparrow(R)) * \pi_{ABC_1}(\uparrow(R)) \subseteq R.$$

(ii) **q is of the form z=w.**

Hence δ is an equality generating dependency. Suppose z and w are of type j. W is in this case $A'_jA''_j$, where A'_j and A''_j are the duplicates of A_j associated with z and w, respectively. We recall the functional dependency (5):

$$\forall\, x, y, z, y_1, z_1\ (p(xyz) \wedge p(xy_1z_1) \Rightarrow y{=}y_1).$$

Here the set of variables of type 1 is $\{x\}$, of type 2 $\{y,y_1\}$ and of type 3 $\{z,z_1\}$. We get k=1, and then we associate x with A, y with B, y_1 with B_1, z with C, and z_1 with C_1. Obviously the algebraic dependency now takes the form (9), which we repeat below:

$$\pi_{BB_1}(\pi_{ABC}(\uparrow(R)) * \pi_{AB_1C_1}(\uparrow(R))) \subseteq \pi_{BB_1}(\uparrow(R)).$$

It should now be clear that the following simplifying notations can be applied:

Corollary 2.1. For any dependency δ there exists an algebraic dependency ρ, such that *Sat*(δ) = *Sat*(ρ), and

(i) ρ is of the form $f(\uparrow^n(R)) \subseteq R$, $n \geq 0$, if δ is a tuple generating dependency, and

(ii) ρ is of the form $\pi_{B_1B_2}(f(\uparrow^n(R)) \subseteq \pi_{B_1B_2}(\uparrow^n(R))$, for some $B \in R$ and $n \geq 1$, if δ is an equality generating dependency.

The mappings $f(\uparrow^n(R))$ used in the algebraic versions of tuple generating dependencies have some interesting properties that we will need later on. First of all, they are monotonous. This follows from the fact that mappings involving projects and joins are monotonous [Ull82], and that the duplicate operator obviously preserves monotonicity. A less trivial property is stated in the next lemma.

Lemma 2.2. For any PJ-expression f, and $n \geq 0$,

$$\pi_{\beta(f)}(\uparrow^n(R)) \subseteq f(\uparrow^n(R))$$

is satisfied by any relation in $Rel(\alpha(R))$, i.e. the equation is trivial.

Proof. The proof is an induction on the structure of f. In the basis f is the identity, and the claim holds trivially. For the induction step we suppose that $\pi_{\beta(f)}(\uparrow^n(r)) \subseteq f(\uparrow^n(r))$ and $\pi_{\beta(g)}(\uparrow^n(r)) \subseteq g(\uparrow^n(r))$, for some relation r, and $n \geq 0$. Now there are two cases to consider.

(i) (*Projection*). Let $Z \subseteq \beta(f)$. Now the fact $\pi_Z(\pi_{\beta(f)}(\uparrow^n(r)) \subseteq \pi_Z(f(\uparrow^n(r)))$ follows directly from the monotonicity of the projection operator (cf. [Ull82]).

(ii) (*Join*).We claim that $\pi_{\beta(f) \cup \beta(g)}(\uparrow^n(r)) \subseteq f(\uparrow^n(r)) * g(\uparrow^n(r))$. Let t be a tuple in the left-hand side of this equation. Then there is a tuple t' in $\uparrow^n(r)$, such that $t'(\beta(f) \cup \beta(g)) = t$. Now $t'(\beta(f))$ belongs to $\pi_{\beta(f)}(\uparrow^n(r))$ and $t'(\beta(g))$ to $\pi_{\beta(g)}(\uparrow^n(r))$, and thus, by the induction hypothesis, $t'(\beta(f)) \in f(\uparrow^n(r))$ and $t'(\beta(g)) \in g(\uparrow^n(r))$. By the definition of the join, $t'(\beta(f) \cup \beta(g)) = t$ is in $f(\uparrow^n(r)) * g(\uparrow^n(r))$. *Q.E.D.*

In addition to multivalued dependencies, there is another special case of tuple generating dependencies: let $S_1, ..., S_n$ and R be relational variables, such that $\alpha(S_1) \cup ... \cup \alpha(S_n) = \alpha(R)$. Suppose that $\alpha(S_i)$ is S_i. Then $\pi_{S_1}(R) * ... * \pi_{S_n}(R) \subseteq R$ is called a *join dependency* on $\alpha(R)$. This dependency is sometimes denoted by $*[S_1, ..., S_n]$. We note that the multivalued dependency $X \rightarrow\rightarrow Y$ on R is equivalent to the (binary) join dependency $*[XY, X \cup (R-Y)]$. The notation $X \rightarrow\rightarrow Y | R-Y$, sometimes used, reflects this fact.

In the sequel we shall speak of sets of dependencies. By this we will mean a set of algebraic dependencies that are either tuple generating, and of form (i) of Corollary 2.1, or equality generating, and of form (ii) of the corollary. Given a set Σ of dependencies we can partition it into two disjoint sets Σ_T and Σ_E. The set Σ_T contains all the tuple generating dependencies, and Σ_E contains all the equality generating ones. If an equality generating dependency happens to be a functional one, we will for simplicity sometimes use the classical notation $X \rightarrow Y$. Similarly, we will sometimes write $X \rightarrow\rightarrow Y$ and $*[S_1,...,S_n]$ for multivalued resp. join dependencies.

We are now able to characterize satisfaction of a set of tuple generating dependencies in terms of least fixpoints.

Theorem 2.2. For any finite set Σ of tuple generating dependencies, and finite relation $r \in Rel(\alpha(\Sigma))$, there is a mapping $g(\Sigma)_r : Rel(\alpha(\Sigma)) \rightarrow Rel(\alpha(\Sigma))$, such that $r \in Sat(\Sigma)$ if and only if $r = \psi(g(\Sigma)_r)$.

Proof. Let $\Sigma = \{f_1(\uparrow^{m_1}(R)) \subseteq R, \ldots, f_n(\uparrow^{m_n}(R)) \subseteq R\}$. We denote $f_i(\uparrow^{m_i}(R))$ by $g_i(R)$, $1 \leq i \leq n$. Then the mapping $g(\Sigma)_r$ is $g_1(...(g_n(R))...) \cup r$. From Lemma 2.1 it should be clear that $\psi(g_1(...(g_n(R))...) \cup r) = \psi(g_{j_1}(...(g_{j_n}(R))...) \cup r)$, where $<j_1,...,j_n>$ is any permutation of $<1,...,n>$.

(Only if). Suppose $r \in Sat(\Sigma)$. This means that $g_i(r) \subseteq r$, for all $g_i(R) \subseteq R \in \Sigma$. From Lemma 2.2 we can conclude that $r = g_i(r)$. Hence

$$r = g_n(r) = g_{n-1}(g_n(r)) = ... = g_1(...(g_{n-1}(g_n(r)))...) = g_1(...(g_{n-1}(g_n(r)))...) \cup r.$$

Thus r is a fixpoint of $g(\Sigma)_r$. By the definition of $g(\Sigma)_r$, any fixpoint of $g(\Sigma)_r$ must contain r. We conclude that r is the least fixpoint of $g(\Sigma)_r$.

(If). Suppose that $r = \psi(g(\Sigma)_r)$. Suppose then to the contrary that r is <u>not</u> in $Sat(\Sigma)$. Then there must be some $g_i(R) \subseteq R \in \Sigma$, such that $g_i(r) \not\subseteq r$. By Lemma 2.2, $r \subseteq g_i(r)$. Hence $r \subsetneq g_i(r)$. Using this, and Lemma 2.2, we get

(12) $$r \subsetneq g_i(r) \subseteq g_1(...(g_{i-1}(g_{i+1}(...(g_n(g_i(r)))...)))...) \subseteq g_1(...(g_{i-1}(g_{i+1}(...(g_n(g_i(r)))...)))...) \cup r.$$

By Lemma 2.1, the rightmost part of (12) is the mapping $g(\Sigma)_r$. Alas, r cannot be the least fixpoint of $g(\Sigma)_r$; a contradiction. The counter assumption is thus wrong and r must be in $Sat(\Sigma)$. *Q.E.D.*

The following corollary is obvious by the construction of $g(\Sigma)_r$.

Corollary 2.2. Let Σ be a set of tuple generating dependencies, and r and s finite relations in *Rel*($\alpha(\Sigma)$). Then $r \subseteq s$ implies that $\psi(g(\Sigma)_r) \subseteq \psi(g(\Sigma)_s)$.

Concerning equality generating dependencies, the next lemma will lead to a useful little theorem, which is needed later on.

Lemma 2.3. Let r be a relation, and $\rho = \pi_{B_1B_2}(f(\uparrow^n(R))) \subseteq \pi_{B_1B_2}(\uparrow^n(R))$ an equality generating dependency, where $\alpha(r) = \alpha(\rho)$. Then $r \in Sat(\rho)$ if and only if for all tuples $t \in \pi_{B_1B_2}(f(\uparrow^n(r))$ it is true that $t(B_1) = t(B_2)$.

Proof. (*Only if*). Obviously, for any relation s, $n \geq 1$, and $t \in \pi_{B_1B_2}(\uparrow^n(s))$, it is true that $t(B_1) = t(B_2)$. By Lemma 2.2, $\pi_{B_1B_2}(\uparrow^n(R)) \subseteq \pi_{B_1B_2}(f(\uparrow^n(R)))$. Suppose $r \in Sat(\rho)$. Then $\pi_{B_1B_2}(f(\uparrow^n(r)) \subseteq \pi_{B_1B_2}(\uparrow^n(r))$, and consequently $\pi_{B_1B_2}(f(\uparrow^n(r))) = \pi_{B_1B_2}(\uparrow^n(r))$. Now, if t belongs to $\pi_{B_1B_2}(f(\uparrow^n(r)))$, t also belongs to $\pi_{B_1B_2}(\uparrow^n(r))$, and thus $t(B_1) = t(B_2)$.

(*If*). Suppose $r \notin Sat(\Sigma)$. Then by Lemma 2.2, $\pi_{B_1B_2}(\uparrow^n(r)) \not\subseteq \pi_{B_1B_2}(f(\uparrow^n(r)))$. Let t be a tuple in $\pi_{B_1B_2}(f(\uparrow^n(r))) - \pi_{B_1B_2}(\uparrow^n(r))$. Since the mapping $\pi_{B_1B_2}(f(\uparrow^n(R)))$ does not introduce any new values, t is a combination of values in r. If $t(B_1) = t(B_2)$, then $t \in \pi_{B_1B_2}(\uparrow^n(r))$. Thus the only remaining possibility is that $t(B_1) \neq t(B_2)$. *Q.E.D.*

Theorem 2.3. Let Σ be a set of equality generating dependencies, and r and s relations in *Rel*($\alpha(\Sigma)$), such that $s \subseteq r$. Then $r \in Sat(\Sigma)$ only if $s \in Sat(\Sigma)$.

Proof. Let $r \in Sat(\Sigma)$, and suppose that $s \notin Sat(\Sigma)$, i.e there is a $\rho = \pi_{B_1B_2}(f(\uparrow^n(r))) \subseteq \pi_{B_1B_2}(\uparrow^n(r)) \in \Sigma$, such that $s \notin Sat(\rho)$. Then, by Lemma 2.3, there is a tuple $t \in \pi_{B_1B_2}(f(\uparrow^n(s)))$, such that $t(B_1) \neq t(B_2)$. Now $s \subseteq r$ implies $\pi_{B_1B_2}(f(\uparrow^n(s)) \subseteq \pi_{B_1B_2}(f(\uparrow^n(r))$. Thus $t \in \pi_{B_1B_2}(f(\uparrow^n(r))$. Then Lemma 2.3 implies that $r \notin Sat(\rho)$. Consequently $r \notin Sat(\Sigma)$; a contradiction. We conclude that $s \in Sat(\Sigma)$. *Q.E.D.*

Dependency enforcement

The extension of a database changes when we regard dependencies as a part of the specification of the database. For an example, consider a relation r on ABC and the dependency $A \rightarrow\rightarrow B$. Let $r = \{(a,b,c), (a,e,f)\}$. Now, if r is to be in *Sat* ($A \rightarrow\rightarrow B$), then the tuples (a,e,c) and (a,b,f) also have to be in r. This argumentation is in fact a deduction. With respect to querying the database there are two strategies that can be adopted:

- do the necessary deduction in connection with each query,

- store all the deduced facts.

The first strategy is used in Prolog [Llo85] and in deductive databases [GMN84]. Our scope is different. We want to process the database (be it complete or incomplete) in an algebraic way. Thus we are going to adopt the second strategy.

The problem is thus to characterize the meaning of a database specified by a finite relation r and a set $\Sigma = \Sigma_E \cup \Sigma_T$ of equality and tuple generating dependencies. This meaning is called the *completion of* r *w.r.t.* Σ, and it is denoted by $comp_\Sigma(r)$. If we think of the completion as a relation s, it should obviously satisfy the following three requirements (cf. [Mai83, p.182]).

(i) $r \subseteq s$,

(ii) $s \in Sat(\Sigma)$,

(iii) for any s' that satisfies (i) and (ii), $s \subseteq s'$.

The intuition is that we should increase the original information (requirement (i)), the completion should satisfy the dependencies (req. (ii)), and that the increase should be minimal (in the ordering of the lattice, requirement (iii)).

An alternative way of defining $comp_\Sigma(r)$ is through a set of recursive equations, in analogue with the fixpoint operator ψ on pages 14-15. Let

$$\Sigma \;=\; \{f_i(\uparrow m_i(R)) \subseteq g_i(\uparrow m_i(R)) : 1 \leq i \leq n\}.$$

Then $comp_\Sigma(r)$ is the smallest (w.r.t. $\subseteq$) solution to the equation set Φ, where

$$\Phi = \begin{cases} r \subseteq R \\ f_i(\uparrow m_i(R)) \subseteq g_i(\uparrow m_i(R)) \quad 1 \leq i \leq n. \end{cases}$$

We note that if the solution exist, it is unique, and if it does not exist, then the database is "inconsistent". The two specifications of the completion are obviously equivalent. Now we define the completion procedurally as

$$comp_\Sigma(r) = \begin{cases} \psi(g(\Sigma_T)_r) & \text{if } \psi(g(\Sigma_T)_r) \in Sat(\Sigma_E) \\ \text{does not exist} & \text{otherwise.} \end{cases}$$

If the completion does not exist, we say that the database is *inconsistent*. If the completion exists, it is finite. The mapping $g(\Sigma_T)_r$ is constructed from the set of tuple generating dependencies Σ_T as in the proof of Theorem 2.2. Consider the previous example. There $comp_{\{A \to\to B\}}(\{(a,b,c), (a,e,f)\}) = \{(a,b,c), (a,e,f), (a,b,f), (a,e,c)\}$, i.e. a relation that contains r and all the implied tuples. The relation s specified in the requirements (i) - (iii) is uniquely defined by $comp_\Sigma(r)$. For an example where the completion does not exist we add $C \to B$ to Σ in the example above. The initial relation satisfies $C \to B$, but the additional tuples cause a violation.

Theorem 2.4. For any set Σ of dependencies, and finite relation $r \in Rel(\alpha(\Sigma))$, if $comp_\Sigma(r)$ exists, then $comp_\Sigma(r)$ satisfies requirements (i) - (iii) above. If the completion does not exist, then there is no relation satisfying (i) - (iii).

Proof. Suppose the completion exists. Since $r \subseteq \psi(g(\Sigma_T)_r)$ (inductively by Lemma 2.2), requirement (i) is fulfilled. From the construction of the mapping $g(\Sigma_T)_r$ (see the proof of Theorem 2.2) it should be clear that $g_i(\psi(g(\Sigma_T)_r)) \subseteq \psi(g(\Sigma_T)_r)$, for any $g_i(R) \subseteq R \in \Sigma_T$. Thus $\psi(g(\Sigma_T)_r) \in Sat(\Sigma_T)$. By definition the completion is a member of $Sat(\Sigma_E)$. Obviously $Sat(\Sigma_T) \cap Sat(\Sigma_E) = Sat(\Sigma_T \cup \Sigma_E) = Sat(\Sigma)$. Consequently $comp_\Sigma(r) \in Sat(\Sigma)$; requirement (ii) is fulfilled. Suppose then that $s' \in Sat(\Sigma)$ and $r \subseteq s'$. By Theorem 2.2, $s' = \psi(g(\Sigma_T)_{s'})$. Since $r \subseteq s'$, Corollary 2.2 gives us $\psi(g(\Sigma_T)_r) \subseteq \psi(g(\Sigma_T)_{s'})$, which is requirement (iii).

For the second part of the proof, suppose that the completion does not exist, i.e. that $\psi(g(\Sigma_T)_r) \notin Sat(\Sigma_E)$. Suppose then to the contrary that a relation s satisfying (i) - (iii) exists. Thus $s \in Sat(\Sigma)$. Then, by Theorem 2.2, $s = \psi(g(\Sigma_T)_s)$. In particular $s \in Sat(\Sigma_E)$. Now $r \subseteq s$, so from Corollary 2.2 we conclude that $\psi(g(\Sigma_T)_r) \subseteq \psi(g(\Sigma_T)_s)$. By Theorem 2.3 $\psi(g(\Sigma_T)_r) \in Sat(\Sigma_E)$. But this is a contradiction. It means that no such relation s can exist. *Q.E.D.*

Given r and Σ, the relation $comp_\Sigma(r)$ can be computed in the following way. First, compute $s = \psi(g(\Sigma_T)_r)$, by folding. Then, for each $f_i(\uparrow^{n_i}(R)) \subseteq g_i(\uparrow^{n_i}(R)) \in \Sigma_E$, check whether $f_i(\uparrow^{n_i}(s)) \subseteq g_i(\uparrow^{n_i}(s))$. If some equality generating dependencies are not satisfied, the completion does not exist, otherwise it is s.

On the other hand, if we want to adopt a Prolog-like solution, i.e. if we choose not to store the deduced facts, these facts could be generated in connection with a query. Let $f(\boldsymbol{R})$ be the query, r a relation, and Σ the set of dependencies. Here $\alpha(r) = \alpha(\Sigma) = \alpha(R)$, where R is one of the relational variables in $\boldsymbol{R}$. When $f(\boldsymbol{R})$ is evaluated, we substitute R by $\psi(g(\Sigma_T)_r)$, and not by r. Thus we take all deduced facts into account. This approach has the disadvantage that it is possible that $\psi(g(\Sigma_T)_r) \notin Sat(\Sigma_E)$, even if $r \in Sat(\Sigma_E)$ (see the example on top of this page). Thus $\psi(g(\Sigma_T)_r)$ has to be computed anyway, if we want to detect possible inconsistencies before answering queries. We conclude that it is a better solution to store $\psi(g(\Sigma_T)_r)$. The problem is of course a classical time-space tradeoff situation. The frequency of queries versus updates should guide the choice in a particular application.

2.3. Updates to databases

For updating a relation there are three types of operations (see [AV84, Mai83]).

(i) *Insertions*. This means appending a tuple or a set of tuples to a relation.

(ii) *Deletions*. Suppress from a relation all tuples satisfying a given condition.

(iii) *Modifications*. Modify in a relation all tuples satisfying a given condition.

Since modifications can be achieved through a sequence of deletions and insertions, we shall be content with formalizing only insertions and deletions. Also, the insertion of a set of tuples can be achieved through a sequence of insertions of single tuples. Thus we restrict ourselves to insertions of single tuples.

In the insertion we want to add a tuple t to a relation r. Let ϕ be an equation of the form $\{t\} \subseteq R$, where $\alpha(t) = \alpha(r) = \alpha(R)$. The left-hand side of ϕ is really the constant mapping $f_{\{t\}}(R) = \{t\}$. The *insertion* into $r \in Rel(R)$ by ϕ is a relation $s \in Rel(R)$, such that

(i) $r \subseteq s$,

(ii) $s \in Sat(\phi)$, and

(iii) for any s' that fulfills (i) and (ii), $s \subseteq s'$.

Intuitively, condition (i) says that we should keep all the old information, condition (ii) that the new relation should satisfy the insertion equation, and the last condition means that we should insert as little as possible. If ϕ is the equation $\{t\} \subseteq R$ it is obvious that s is uniquely defined by $r \cup \{t\}$. This relation is denoted by $ins_\phi(r)$.

An alternative way of defining the insertion is through a set of equations. Then $r \cup \{t\}$ would be the smallest solution (w.r.t. $\subseteq$) to the set Φ below.

$$\Phi = \begin{cases} r \subseteq R \\ \{t\} \subseteq R. \end{cases}$$

In the deletion we want to suppress all tuples satisfying a condition E from a relation r. Consider an equation ϕ of the form $\sigma_E(R) \subseteq \emptyset$, where $\alpha(R) = \alpha(\emptyset) = R$. The right-hand side of ϕ is a shorthand for the constant mapping $g_\emptyset(R) = \emptyset$. Now the *deletion* from $r \in Rel(R)$ by ϕ is a relation $s \in Rel(R)$, such that

(i) $s \subseteq r$,

(ii) $s \in Sat(\phi)$, and

(iii) for any s' that fullfills (i) and (ii), $s' \subseteq s$.

The intuition of the conditions are similar to those of the insertion, except that we want to keep as much of the old information as possible. Requirements (i) -(iii) above obviously uniquely define the relation $del_\phi(r) = r - \sigma_E(r)$. Defined through a set of equations, $r - \sigma_E(r)$ is the unique largest (w.r.t. $\subseteq$) solution to Φ below.

$$\Phi = \begin{cases} r \subseteq R \\ \sigma_E(R) \subseteq \emptyset. \end{cases}$$

Updates in the presence of dependencies

In Section 2.2 we argued that if there is a set of dependencies defined for the scheme, then these dependencies must be regarded as a part of the database intension. The same is certainly true when it comes to updating the database. That is, the updated state should satisfy the dependencies. Of course we must assume that the old state does not violate the dependencies. In the case of insertions we can therefore reformulate the requirements as follows:

Let ϕ be an equation of the form $\{t\} \subseteq R$, and Σ a set of dependencies, where $\alpha(t) = \alpha(\Sigma) = \alpha(R) = R$. Let r be a relation on R, such that $r \in Sat(\Sigma)$. Then the *insertion* by ϕ to r *under* Σ is a relation $s \in Rel(R)$, such that

(i) $r \subseteq s$,

(ii) $s \in Sat(\phi)$,

(iii) $s \in Sat(\Sigma)$, and

(iv) for any s' that fulfils (i) - (iii), $s \subseteq s'$.

The result, denoted by $ins_\phi(r, \Sigma)$, will be $comp_\Sigma(r \cup \{t\})$, provided that the completion exists. Obviously $comp_\Sigma(r \cup \{t\})$ satisfies (i) - (iii). The minimality (req. (iv)) follows directly from Theorem 2.4. If the completion of $r \cup \{t\}$ does not exist, we can regard the insertion as *illegal*, since the addition of the tuple t has caused a violation of an equality generating dependency (in this case $ins_\phi(r, \Sigma)$ is undefined).

When we make a deletion in the presence of dependencies, we have the following requirements.

Let ϕ be an equation of the form $\sigma_E(R) \subseteq \emptyset$, and Σ a set of dependencies, where $\alpha(t) = \alpha(\Sigma) = \alpha(R) = R$. Let r be a relation on R, such that $r \in Sat(\Sigma)$. Then the *deletion* with ϕ from r *under* Σ is a relation $s \in Rel(R)$, such that

(i) $s \subseteq r$,

(ii) $s \in Sat(\phi)$,

(iii) $s \in Sat(\Sigma)$, and

(iv) for any s' that fulfils (i) - (iii), $s' \subseteq s$.

If s exists and is unique, it is denoted by $del_\phi(r, \Sigma)$. The problem is that there may be several incomparable relations satisfying (i) - (iv). Consider the relation r below. The set Σ of dependencies is {EMPLOYEE $\rightarrow\rightarrow$CHILD}. Intuitively, this means that the children of an employee are independent of the departments the employee works for.

r =

	EMPLOYEE	CHILD	DEPARTMENT
t_1	Jones	Sue	Toys
t_2	Jones	Bill	Cars
t_3	Jones	Sue	Cars
t_4	Jones	Bill	Toys

Now r satisfies Σ. Suppose we want to delete the fourth tuple, i.e. the fact "Bill is the child of Jones, and Jones works for the Toys department". The equation is

$$\sigma_{\text{EMPLOYEE=Jones} \wedge \text{CHILD=Bill} \wedge \text{DEPARTMENT=Toys}}(R) \subseteq \emptyset.$$

If we delete tuple t_4 only, the completion will reproduce that tuple. Thus we will have to delete the first or the second tuple also. This means that the result of the deletion is not uniquely defined, since both $\{t_1, t_3\}$ and $\{t_2, t_3\}$ satisfy (i) - (iv). Note that the problem does not appear if there are equality generating dependencies only.

In general, this problem can be seen as an instance of the view update problem. In our case the view would be $\pi_{\text{EMPLOYEE CHILD}}(r)*\pi_{\text{EMPLOYEE DEPARTMENT}}(r)$. The solution suggested in e.g. [BS81, CP84] is to give an additional constraint, called a complementary view, yielding uniqueness. We shall take another direction that will fit better into our framework.

Fagin, Mendelzon and Ullman [FMU82] argue that every relation in a real world application can be sufficiently constrained by a single join dependency and a set of functional dependencies. In particular, the join dependency is determined by how we explain the basic constituents of the relation. The following example is offered in [FMU82]. Suppose the attributes in a scheme are COURSE, TEACHER, ROOM, HOUR, STUDENT, and GRADE, and that the informal description of a tuple (c, t, r, h, s ,g) on these attributes is t "teaches" c, c "meets in" r "at hour" h, and s "is getting" g "in" c. The informal description is seen as a definition of three abstract predicates, such as "teaches", and these predicates determine the parts of a tuple that is an "irreducible" fact. Now a relation can be defined by some values of these predicates exactly when it satisfies the join dependency *[COURSE TEACHER, COURSE ROOM HOUR, COURSE STUDENT GRADE]. The attribute sets COURSE TEACHER, COURSE ROOM HOUR, and COURSE STUDENT GRADE are called the *objects* of the join dependency.

Let us return to our example. The dependency EMPLOYEE →→CHILD is equivalent to the join dependency *[EMPLOYEE CHILD, EMPLOYEE DEPARTMENT]. The objects of the join dependency are EMPLOYEE CHILD, and EMPLOYEE DEPARTMENT. This means that a tuple (e, c, d) has the informal description c "is a child of" e, and e "works for" d. If we want to delete that fact "Bill is the child of Jones, and Jones works for the Toys department", it is not clear if we want to delete Bill "is a child of" Jones, or Jones "works for" Toys. If we delete the second and the fourth tuple, we delete the "is a child of" fact, and if we delete the first and the fourth tuple, we delete the "works for" fact. To obtain uniqueness, we shall therefore require that a deletion *specifies an object* for the join dependency. (We note that the choice of the so called view complement in the method of [BS81] determines which of the two facts is to be deleted.) In general, the above means that if the join dependency is $*[R_1,\ldots,R_n]$, and the deletion equation is $\sigma_E(R) \subseteq \emptyset$, then E is of the forrm

$$\bigwedge_{A_j \in R_i} (A_j = a_j), \text{ for some i, where } 1 \leq i \leq n.$$

In our example database this would correspond to the deletion of facts of the type "c is a child of e" and facts of the type "e works for d". We can now state

Theorem 2.5. Let Σ consist of a join dependency $*[R_1,\ldots,R_n]$, and a set of equality generating dependencies, and let ϕ be an equation $\sigma_E(R) \subseteq \emptyset$, where E specifies an object for the join dependency. If r is a relation in *Sat*(Σ), then $\sigma_{\neg E}(r)$ is the unique result of the deletion by ϕ from r under Σ.

Proof. Suppose that E specifies an object on R_i, for some i. We shall show that the requirements (i) - (iv) hold. The first two requirements are obviously satisfied. For (iii), suppose that $\sigma_{\neg E}(r)$ is not in *Sat*(Σ). Since $\sigma_{\neg E}(r)$ is a subset of r, and since r is in *Sat*(Σ), it follows from Theorem 2.3 that $\sigma_{\neg E}(r)$ satisfies all equality generating dependencies in Σ. If $\sigma_{\neg E}(r)$ is not in *Sat*(Σ) it must then violate the join dependency $*[R_1,\ldots,R_n]$, meaning that $\pi_{R_1}(\sigma_{\neg E}(r))*\ldots*\pi_{R_n}(\sigma_{\neg E}(r)) \not\subset \sigma_{\neg E}(r)$.

Let t be a in tuple $\pi_{R_1}(\sigma_{\neg E}(r))*\ldots*\pi_{R_n}(\sigma_{\neg E}(r)) - \sigma_{\neg E}(r)$. Since $\sigma_{\neg E}(r)$ is a subset of r, it follows from the monotonicity of the Project-Join expression that $\pi_{R_1}(\sigma_{\neg E}(r))*\ldots*\pi_{R_n}(\sigma_{\neg E}(r))$ is a subset of $\pi_{R_1}(r)*\ldots*\pi_{R_n}(r)$. Since r is in *Sat*($\Sigma$), we have $\pi_{R_1}(r)*\ldots*\pi_{R_n}(r) \subseteq r$. Thus the tuple t is in r. Since we assumed that t is not in $\sigma_{\neg E}(r)$, it must be the case that $\neg E(t)$ is **false**. We can now derive a contradiction, since the assumption that t is in $\pi_{R_1}(\sigma_{\neg E}(r))*\ldots*\pi_{R_n}(\sigma_{\neg E}(r))$ implies that there is a tuple t_i in $\pi_{R_i}(\sigma_{\neg E}(r))$, such that $t(R_i) = t_i$. Now $t_i \in \pi_{R_i}(\sigma_{\neg E}(r))$ means that there is a tuple u in $\sigma_{\neg E}(r)$, such that $u(R_i) = t_i = t(R_i)$. Since u is in $\sigma_{\neg E}(r)$, it must be the case that $\neg E(u)$ = **true**. But the selection expression E involves exactly the attributes of R_i, and $\neg E(t)$ = **false,** $t(R_i) = u(R_i)$; a contradiction. We conclude that $\sigma_{\neg E}(r)$ therefore must satisfy the join dependency. Consequently $\sigma_{\neg E}(r) \in$ *Sat*(Σ).

To show maximality (req. (iv)), suppose that there is a relation s' that satisfies (i) - (iii). In particular we have $s' \subseteq r$, and consequently $\sigma_{\neg E}(s') \subseteq \sigma_{\neg E}(r)$. Since s' is in *Sat*($\phi$), we have $\sigma_{\neg E}(s') = s'$. Thus $s' \subseteq \sigma_{\neg E}(r)$. *Q.E.D.*

Corollary 2.3. Let r, ϕ and Σ be as in Theorem 2.5. Then $comp_\Sigma(\sigma_{\neg E}(r)) = \sigma_{\neg E}(r)$.

The situation where the update objects are defined independently of the join dependency is studied in among others [BrVo84, Sci81].

2.4. Computational complexity

We shall now look at the complexity of query evaluation, dependency enforcement and update operations. We shall see that all of these operations can be done in time polynomial in the size of the database extension. This measure is called *data complexity* [Var82]. It assumes that the length of the operation in question is fixed, i.e. that we have a fixed size query, a fixed set of dependencies, or an update operation of fixed size.

The motivation for considering data complexity is that the size of the database extension is the dominating factor in any application. Also, in a particular application, once the scheme is defined the arities of the relations are fixed. The length of a query is closely related to the arities of the relations. With respect to dependencies, we argue that the set of dependencies is time-invariant, and thus fixed, while the extension of the database changes with time. In the update operations we typically insert one tuple, or make a deletion according to a fixed size selection condition.

In the sequel we shall use the following notation: Let r be a relation. Then $|r|$ stands for the number of tuples in r. If we have a multirelation $\mathbf{r} = \langle r_1, \ldots, r_n \rangle$, then $|\mathbf{r}| = |r_1| + \ldots + |r_n|$. We assume that all relations and multirelations are finite.

Query evaluation

Theorem 2.6. Let Ω be the set of all PSUJRDY-expressions. Then for all multirelations $\mathbf{r}$, and $f \in \Omega$, the answer $f(\mathbf{r})$ can be computed in time polynomial in $|\mathbf{r}|$.

Proof. Let k denote the sum of the arities in the relations in $\mathbf{r}$. Since the mapping f does not introduce any new values, there are at most $|\mathbf{r}|^k$ candidate tuples for $f(\mathbf{r})$ (k is the sum of the arities of the relations in $\mathbf{r}$, and thus k is fixed). For each candidate tuple t, we test if $t \in f(\mathbf{r})$. The time it takes to do this test is polynomial in $|\mathbf{r}|$ [CH82, Var82]. *Q.E.D.*

From a practical viewpoint efficient query evaluation is a question of transforming the query into a form that eases the evaluation (query optimization), and of choosing suitable indices. See [Ull82] for a discussion of these topics. For least fixpoint queries there now exists a variety of algorithms, each being suitable for particular types of least fixpoint queries. The reader is referred to [BR86].

Dependency enforcement

Theorem 2.7. For all relations r and sets of dependencies Σ, with $\alpha(r) = \alpha(\Sigma)$, the relation $comp_\Sigma(r)$ can be computed in time polynomial in $|r|$.

Proof. Let $\Sigma = \Sigma_T \cup \Sigma_E$, where Σ_T is the set of tuple generating, and Σ_E is the set of equality generating dependencies. As suggested on page 24, we first compute $lfp(g(\Sigma_T)_r)$ (the notation is explained on page 21). By Theorem 2.6, $s = lfp(g(\Sigma_T)_r)$ can be computed in time polynomial in $|r|$. Then we check if $s \in Sat(\Sigma_E)$, i.e. for each $f_i(\uparrow m_i(R)) \subseteq g_i(\uparrow m_i(R)) \in \Sigma_E$, we check whether $f_i(\uparrow m_i(s)) \subseteq g_i(\uparrow m_i(s))$. It follows directly from Theorem 2.6 that this test can be done in time polynomial in $|lfp(g(\Sigma_T)_r)|$. Since there is a fixed number of equality generating dependencies, $lfp(g(\Sigma_T)_r) \in Sat(\Sigma_E)$ can be tested in time polynomial in $|lfp\ g(\Sigma_T)_r)|$. Since $|lfp(g(\Sigma_T)_r)|$ is polynomial in $|r|$, the whole process can be carried out in time polynomial in $|r|$.
Q.E.D.

In practice the most important dependencies are the functional ones [FMU82]. In this case we propose the following algorithm. Let Σ stand for a set of functional dependencies. We want to know if a given relation r satisfies Σ.

For each $X \rightarrow Y \in \Sigma$ we sort the relation r on its X-columns to bring tuples with equal X-values together. If no set of tuples with equal X-values has unequal Y-values, then $r \in Sat(\Sigma)$, otherwise $r \notin Sat(\Sigma)$. Since sorting takes time proportional to $|r| \cdot \log(|r|)$, the whole process can obviously be carried out in time $O(|\Sigma| \cdot |r| \cdot \log(|r|))$. If we regard Σ as fixed, the time complexity will be $O(|r| \cdot \log(|r|))$.

Update operations

Theorem 2.8. For all relations r, and equations ϕ of the form $\{t\} \subseteq R$, and equations γ of the form $\sigma_E(R) \subseteq \emptyset$, the relations $ins_\phi(r)$ and $del_\gamma(r)$ can be computed in time linear in $|r|$.

Proof. Obviously $ins_\phi(r) = r \cup \{t\}$ can be computed in time $O(|r|)$. We simply scan through r to see if the tuple t is already there. If the tuple t is not found, it is added. Thus the time spent is $O(|r|)$.

The deletion operation is defined by $del_\gamma(r) = \sigma_{\neg E}(r)$, which we can compute in time $O(|r|)$. We scan through r and delete all tuples t for which E(t) = **true**. E(t) can be evaluated in time polynomial in the length of E, i.e. in constant time. The total time is thus $O(|r|)$. *Q.E.D.*

When we take the dependencies into account, we note that under the restrictions of Theorem 2.5, the result of the deletion is still $\sigma_{\neg E}(r)$. Thus the time complexity remains the same. For the insertions the result is given by $comp_{\Sigma}$ $(r \cup \{t\})$. It follows from Theorem 2.7 and 2.8 that this set can be computed in time polynomial in $|r|$.

Corollary 2.4. For all relations r, and equations ϕ of the form $\{t\} \subseteq R$, and equations γ of the form $\sigma_E(R) \subseteq \emptyset$, and sets Σ consisting of one join dependency and a set of equality generating dependencies, the relation $ins_{\phi}(r, \Sigma)$ can be computed in time polynomial in $|r|$, and the relation $del_{\gamma}(r, \Sigma)$ can be computed in time linear in $|r|$, provided that the selection formula E specifies an object for the join dependency.

3. Semantic aspects of incomplete information

This chapter lays the foundation for treating incomplete information. We introduce the necessary semantic concepts for databases containing incomplete information. We define incomplete information databases, and two types of answers to queries applied to such databases. There will be two different lattices in incomplete information databases. The completion of an incomplete information database w.r.t. a set of dependencies is an operation on one of the lattices. Update operations can be defined on both lattices, thus capturing distinct intuitions.

This chapter is a generalization of Chapter 2 for the case of incomplete information databases.

3.1. Incomplete databases and queries

Basic notions

On the semantic level an incomplete database is a set of possible (complete) databases, one of which corresponds to the true state of the real world. For an intuitive justification of this interpretation we give a simple example of a relation containing syntactic characters "ω", denoting null-values of the type "value exists, but is unknown".

NAME	ACTIVITY
Toto	Siesta
Lulu	ω
ω	Music

The intended meaning of this kindergarten database is that Toto is taking part in the Siesta activity, Lulu is involved in some activity, but we do not know which one, and there is someone with an unknown name playing music. If we now assume that the domain of the attribute NAME is {Toto, Lulu, Zaza}, and *Dom*(ACTIVITY) = {Siesta, Music}, and furthermore that the symbol "ω" stands for an unknown value from the domain of the corresponding attribute, the database can be seen as a shorthand for the following set of possible states of the real world (cf. the "null- substitution principle" in [Cod79]). (To save space, we abbreviate NAME and ACTIVITY by N and A, and we use t, l, z, s and m for the various names and activities.)

NA	NA	NA	NA	NA	NA
t s	t s	t s	t s	t s	t s
l s	l s	l s	l m	l m	l m
t m	l m	z m	t m	z m	

One of the relations in this set corresponds to the true state of the real world, but our knowledge is restricted to the set. In the case where the set happens to be a singleton we have an ordinary (complete) database.

We shall denote sets of relations by $\mathcal{X}$, $\mathcal{Y}$, ..., and sets of multirelations by $\mathcal{X}$, $\mathcal{Y}$, ... The set of all sets of multirelations on a scheme **R** is denoted by *Inc*(**R**). Obviously *Inc*(**R**) is the powerset of *Rel*(**R**). For an $\mathcal{X} \in$ *Inc*(**R**), we define $\alpha(\mathcal{X})$ = **R.** Note that an incomplete database $\mathcal{X}$ can contain infinitely many elements (as a consequence of the infinite domains). A finite or an infinite set of incomplete databases of the same type is denoted by $\{\mathcal{X}_i : i \in I\}$, where I is a finite or an infinite index set. In our examples we shall usually use finite sets of finite relations. Then the incomplete database is listed either in tabular form, as above, or in set form, e.g. $\mathcal{X} = \{\{(a,b), (a,c)\}, \{(a,e)\}\}$ contains two relations consisting of two tuples and one tuple, respectively.

Querying an incomplete database

What is now the answer to a query f(***R***) applied to an incomplete database $\mathcal{X}$? Since our knowledge of the real world is represented by $\mathcal{X}$, it is quite natural that the knowledge of the answer to a query f is represented by the set

(1) $\{f(\mathbf{r}) : \mathbf{r} \in \mathcal{X}\}$,

as defined in [IL84]. This is the *elementwise extension* of the query f. The set (1) is called the *possible answer*, and it will be denoted by f($\mathcal{X}$). To put (1) differently, we get a set of possible answers, each computed from one possible state of the real world. Thus the answer is another incomplete database, just as the answer to a relational query in the complete case is a relation. This means that the mapping f(***R***) : *Rel*(α(f)) $\rightarrow$ *Rel*(β(f)) is generalized to a mapping f : *Inc*(α(f)) $\rightarrow$ *Inc*(β(f)). Thus the elementwise extension of the answer to a query defines a query on incomplete databases. To emphasize that the variable ***R*** now ranges over sets of relations, we shall sometimes use the notation $\underline{\boldsymbol{R}}$. That is, $\underline{\boldsymbol{R}}$ is a variable ranging over *Inc*($\alpha(\underline{\boldsymbol{R}})$), where $\alpha(\underline{\boldsymbol{R}}) = \alpha(\boldsymbol{R})$.

As an illustration of the possible answer, consider the kindergarten database above. If we want to know the activities of Toto, we apply the selection $\sigma_{N=Toto}(\underline{R})$, $\alpha(\underline{R})$ = NA. The answer is given below.

NA	NA
t s	t s
t m	

From this we see that no matter what the true state of the real world is, Toto is involved in the Siesta activity. This observation motivates the notion of the *certain answer*. The certain answer is given by

(2) $\bigcap_{\mathbf{r} \in \mathcal{X}} f(\mathbf{r})$,

denoted by $\cap f(\mathcal{X})$ ([IL84]). The certain answer contains the tuples that are in f(**r**), no matter which **r** happens to be the true state of the real world.[1] Since $f(\mathcal{X})$ is a set of elements in the lattice of complete relations, we regard the certain answer as an approximation from below, i.e. as $glb(f(\mathcal{X}))$, which is equal to $\cap f(\mathcal{X})$. [2]

In a complete database the answer f(**r**) is equal to the declaratively characterized set $\|\phi_f\|_{\mathbf{r}} = \{t : \mathbf{r} \models \phi(t)\}$, by the Codd completeness theorem [Cod72b]. Here **r** is interpreted as a structure, and ϕ_f is the calculus query equivalent to the algebraic query f (f_ϕ will denote the algebraic query equivalent to a calculus query ϕ). In the incomplete case we have a set $\mathcal{X}$ of structures, and the certain and possible answers to queries. We shall sketch a declarative characterization of the answers. The characterization will be in a "modal" fashion.

A *modal structure* is a couple $<\mathcal{X}, \mathbf{r}>$, where $\mathcal{X}$ is a set of relations, and **r** is a member of $\mathcal{X}$. We say that a sentence ϕ is true in a modal structure $<\mathcal{X}, \mathbf{r}>$, denoted by $<\mathcal{X}, \mathbf{r}> \models \phi$, if $\mathbf{r} \models \phi$.

The sentence ϕ is *surely* true in a modal structure $<\mathcal{X}, \mathbf{r}>$, denoted by $<\mathcal{X}, \mathbf{r}> \models \Box(\phi)$, if $\mathbf{s} \models \phi$, for all **s** in $\mathcal{X}$. Obviously ϕ is surely true in $<\mathcal{X}, \mathbf{r}>$ if and only if ϕ is surely true in all structures $<\mathcal{X}, \mathbf{s}>$, where **s** is in $\mathcal{X}$. Thus the parameter **r** is irrelevant in this case.

The sentence ϕ is *maybe* true in $<\mathcal{X}, \mathbf{r}>$, denoted by $<\mathcal{X}, \mathbf{r}> \models \Diamond(\phi)$, if $\mathbf{s} \models \phi$, for at least one **s** in $\mathcal{X}$. We see that the parameter **r** is irrelevant in this case also.

We can now define the answer to a calculus query $x.\phi(x)$ on an incomplete database $\mathcal{X}$. The *sure* answer is

$$_*\|\phi\|_{\mathcal{X}} = \{t : <\mathcal{X}, \mathbf{r}> \models \Box(\phi(t))\},$$

---

[1] Note that if $\mathcal{X} = \emptyset$, then $f(\mathcal{X}) = \emptyset$ and consequently $\cap f(\mathcal{X}) = r_\infty$, where $\alpha(r_\infty) = \beta(f)$.

[2] Note that $\bigcap_{\mathbf{r} \in \mathcal{X}} f(\mathbf{r})$ is <u>not</u> in general equal to $f(\bigcap_{\mathbf{r} \in \mathcal{X}} \mathbf{r})$. As an example, take $\mathcal{X} = \{\{(a,b)\}, \{(a,c)\}\}$, $\alpha(\mathcal{X}) = AB$. Then $\bigcap_{\mathbf{r} \in \mathcal{X}} \pi_A(\mathbf{r}) = \{(a)\}$, while $\pi_A(\bigcap_{\mathbf{r} \in \mathcal{X}} \mathbf{r}) = \emptyset$.

and the *maybe* answer is

$$^{*}\|\phi\|_{\mathcal{X}} = \{t : \langle \mathcal{X}, r\rangle \models \Diamond(\phi(t))\}.$$

The sure answer is obviously equal to the certain answer $\cap f_{\phi}(\mathcal{X})$, and the maybe answer is equal to $\cup f_{\phi}(\mathcal{X}) = \bigcup_{r \in \mathcal{X}} f_{\phi}(r)$. But note that the maybe answer is a set of tuples, and that some of the tuples come from different possible relations in $\mathcal{X}$. Thus some information is lost in the maybe answer. To recover this information, we can refine the maybe answer to the *exact* answer, denoted by $\|\phi\|_{\mathcal{X}}$, and defined as

$$\|\phi\|_{\mathcal{X}} = \{\{t : \langle \mathcal{X}, r\rangle \models \phi(t)\} : r \in \mathcal{X}\}.$$

The exact answer is obviously what we in the elementwise extension called the possible answer, i.e.

$$\|\phi\|_{\mathcal{X}} = f_{\phi}(\mathcal{X}).$$

The structure of incomplete information

We are now ready to start the construction of the promised two lattices. We begin by studying the question of when a database is more (or less) incomplete than another database. Thus we need some partial orders. The first intuition is that a database $\mathcal{X}$ is more incomplete than a database $\mathcal{Y}$, if $\mathcal{X}$ contains <u>more possible states</u> of the real world, i.e. if each element of $\mathcal{Y}$ is an element of $\mathcal{X}$.

Formally, let $\mathcal{X}$ and $\mathcal{Y}$ be in *Inc* (**R**), for some **R**. Then we say that $\mathcal{X}$ is (absolutely) *less informative* than $\mathcal{Y}$, denoted by $\mathcal{X} < \mathcal{Y}$, if $\mathcal{Y} \subseteq \mathcal{X}$. If we have both $\mathcal{X} < \mathcal{Y}$ and $\mathcal{Y} < \mathcal{X}$, then $\mathcal{X}$ and $\mathcal{Y}$ are (absolutely) *equivalent*. This fact is denoted by $\mathcal{X} = \mathcal{Y}$. It is indeed an equivalence relation, since $\mathcal{X} = \mathcal{Y}$ means that $\mathcal{X}$ and $\mathcal{Y}$ are the same set.

The containment $\subseteq$ is obviously antisymmetric, transitive and reflexive; thus the relationship $<$ is a partial order.[1] Furthermore, for a set $\{\mathcal{X}_i : i \in I\}$ of incomplete databases, the least upperbound is $\bigcap_{i \in I} \mathcal{X}_i = \{\mathbf{r} : \mathbf{r} \in \mathcal{X}_i \text{ for all } i \in I\}$ and the greatest lower bound is $\bigcup_{i \in I} \mathcal{X}_i = \{\mathbf{r} : \mathbf{r} \in \mathcal{X}_i \text{ for some } i \in I\}$. It is also easy to see that $\mathcal{X} < \emptyset$, and that $Rel(\mathbf{R}) < \mathcal{X}$, for any $\mathcal{X}$ in *Inc* (**R**). The top element is thus $\emptyset$, and the bottom element is $Rel(\mathbf{R})$.

---

[1] In the sequel we shall repeatedly make use of the following obvious fact: If $\mathcal{Y} \subseteq \mathcal{X}$, then $\cap\mathcal{X} \subseteq \cap\mathcal{Y}$.

We have argued our way to the following result.

Theorem 3.1. For any **R**, the couple $\langle Inc(\mathbf{R}), < \rangle$ is a complete lattice.

An example of a lattice $\langle Inc(\mathrm{R}), < \rangle$ is given in Figure 3.2 on page 42.

The partial order < is defined in terms of the elements of the databases. We shall now look for a more semantic characterization of $\langle Inc\ (\mathbf{R}), < \rangle$, i.e. a characterization of < in terms of the information content of the databases. Consider databases $\mathcal{X}$ and $\mathcal{Y}$. If any query posed to $\mathcal{X}$ produces as certain answer a subset of the certain answer obtained from $\mathcal{Y}$, we have good justification for saying that $\mathcal{X}$ is less informative than $\mathcal{Y}$.

Formalized, and relativized to a set of operations Ω, we get the following: Let $\mathcal{X}$ and $\mathcal{Y}$ be in $Inc(\mathbf{R})$, for some **R**. Then $\mathcal{X}$ is said to be Ω-*less* than $\mathcal{Y}$, if for all Ω-expressions f, with $\alpha(f) = \mathbf{R}$, it is true that $\cap f(\mathcal{X}) \subseteq \cap f(\mathcal{Y})$. The relationship is denoted by $\mathcal{X} <_{\Omega} \mathcal{Y}$.

The relationship $<_{\Omega}$ is a quasiorder since it obviously is reflexive and transitive. It is however <u>not</u> antisymmetric, as can be seen from the following example. Let $\mathcal{X}$ be $\{\{(a,b)\}, \{(a,d)\}\}$, and $\mathcal{Y}$ be $\{\{(a,d)\}, \{(a,e)\}\}$, with $\alpha(\mathcal{X}) = \alpha(\mathcal{Y}) = AB$. Now $\mathcal{X} \neq \mathcal{Y}$, but as it is easily seen, any P-expression produces at most $\{(a)\}$ as a certain answer (for example, the P-expression $\pi_A(AB)$). It is not a difficult exercise to formally prove that $\cap f(\mathcal{X}) = \cap f(\mathcal{Y})$, for all P-expressions f. Thus we have $\mathcal{X} <_P \mathcal{Y}$, and $\mathcal{Y} <_P \mathcal{X}$. Since $\mathcal{X} \neq \mathcal{Y}$ we have produced a counter example to the antisymmetricity of $<_{\Omega}$.

If both $\mathcal{X} <_{\Omega} \mathcal{Y}$ and $\mathcal{Y} <_{\Omega} \mathcal{X}$, we say that $\mathcal{X}$ and $\mathcal{Y}$ are Ω-*equivalent*. This fact is denoted by $\equiv_{\Omega}$. Since $<_{\Omega}$ is reflexive and transitive, $\equiv_{\Omega}$ is also reflexive and transitive. By definition $\equiv_{\Omega}$ is symmetric. The relationship $\equiv_{\Omega}$ is thus an equivalence relation. (We make here the bibliographic note that $\equiv_{\Omega}$ was introduced in [IL84], but without any reference to $<_{\Omega}$.)

The relationship $<_{\Omega}$ is a quasiorder, but not a partial order. There is something to be rescued though. In the case where Ω is PSUJRD we get a partial order. The following theorem will be needed.

Theorem 3.2. Let $\mathcal{X}$ and $\mathcal{Y}$ be in $Inc(\mathbf{R})$, for some **R**. Then $\mathcal{X} <_{PSUJRD} \mathcal{Y}$ if and only if $\mathcal{X} < \mathcal{Y}$.

Proof. *(If)*. Suppose $\mathcal{X} < \mathcal{Y}$, i.e. $\mathcal{Y} \subseteq \mathcal{X}$. Let f be a PSUJRD-expression. We have $f(\mathcal{Y}) \subseteq f(\mathcal{X})$, and thus $\cap f(\mathcal{X}) \subseteq \cap f(\mathcal{Y})$, which is the claim.

(Only if). Without loss of generality we prove the claim for sets of unirelations $\mathcal{X}$ and $\mathcal{Y}$ in $Inc(\mathrm{R})$, for some R. Suppose that $\mathcal{X} \not< \mathcal{Y}$, i.e. that $\mathcal{Y} \not\subseteq \mathcal{X}$. We shall show that $\mathcal{X} \not<_{PSUJRD} \mathcal{Y}$.

Since $\mathcal{Y} \not\subset \mathcal{X}$, there is a relation r in $\mathcal{Y} - \mathcal{X}$. Suppose $r = \{t_1,..., t_n\}$, $n \geq 0$. We construct an expression f(*R*), such that for all $s \in Rel(R)$

$$(3) \qquad f(s) = \begin{cases} \varepsilon & \text{if } r \neq s \\ \emptyset & \text{if } r = s. \end{cases}$$

If r = ø, then f(*R*) is $\pi_\emptyset(R)$. Then clearly (3) holds.

Suppose $r = \{t_1, ..., t_n\}$, $n \geq 1$. Then, by $\sigma_{t_i}(R)$ we mean a selection expression that picks the tuple t_i, i.e. the formula is $(A_1=t_i(A_1) \wedge ... \wedge A_k=t_i(A_k))$ (assuming $R = A_1... A_k$). Now

$$(4) \qquad f(R) = \varepsilon - \Big((\pi_\emptyset(\sigma_{t_1}(R)) \cap ... \cap \pi_\emptyset(\sigma_{t_n}(R))) \cap (\varepsilon - \pi_\emptyset(\sigma_{\neg t_1 \wedge ... \wedge \neg t_n}(R))) \Big).$$

The verification of (3) is a mechanical exercise, and thus omitted.

Note that f(*R*) is a PSJD-expression, and thus a PSUJRD-expression. We return to the original claim that $\mathcal{X} \not<_{PSUJRD} \mathcal{Y}$. This follows from the fact that $\cap f(\mathcal{Y}) = f(r) \cap (\cap(f(\mathcal{Y} - \{r\}))) = \emptyset$. On the other hand, $\cap f(\mathcal{X}) = \varepsilon$. Thus $\cap f(\mathcal{X}) \not\subset \cap f(\mathcal{Y})$. *Q.E.D.*

Corollary 3.1. Let $\mathcal{X}$ and $\mathcal{Y}$ be in *Inc*(**R**), for some **R**. Then $\mathcal{X} = \mathcal{Y}$ if and only if $\mathcal{X} \equiv_{PSUJRD} \mathcal{Y}$.

This corollary can be seen as a characterization of the power of the relational algebra. (It is a sort of completeness theorem for the relational algebra w.r.t. incomplete databases.) The next corollary returns us to the lattice world.

Corollary 3.2. For any **R**, the couple $\langle Inc(\mathbf{R}), <_{PSUJRD} \rangle$ is a complete lattice. For a set $\{\mathcal{X}_i : i \in I\}$ of databases $\mathcal{X}_i$ in *Inc*(**R**), $glb(\{\mathcal{X}_i : i \in I\}) = \bigcup_{i \in I} \mathcal{X}_i$, and $lub(\{\mathcal{X}_i : i \in I\}) = \bigcap_{i \in I} \mathcal{X}_i$. The top element is Ø, and the bottom element is *Rel*(**R**).

The PSUJRD-expressions cover the whole relational algebra. There is though a special interest in *positive* expressions. We define a positive expression to be any PSUJR-expression. Note that we do allow negations in the selection formulas.

We are interested in the quasiordering $<_{PSUJR}$. Intuitively $\mathcal{X} <_{PSUJR} \mathcal{Y}$ means that $\mathcal{X}$ contains less positive information than $\mathcal{Y}$. To begin with, we are going to give a set theoretic characterization of $\mathcal{X} <_{PSUJR} \mathcal{Y}$. The characterization is the elementwise version of the quasiorder $<_{PSUJR}$, and it will ease various proofs.

Let us compare the incomplete databases

$\mathcal{X} =$	A	A	and	$\mathcal{Y} =$	A	A
	a	b			a	b
					d	d

It seems clear that $\mathcal{Y}$ in some sense contains more information than $\mathcal{X}$, but w.r.t. the absolute ordering $\mathcal{X}$ and $\mathcal{Y}$ are incomparable. To capture the intuition we define the following quasiorder.

Let $\mathcal{X}$ and $\mathcal{Y}$ be in *Inc*(**R**), for some **R**. Then $\mathcal{X}$ is said to be *+-less* than $\mathcal{Y}$, if for all $s \in \mathcal{Y}$, there is an $\mathbf{r} \in \mathcal{X}$, such that $\mathbf{r} \subseteq \mathbf{s}$. The relationship is denoted by $\mathcal{X} <_+ \mathcal{Y}$, and it is obviously a quasiorder.

We say that $\mathcal{X}$ is *+-equivalent* to $\mathcal{Y}$, if $\mathcal{X} <_+ \mathcal{Y}$ and $\mathcal{Y} <_+ \mathcal{X}$. This fact is denoted by $\mathcal{X} \equiv_+ \mathcal{Y}$. The +-equivalence is indeed an equivalence relation on *Inc*(**R**). The reflexivity, transitivity and symmetricity of $\equiv_+$ follows directly from the definitions.

Returning to the intuitive viewpoint, the $\mathcal{X} <_+ \mathcal{Y}$ order is interpreted as $\mathcal{Y}$ being more precise than $\mathcal{X}$, since a subset of every possibility in $\mathcal{Y}$ occurs in $\mathcal{X}$. This means that w.r.t. what <u>is</u> in $\mathcal{Y}$ and what <u>is</u> in $\mathcal{X}$, $\mathcal{Y}$ is more precise. Note that this does not mean that $\mathcal{Y}$ has to be more precise when it comes to the question of what is <u>not</u> in the database. Thus we can expect to get more information from $\mathcal{Y}$ than from $\mathcal{X}$ when a certain answer to a positive query is evaluated. The next theorem verifies this intuition.

Theorem 3.3. Let $\mathcal{X}$ and $\mathcal{Y}$ be in *Inc*(**R**), for some **R**. Then $\mathcal{X} <_+ \mathcal{Y}$ if and only if $\mathcal{X} <_{PSUJR} \mathcal{Y}$.

Proof. Without loss of generality we prove the claim for sets of unirelations $\mathcal{X}$ and $\mathcal{Y}$ in *Inc*(R).

(*Only if*). For each $s \in \mathcal{Y}$ we denote by h(s) the relation in $\mathcal{X}$ which is contained in s. Since h(s) is not uniquely defined we choose one of the contained relations in $\mathcal{X}$ to be h(s). Let f be an arbitrary PSUJR-expression. Now $\cap f(\mathcal{Y}) = \cap_{s \in \mathcal{Y}} f(s) \supseteq \cap_{s \in \mathcal{Y}} f(h(s)) \supseteq \cap_{r \in \mathcal{X}} f(r) = \cap f(\mathcal{X})$. The first containment follows from the fact that any PSUJR-expression is monotonous. (If $\mathcal{Y} = \emptyset$, then $\cap f(\mathcal{Y}) = r_\infty \supseteq \cap f(\mathcal{X})$.)

(*If*). Suppose that $\mathcal{X}$ is <u>not</u> $<_+$-less than $\mathcal{Y}$. This means that there is a relation $s \in \mathcal{Y}$, such that s contains no relation in $\mathcal{X}$. Let $s = \{t_1,\ldots,t_n\}$, $n \geq 0$. We define f(*R*) to be the expression

(5) $\pi_{\emptyset}(\sigma_{\neg t_1 \vee \ldots \vee \neg t_n}(R))$.

If s=ø, then $f(R) = \pi_{\emptyset}(R)$. The meaning of the selection formula is similar to the one in the proof of Theorem 3.2. Now

$$(6) \qquad f(r) = \begin{cases} \emptyset & \text{if } r \subseteq s \\ \varepsilon & \text{if } r \not\subseteq s. \end{cases}$$

We see that $\cap f(\mathcal{X}) = \varepsilon$, and that $\cap f(\mathcal{Y}) = \emptyset$. Thus $\mathcal{X}$ is <u>not</u> PSURJ-less than $\mathcal{Y}$. *Q.E.D.*

Corollary 3.3. Let $\mathcal{X}$ and $\mathcal{Y}$ be in *Inc*(**R**), for some **R**. Then $\mathcal{X} \equiv_+ \mathcal{Y}$ if and only if $\mathcal{X} \equiv_{PSUJR} \mathcal{Y}$.

In the process of constructing a lattice we shall identify equivalent elements. For this purpose we denote by $|\mathcal{X}|_{\equiv_+}$ the equivalence class of $\mathcal{X}$, i.e. the set $\{\mathcal{Y} : \mathcal{Y} \equiv_+ \mathcal{X}\}$. Similarly, the *quotient set* of *Inc*(**R**) is denoted by $Inc(\mathbf{R})/_{\equiv_+}$. The quotient set has as elements the equivalence classes generated by the members of *Inc*(**R**). In order not to complicate the notation too much, we shall omit the subscript $\equiv_+$ from the equivalence classes. Thus $|\mathcal{X}|_{\equiv_+}$ is simply denoted by $|\mathcal{X}|$.

Then we define a relation $<_+$ on $Inc(\mathbf{R})/_{\equiv_+}$. We will have $|\mathcal{X}| <_+ |\mathcal{Y}|$ if $\mathcal{X} <_+ \mathcal{Y}$. Since $<_+$ is reflexive and transitive, the relationship $<_+$ on equivalence classes is reflexive and transitive. To see that $<_+$ is antisymmetric, suppose that $|\mathcal{X}| <_+ |\mathcal{Y}|$ and $|\mathcal{Y}| <_+ |\mathcal{X}|$. Then $\mathcal{X} <_+ \mathcal{Y}$ and $\mathcal{Y} <_+ \mathcal{X}$. Thus $\mathcal{X} \equiv_+ \mathcal{Y}$, and so $|\mathcal{X}| = |\mathcal{Y}|$. This means that $<_+$ is a partial order.

The least upper bound will be defined through the *elementwise union*

$$\underline{\cup}_{i \in I} \mathcal{X}_i = \{ \cup_{i \in I} \mathbf{r}_i : \mathbf{r}_i \in \mathcal{X}_i \}.$$

If for instance I = {1, 2, 3, ... }, then $\underline{\cup}_{i \in I} \mathcal{X}_i = \{\mathbf{r}_1 \cup \mathbf{r}_2 \cup \mathbf{r}_3 \cup \ldots : \mathbf{r}_1 \in \mathcal{X}_1, \mathbf{r}_2 \in \mathcal{X}_2, \mathbf{r}_3 \in \mathcal{X}_3, \ldots\}$. In the binary case the elementwise union becomes $\mathcal{X} \underline{\cup} \mathcal{Y} = \{\mathbf{r} \cup \mathbf{s} : \mathbf{r} \in \mathcal{X}$ and $\mathbf{s} \in \mathcal{Y}\}$.

Lemma 3.1. For any set $\{|\mathcal{X}_i| : i \in I\}$, where $|\mathcal{X}_i|$ is in $Inc(\mathbf{R})/_{\equiv_+}$, we have $lub(\{|\mathcal{X}_i| : i \in I\}) = |\underline{\cup}_{i \in I} \mathcal{X}_i|$ and $glb(\{|\mathcal{X}_i| : i \in I\}) = |\cup_{i \in I} \mathcal{X}_i|$.

Proof. (*lub*). Let **p** be in $\underline{\cup}_{i \in I} \mathcal{X}_i$. Since **p** is of the form $\cup_{i \in I} \mathbf{r}_i$, where $\mathbf{r}_i \in \mathcal{X}_i$, we see that $\mathcal{X}_i <_+ \underline{\cup}_{i \in I} \mathcal{X}_i$, for each $i \in I$. Thus $|\mathcal{X}_i| <_+ |\underline{\cup}_{i \in I} \mathcal{X}_i|$. Hence $|\underline{\cup}_{i \in I} \mathcal{X}_i|$ is an upper bound. To see that it is the least upper bound, suppose that for some $\mathcal{Z} \in Inc(\mathbf{R})$, we have

$|\mathcal{X}_i| <_+ |\mathcal{Z}|$, for all $i \in I$. This means that for all $\mathbf{p} \in \mathcal{Z}$, and for all $i \in I$, there is an $\mathbf{r}_i \in \mathcal{X}_i$, such that $\mathbf{r}_i \subseteq \mathbf{p}$. Therefore $\bigcup_{i \in I} \mathbf{r}_i \subseteq \mathbf{p}$. As $\bigcup_{i \in I} \mathbf{r}_i$ is a member of $\underline{\bigcup}_{i \in I} \mathcal{X}_i$ we conclude that $\underline{\bigcup}_{i \in I} \mathcal{X}_i <_+ \mathcal{Z}$, which means that $|\underline{\bigcup}_{i \in I} \mathcal{X}_i| <_+ |\mathcal{Z}|$.

(*glb*). It is obvious that $\bigcup_{i \in I} \mathcal{X}_i <_+ \mathcal{X}_i$, for all $i \in I$. Thus $|\bigcup_{i \in I} \mathcal{X}_i| <_+ |\mathcal{X}_i|$, i.e. we have a lower bound. Suppose then that for some $\mathcal{Z} \in Inc(\mathbf{R})$, it is true that $|\mathcal{Z}| <_+ |\mathcal{X}_i|$, for all $i \in I$. This means that $\mathcal{Z} <_+ \mathcal{X}_i$, for all $i \in I$. Therefore $\mathcal{Z} <_+ \bigcup_{i \in I} \mathcal{X}_i$, and so $|\mathcal{Z}| <_+ |\bigcup_{i \in I} \mathcal{X}_i|$. We have thus established that $|\bigcup_{i \in I} \mathcal{X}_i|$ is the greatest lower bound. *Q.E.D.*

Lemma 3.2. The top element of $Inc(\mathbf{R})/_{\equiv_+}$ is $|\emptyset|$, and the bottom element is $|\{\emptyset\}|$.

Proof. It is quite obvious that $\mathcal{X} <_+ \emptyset$, and that $\{\emptyset\} <_+ \mathcal{X}$ is true for any $|\mathcal{X}| \in Inc(\mathbf{R})/_{\equiv_+}$. *Q.E.D.*

We have now defined a complete lattice. By Theorem 3.3 we are allowed to replace the relationship $<_+$ by the relationship $<_{PSUJR}$. By Corollary 3.3 the equivalence classes $|\mathcal{X}|_{PSUJR} = \{\mathcal{Y} : \mathcal{Y} \equiv_{PSUJR} \mathcal{X}\}$, and $|\mathcal{X}|_{\equiv_+}$ are the same. Thus the quotient sets $Inc(\mathbf{R})/_{\equiv_{PSUJR}}$ and $Inc(\mathbf{R})/_{\equiv_+}$ are also the same. We define $|\mathcal{X}|_{PSUJR} <_{\mathbf{PSUJR}} |\mathcal{Y}|_{PSUJR}$, if $\mathcal{X} <_{PSUJR} \mathcal{Y}$. It then follows from Theorem 3.3 that $<_{\mathbf{PSUJR}}$ is the same partial order as $<_+$, so we can replace the latter with the former in all definitions above. Collecting things together we have established the following result:

Theorem 3.4. For any $\mathbf{R}$, the couple $\langle Inc(\mathbf{R})/_{\equiv_{PSUJR}}, <_{\mathbf{PSUJR}} \rangle$ is a complete lattice. For any set $\{|\mathcal{X}_i| : i \in I\}$, where $\mathcal{X}_i$ is in $Inc(\mathbf{R})$, $lub(\{|\mathcal{X}_i| : i \in I\}) = |\underline{\bigcup}_{i \in I} \mathcal{X}_i|$ and $glb(\{|\mathcal{X}_i| : i \in I\}) = |\bigcup_{i \in I} \mathcal{X}_i|$. The top element of the lattice is $|\emptyset|$, and the bottom element is $|\{\emptyset\}|$.

It has been pointed out to this author, that the $<_+$ order corresponds to a partial order used in the semantics of parallel processes (see [Plo76, Smy78]).

To round off this section we shall illustrate the lattice of complete databases from Chapter 2, and the two lattices of this chapter through a small example. We assume that the scheme is R = {A}, and that *Dom*(A) = {a, b}. Then *Rel*(R) = $\{r_\emptyset, r_a, r_b, r_{ab}\}$, where $r_\emptyset$ is the empty relation, $r_a = \{(a)\}$, $r_b = \{(b)\}$ and $r_{ab} = \{(a), (b)\}$. Figure 3.1 shows *Rel*(A) ordered by $\subseteq$. The set *Inc*(A), ordered by < is shown in Figure 3.2, and $Inc(A)/_{\equiv_+}$ ordered by $<_+$ is displayed in Figure 3.3.

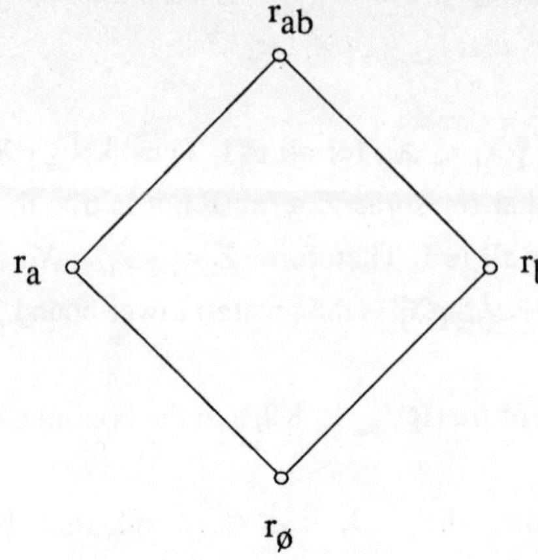

Figure 3.1. The lattice $<Rel(A), \subseteq>$.

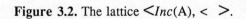

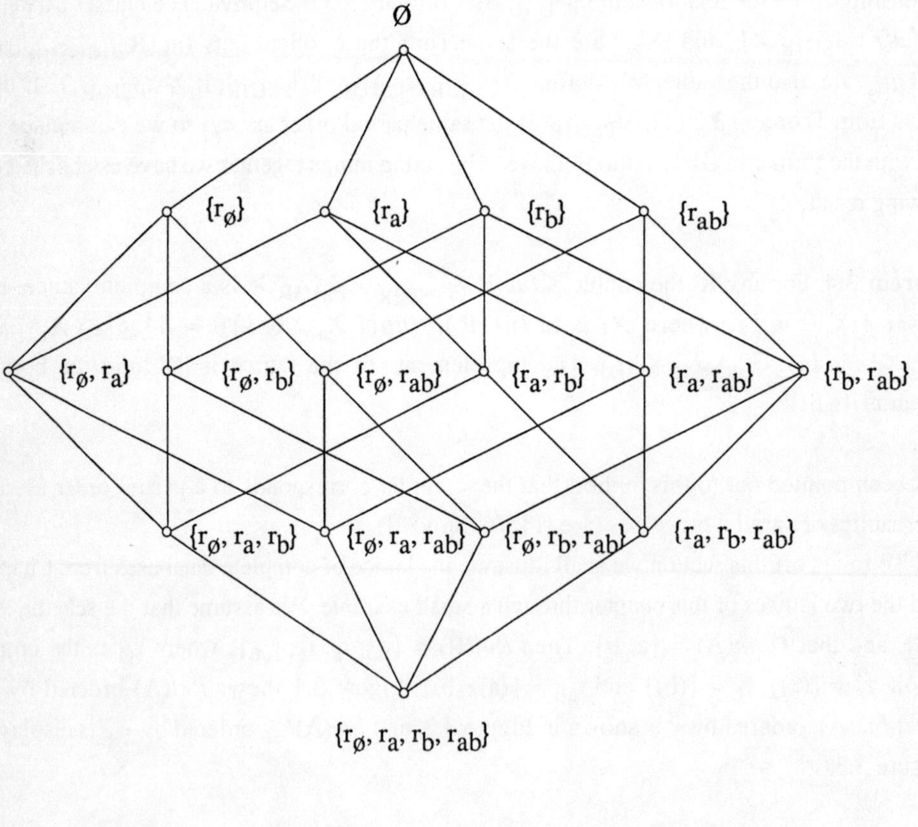

Figure 3.2. The lattice $<Inc(A), < >$.

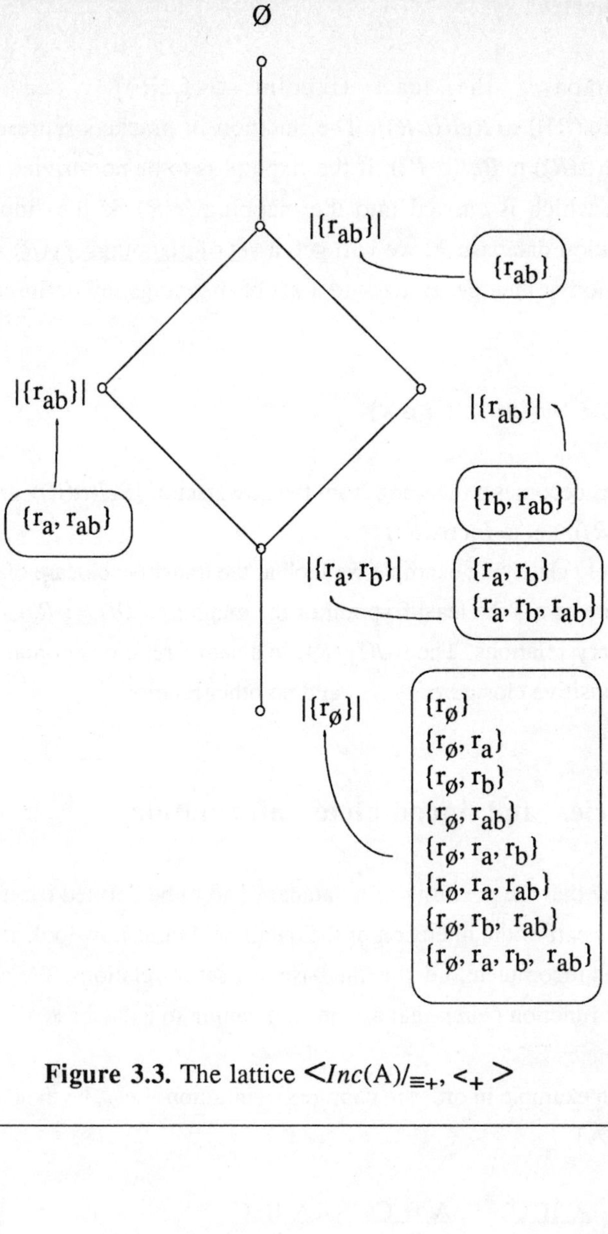

Figure 3.3. The lattice $<Inc(A)/_{\equiv+}, <_+>$

Least fixpoint queries

In complete databases the least fixpoint $\psi(f_r(R))$ is an operation from $[Rel(\alpha(R)) \rightarrow Rel(\alpha(R))]$ to $Rel(\alpha(R))$. The notation in brackets represents the set of all mappings from $Rel(\alpha(R))$ to $Rel(\alpha(R))$. If the fixpoint is to be non-trivial, there has to be an "input" relation **r**, which is curried into the mapping $f_r(R)$. If the "input" relation is an incomplete information database X, we will get a <u>set of mappings</u> $f_X(\underline{R}) = \{f_r(R) : r \in X\}$. The fixpoint operation ψ then generalizes to a set of mappings, by defining the elementwise extension

(7) $\psi(f_X(\underline{R})) = \{\psi(f_r(R)) \ : \ r \in X\}.$

The operation ψ thus becomes a mapping from the powerset of $[Rel(\alpha(R)) \rightarrow Rel(\alpha(R))]$ to the powerset of $Rel(\alpha(R))$, i.e. to $Inc(\alpha(R))$.

As an intuitively clarifying example we look at the transitive closure of a binary relation r. The transitive closure of r is the least fixpoint of the mapping $f_r(R) = r \circ R \cup r$. Let $X = \{r_1, r_2, \ldots\}$ be a set of binary relations. Then $\psi(f_X(\underline{R}))$ is a set of relations containing the transitive closure of r_1, the transitive closure of r_2, ..., and no other relations.

3.2. Dependencies and incomplete information

In Chapter 2 we saw that the meaning of a database had to be defined carefully when a set of data dependencies is part of the intension of the database. Let us now look at the same problem when the database is incomplete, i.e. the database is a set of relations. We are thus faced with defining a semantic function *Comp* that assigns a meaning to a database X in the presence of a set of data dependencies Σ.

We start with an example in order to capture the intuition. Let X be the database below, and $\Sigma = \{A \rightarrow\rightarrow B, B \rightarrow A\}$.

X =

A	B	C
a	b	c
a	b'	c'

A	B	C
e	f	g
e	f'	g'
e	f	g'
e	f'	g

A	B	C
a	b	c
g	b	h

Since an incomplete database is a set of complete databases, the notion of <u>satisfaction</u> of a set of dependencies generalizes to $X \subseteq Sat(\Sigma)$. The question is then what changes we should make to X in order to make it satisfy Σ. Regarding the tuple generating dependency our intuition tells us that we should add the tuples (a, b, c') and (a, b', c) to the first relation in $\mathcal{X}$. But the changes we make to $\mathcal{X}$ should be minimal in some sense. So we replace each relation r in $\mathcal{X}$ by $\psi(g(\Sigma_T)_r)$. The mapping $g(\Sigma_T)_r$ is explained in Section 2.2. The subscript r is a parameter that relates the mapping $g(\Sigma_T)$ to r. (Thus the set of mappings that relates the tuple generating dependencies to an incomplete database $\mathcal{X}$ is $g(\Sigma_T)_{\mathcal{X}} = \{g(\Sigma_T)_r : r \in \mathcal{X}\}$.)

For the equality generating dependency, we see that the third relation in $\mathcal{X}$ violates $B \rightarrow A$. The only possibility is to drop the relation from the completion. When completing an incomplete database $\mathcal{X}$ w.r.t. a set Σ of dependencies, we thus replace each relation in $\mathcal{X}$ by its completion, provided the completion exists. Formally, $Comp_\Sigma(\mathcal{X})$ is the elementwise extension of the completion of relations. i.e.

(8) $$Comp_\Sigma(\mathcal{X}) = \{comp_\Sigma(r) : r \in \mathcal{X}\}.$$

The following fact is obvious.

Lemma 3.3. $Comp_\Sigma(\mathcal{X}) = \psi(g(\Sigma_T)_{\mathcal{X}}) \cap Sat(\Sigma_E)$.

The completion of the example database $\mathcal{X}$ is shown below.

$Comp_\Sigma(\mathcal{X}) =$

A	B	C
a	b	c
a	b'	c'
a	b	c'
a	b'	c

A	B	C
e	f	g
e	f'	g'
e	f	g'
e	f'	g

Now we can see that the transformation from $\mathcal{X}$ to $Comp_\Sigma(\mathcal{X})$ is an increase of positive information, since some possibilities are dropped and tuples are added to the remaining possibilities. This transformation is indeed minimal in the $<_+$ (or $<_{PSUJR}$) ordering, as verified by the following theorem.

Theorem 3.5. For all $\mathcal{X}$ and $\Sigma = \Sigma_T \cup \Sigma_E$, with $\alpha(\mathcal{X}) = \alpha(\Sigma)$

(i) $|\mathcal{X}| <_+ |Comp_\Sigma(\mathcal{X})|$,

(ii) $Comp_\Sigma(\mathcal{X}) \subseteq Sat(\Sigma)$, and

(iii) for any $\mathcal{Y} \in Inc(\alpha(\Sigma))$, such that $|\mathcal{X}| <_+ |\mathcal{Y}|$ and $\mathcal{Y} \subseteq Sat(\Sigma)$, it is true that $|Comp_\Sigma(\mathcal{X})| <_+ |\mathcal{Y}|$.

Proof. Suppose that $Comp_{\Sigma}(\mathcal{X}) \neq \emptyset$. We show that (i) - (iii) hold.

(i) Each $s \in Comp_{\Sigma}(\mathcal{X})$ is of the form $\psi(g(\Sigma_T)_r)$, where $r \in \mathcal{X}$. By Lemma 2.2, we have $r \subseteq g(\Sigma_T)_r$, and thus (i) holds.

(ii) By definition every $s \in Comp_{\Sigma}(\mathcal{X})$ satisfies all equality generating dependencies. Since s is of the form $\psi(g(\Sigma_T)_r)$, where $r \in \mathcal{X}$, Theorem 2.2 states that s satisfies all tuple generating dependencies.

(iii) Suppose that there is an $\mathcal{Y} \in Inc(\alpha(\Sigma))$ such that $|\mathcal{X}| <_+ |\mathcal{Y}|$ and $\mathcal{Y} \subseteq Sat(\Sigma)$. Take a relation s in $\mathcal{Y}$. By the fact that $|\mathcal{X}| <_+ |\mathcal{Y}|$, there is an $r \in \mathcal{X}$, such that $r \subseteq s$. Since $s \in Sat(\Sigma_T)$, Theorem 2.2 implies that $s = \psi(g(\Sigma_T)_s)$. By Corollary 2.2 $\psi(g(\Sigma_T)_s) \supseteq \psi(g(\Sigma_T)_r) \in Comp_{\Sigma_T}(\mathcal{X})$. Since $\psi(g(\Sigma_T)_s) \in Sat(\Sigma_E)$, Theorem 2.3 gives us $\psi(g(\Sigma_T)_r) \in Sat(\Sigma_E)$. Thus $\psi(g(\Sigma_T)_r) \in Comp_{\Sigma}(\mathcal{X})$ and consequently $Comp_{\Sigma}(\mathcal{X}) <_+ \mathcal{Y}$. Then (iii) follows.

Suppose then that $Comp_{\Sigma}(\mathcal{X}) = \emptyset$. Then obviously (i) and (ii) hold (recall that $|\emptyset|$ is the top element in the lattice $Inc(\alpha(\Sigma))/_{\equiv_+}$). For (iii), we claim that there can be no $\mathcal{Y} \neq \emptyset$ such that (a): $|\mathcal{X}| <_+ |\mathcal{Y}|$, and (b): $\mathcal{Y} \subseteq Sat(\Sigma)$. Suppose to the contrary that such a $\mathcal{Y}$ exists. Let s be a relation in $\mathcal{Y}$. By (a), there is then a relation r in $\mathcal{X}$, such that $r \subseteq s$. By (b), s is in $Sat(\Sigma)$, contradicting the fact that the completion of r does not exist. Thus the assumption that $\mathcal{Y} \neq \emptyset$ is wrong, and consequently $Comp_{\Sigma}(\mathcal{X})$ fulfills (iii). *Q.E.D.*

We note that one could consider another possibility to define the completion, by requiring that $Comp_{\Sigma}(\mathcal{X}) \subseteq \mathcal{X}$, $Comp_{\Sigma}(\mathcal{X}) \subseteq Sat(\Sigma)$, and that $Comp_{\Sigma}(\mathcal{X})$ is maximal w.r.t. $\subseteq$. Then $Comp_{\Sigma}(\mathcal{X})$ would be uniquely defined by $\mathcal{X} \cap Sat(\Sigma)$. In the example database $\mathcal{X}$, the completion would consist of the second relation only. Such an approach is taken by Vardi [Var86a], in connection with the "closed world assumption". The closed world assumption [Rei78, Rei84] states intuitively that a fact not implied by the database is false. Since the dependencies are deductive rules that are a part of the database, and the two tuples added to the first relation in the example above are *nota bene* implied by the database, we regard a completion $\mathcal{X} \cap Sat(\Sigma)$ as counterintuitive. In such a completion the closed world assumption is made w.r.t. the basic facts only.

3.3. Updating incomplete databases

Updating an incomplete database will be similar to the complete case. We specify an equation that the new database should satisfy. The change should be minimal. But in the incomplete case there will be two partial orders to choose between. If the change is made in the < (or, equivalently $<_{PSUJRD}$) order, then the update reflects such a change of knowledge, that the set of possible states have increased or decreased. On the other hand, if the change is made with respect to the $<_+$ (or $<_{PSUJR}$) order, then each state may be altered. We shall give some examples to intuitively explain the differences of the two update semantics. The examples resemble the examples of Biskup [Bis83, pp.632-634], who intuitively discusses different update strategies.

We shall work with the kindergarten database of Section 3.1. Suppose that the database X consists of the fact "somebody (unknown) is taking part in the Siesta activity". As a set of states the database is the following.

NAME	ACTIVITY	NAME	ACTIVITY	NAME	ACTIVITY
Toto	Siesta	Lulu	Siesta	Zaza	Siesta

Now the user wants to enter the information that Zaza is taking part in the Siesta activity. This fact can be specified as the equation $\{(\text{Zaza, Siesta})\} \subseteq R$. There are two possible interpretations of the change to be made.

In the first interpretation we regard the insertion as a new piece of information that is to be added to what we already know. Thus each state of the database may be altered. The following inference is made:

someone is taking part in the Siesta activity
Zaza is taking part in the Siesta activity

Zaza and possibly another child are taking part in the Siesta activity

Consequently we change each state of the database to reflect the new knowledge. In other words, the update is done by elementwise extension of the update to each relation. We shall see that this corresponds to a change made w.r.t. the $<_+$ (or $<_{PSUJR}$) order. The resulting database is the following

NAME	ACTIVITY	NAME	ACTIVITY	NAME	ACTIVITY
Toto	Siesta	Lulu	Siesta	Zaza	Siesta
Zaza	Siesta	Zaza	Siesta		

Since we want to be able to obtain incomplete databases as a result of updates we shall work with equations of the form $\{t\} \subseteq \pi_X(R)$, where t is a tuple on X and $X \subseteq \alpha(R)$. Note that in the complete case this equation does not specify a unique update. The phenomenon is an instance of the view update problem. The solution offered in e.g. [BS81, CP84] is to give an additional constraint yielding uniqueness. Our approach is to regard the insertion as incompletely specified, and thus as a <u>set</u> of completely specified updates. Now $\{t\} \subseteq \pi_X(R)$ can be seen as a shorthand for the set of equations $\Phi = \{\ \{t'\} \subseteq R\ : t'(X) = t\}$. Clearly $Sat(\{t\} \subseteq \pi_X(R)) = \cup Sat(\Phi)$. Then the elementwise extension of an incompletely specified update Φ to an incomplete database $\mathcal{X}$ is $\{ins_\phi(r) : r \in \mathcal{X}$ and $\phi \in \Phi\}$. The insertion is called a *positive insertion*, and the result is denoted by p-ins$_\Phi(\mathcal{X})$. Obviously p-ins$_\Phi(\mathcal{X}) = \mathcal{X} \uplus \{t' : \pi_X(t') = t\}$. (Recall that $\uplus$ stands for the elementwise union.) Now the transformation from $\mathcal{X}$ to p-ins$_\Phi(\mathcal{X})$ is an increase in positive information, since each relation in the result is obtained by adding a tuple to a relation in $\mathcal{X}$. As in the completion, the change made is minimal w.r.t. the $<_+$ order. Formally, we have

Theorem 3.6. Let Φ be a set of equations of the form $\{t'\} \subseteq R$, such that $\cup Sat(\Phi) = Sat(\{t\} \subseteq \pi_X(R))$, and let $\mathcal{X}$ be an incomplete database, where $\alpha(\mathcal{X}) = \alpha(R)$. Then

(i) $|\mathcal{X}| <_+ |$p-ins$_\Phi(\mathcal{X})|$,

(ii) p-ins$_\Phi(\mathcal{X}) \subseteq \cup Sat(\Phi)$, and

(iii) for any $\mathcal{Y} \in Inc(\alpha(R))$ that $|\mathcal{X}| <_+ |\mathcal{Y}|$ and $|\mathcal{Y}| \subseteq \cup Sat(\Phi)$, it is true that $|$p-ins$_\Phi(\mathcal{X})| <_+ |\mathcal{Y}|$.

Proof. (i) and (ii) are obvious. For (iii), suppose that a $\mathcal{Y}$ fulfilling the assumptions exists. Let p be a relation in $\mathcal{Y}$. By the first assumption, there is a relation r in $\mathcal{X}$, such that $r \subset p$. By the second assumption, there is a tuple t' in p, such that t'(X) =t. Thus $r \cup \{t'\} \subseteq p$. Since $r \cup \{t'\}$ is a member of p-ins$_\Phi(\mathcal{X})$, we have p-ins$_\Phi(\mathcal{X}) <_+ \mathcal{Y}$. Consequently $|$p-ins$_\Phi(\mathcal{X})| <_+ |\mathcal{Y}|$. *Q.E.D.*

To give another example of the positive insertion, we note that the original database in our example is obtained from the empty state by specifying (the set of equations) $\{(\text{Siesta})\} \subseteq \pi_{ACTIVITY}(R)\}$, and making the insertions elementwise. We do not claim to capture <u>all</u> updates by these insertions, but we do believe that the ability to state a partial fact is the <u>main</u> <u>source</u> of incompleteness in a relational database. This source of incompleteness is also discussed in Chapter 6, in connection with the "dangling tuple" problem.

In the second strategy for inserting the information that Zaza is taking part in the Siesta activity into the database

NAME	ACTIVITY	NAME	ACTIVITY	NAME	ACTIVITY
Toto	Siesta	Lulu	Siesta	Zaza	Siesta

we make the following inference:

someone is taking part in the Siesta activity
Zaza is taking part in the Siesta activity

---

the child taking part in the Siesta activity is Zaza.

Consequently we change the database so that only the states where Zaza is taking part in the Siesta activity are kept. In our case the result consists of the third state. Thus the update reflects a change in our knowledge, where the set of possible states has shrunk, i.e. we increase information w.r.t. the $<$ (or, equivalently $<_{PSUJRD}$) order.

Formally, let ϕ be an equation of the form $\{t\} \subseteq \pi_X(R)$, where t is a tuple on X, and $X \subseteq \alpha(R)$. Let $\mathcal{X}$ be an incomplete database, where $\alpha(\phi) = \alpha(\mathcal{X})$. Then an *absolute insertion* into $\mathcal{X}$ by ϕ is a $\mathcal{Y} \in Inc(\alpha(\phi))$, such that

(i) $\mathcal{X} < \mathcal{Y}$,

(ii) $\mathcal{Y} \subseteq Sat(\phi)$, and

(iii) for any $\mathcal{Z} \in Inc(\alpha(\phi))$ such that $\mathcal{X} < \mathcal{Z}$, and $\mathcal{Z} \subseteq Sat(\phi)$, it is true that $\mathcal{Y} < \mathcal{Z}$.

Obviously the result of the absolute insertion is $\mathcal{X} \cap Sat(\phi)$, denoted by a-ins$_\phi(\mathcal{X})$.

The main difference between specifying an insertion for a complete and an incomplete database is that in the latter we are allowed to specify partial facts (corresponding to a set of equations). In the deletion operation we will not have this distinction. We simply give a selection expression, stating the values of the facts that we want to delete. Working with the two partial orders will however allow us to capture two fundamental semantics for doing the deletion. Let us take the kindergarten database "an unknown child is taking part in the Siesta activity" :

NAME	ACTIVITY	NAME	ACTIVITY	NAME	ACTIVITY
Toto	Siesta	Lulu	Siesta	Zaza	Siesta

Suppose that the user states that "Zaza is not in the kindergarten". As an equation this deletion is specified as $\sigma_{NAME=Zaza}(R) \subseteq \emptyset$. The first possible way of interpreting the deletion is to make deletions in each state in order to get them to satisfy the equation. Thus we perform the elementwise extension of the deletion. This will correspond to a change according to the $<_+$ order. The inference made is the following:

someone is taking part in the Siesta activity
Zaza is not in the kindergarten

---

either nobody is taking part in the Siesta activity
or someone other than Zaza is taking part in the Siesta activity.

The resulting set of states would in this case be

NAME	ACTIVITY
Toto	Siesta

NAME	ACTIVITY
Lulu	Siesta

NAME	ACTIVITY
	ø

Formally, let ϕ be an equation of the form $\sigma_E(R) \subseteq \emptyset$, and let $\mathcal{X}$ be an incomplete database, where $\alpha(\phi) = \alpha(\mathcal{X})$. Then the *positive deletion* with ϕ from $\mathcal{X}$, denoted by p-del$_\phi(\mathcal{X})$, is $\{\text{del}_\phi(r) : r \in \mathcal{X}\}$. Obviously p-del$_\phi(\mathcal{X}) = \{\sigma_{\neg E}(r) : r \in \mathcal{X}\} = \sigma_{\neg E}(\mathcal{X})$. As in the positive insertion, the update is a change according to the $<_+$ order. Since tuples are deleted, the positive information is decreased. The transformation will be minimal, as verified by the next theorem.

Theorem 3.7. Let p-del$_\phi(\mathcal{X})$ be the result of a positive deletion. Then

(i) $|$p-del$_\phi(\mathcal{X})| <_+ |\mathcal{X}|$,

(ii) p-del$_\phi(\mathcal{X}) \subseteq Sat(\phi)$, and

(iii) if there is a $\mathcal{Y} \in Inc(\alpha(\phi))$, such that $|\mathcal{Y}| <_+ |\mathcal{X}|$ and $\mathcal{Y} \subseteq Sat(\phi)$, then $|\mathcal{Y}| <_+ |$p-del$_\phi(\mathcal{X})|$.

Proof. (i) and (ii) are obvious. For (iii) suppose that a $\mathcal{Y}$ mentioned in (iii) exists, and let p be a relation in p-del$_\phi(\mathcal{X})$. Then $p = \sigma_{\neg E}(r)$, where r is in $\mathcal{X}$. Since $|\mathcal{Y}| <_+ |\mathcal{X}|$, $\mathcal{Y}$ contains a relation s, such that $s \sqsubseteq r$. Consequently $\sigma_{\neg E}(s) \subseteq \sigma_{\neg E}(r)$. Since s is in $Sat(\phi)$, we have $\sigma_{\neg E}(s) = s$. Thus $s \subseteq \sigma_{\neg E}(r)$. This means that $|\mathcal{Y}| <_+ |$p-del$_\phi(\mathcal{X})|$. *Q.E.D.*

The second interpretation of the deletion by $\sigma_{NAME=Zaza}(R) \subseteq \emptyset$ from the database

NAME	ACTIVITY	NAME	ACTIVITY	NAME	ACTIVITY
Toto	Siesta	Lulu	Siesta	Zaza	Siesta

is to delete the states where the equation does not hold. The change is then made w.r.t. the < order. The result consists of the first two states. We have then made the following inference:

someone is taking part in the Siesta activity
Zaza is not in the kindergarten

---

there is someone other than Zaza taking part in the Siesta activity.

Formally, let ϕ be an equation of the form $\sigma_E(R) \subseteq \emptyset$, and let $\mathcal{X}$ be an incomplete database, where $\alpha(\phi) = \alpha(\mathcal{X})$. Then the *absolute deletion* from $\mathcal{X}$ by ϕ is a $\mathcal{Y} \in Inc(\alpha(\phi))$, such that

(i) $\mathcal{X} < \mathcal{Y}$,

(ii) $\mathcal{Y} \subseteq Sat(\phi)$, and

(iii) for any $\mathcal{Z} \in Inc(\alpha(\phi))$, such that $\mathcal{X} < \mathcal{Z}$, and $\mathcal{Z} \subseteq Sat(\phi)$, it is true that $\mathcal{Y} < \mathcal{Z}$.

Clearly the result of the absolute deletion is $\mathcal{X} \cap Sat(\phi)$, which will be denoted by a-$del_\phi(\mathcal{X})$. Note that there is a difference between the positive deletion and the absolute deletion. In the first case the positive information <u>decreased</u>, and in the second case the absolute information is <u>increased</u>. This is due to the fact that in the first case we delete tuples from each state, while in the second case we delete states.

A preliminary study of updating databases with incomplete information was done by this author and Abiteboul in [AG85].

Updates in the presence of dependencies

As in the complete case, we also have to take the dependencies into account, when updating an incomplete database $\mathcal{X}$. We suppose that $\mathcal{X} \subseteq Sat(\Sigma)$, and we require that the result of the update is also a subset of $Sat(\Sigma)$.

Let us begin with the positive insertion. We had p-ins$_\Phi(\mathcal{X}) = \{ins_\phi(r) : r \in \mathcal{X}$ and $\phi \in \Phi\} = \mathcal{X} \uplus \{t' : \pi_X(t') = t\}$, where Φ was a set of equations, such that $\cup Sat(\Phi) = Sat(\{t\} \subseteq \pi_X(R))$. If we have a set Σ of dependencies present, ins$_\phi(r, \Sigma)$ generalizes elementwise to

$$\begin{aligned}
&\text{p-ins}_\Phi(\mathcal{X}, \Sigma) = \{ins_\phi(r, \Sigma) : r \in \mathcal{X} \text{ and } \phi \in \Phi\} \quad = \\
&Comp_\Sigma(\mathcal{X} \uplus \{t' : \pi_X(t') = t\}) \quad = \\
&Comp_\Sigma(\text{p-ins}_\Phi(\mathcal{X})).
\end{aligned}$$

Now p-ins$_\Phi(\mathcal{X}, \Sigma)$ satisfies the requirements stated in the next theorem.

Theorem 3.8. Let Φ be a set of equations of the form $\{t'\} \subseteq R$, such that $\cup Sat(\Phi) = Sat(\{t\} \subseteq \pi_X(R))$, let Σ be a set of dependencies, and let $\mathcal{X}$ be an incomplete database, where $\alpha(\mathcal{X}) = \alpha(R) = \alpha(\Sigma) = R$. Then

(i) $|\mathcal{X}| <_+ |$p-ins$_\Phi(\mathcal{X}, \Sigma)|$,

(ii) p-ins$_\Phi(\mathcal{X}, \Sigma) \subseteq \cup Sat(\Phi)$,

(iii) p-ins$_\Phi(\mathcal{X}, \Sigma) \subseteq Sat(\Sigma)$, and

(iv) for any $\mathcal{Y} \in Inc(\alpha(R))$, such that $|\mathcal{X}| <_+ |\mathcal{Y}|$, $\mathcal{Y} \subseteq \cup Sat(\Phi)$, and $\mathcal{Y} \subseteq Sat(\Sigma)$, it is true that $|$p-ins$_\Phi(\mathcal{X}, \Sigma)| <_+ |\mathcal{Y}|$.

Proof. Requirements (i) - (iii) clearly hold. For (iv), suppose that there is a $\mathcal{Y}$ such that (a): $|\mathcal{X}| <_+ |\mathcal{Y}|$, (b): $\mathcal{Y} \subseteq \cup Sat(\Phi)$, and (c): $\mathcal{Y} \subseteq Sat(\Sigma)$. Let s be a relation in $\mathcal{Y}$. By (a), there is a relation r in $\mathcal{X}$, such that $r \subseteq s$. By (b), $\{t\} \subseteq \pi_X(s)$. Thus there is a tuple t' on R, such that $t' \in s$, and $t'(X) = t$. Consequently $r \cup \{t'\} \subseteq s$. Denote $r \cup \{t'\}$ by p. By (c), $s \in Sat(\Sigma_T)$. Then Theorem 2.2. implies that $s = \psi(g(\Sigma_T)_s)$, and from Corollary 2.2 it follows that $\psi(g(\Sigma_T)_p) \subseteq \psi(g(\Sigma_T)_s)$. By (c), we have $\psi(g(\Sigma_T)_s) \in Sat(\Sigma_E)$. Then Theorem 2.3 gives us $\psi(g(\Sigma_T)_p) \in Sat(\Sigma_E)$. Now $\psi(g(\Sigma_T)_p)$ is obviously a member of p-ins$_\Phi(\mathcal{X}, \Sigma)$. Thus $|$p-ins$_\Phi(\mathcal{X}, \Sigma)| <_+ |\mathcal{Y}|$. *Q.E.D.*

The result of a positive deletion by an equation ϕ of the form $\sigma_E(R) \subseteq \emptyset$ from a complete relation r under a set Σ of dependencies, is $\sigma_{\neg E}(r)$, provided $r \in Sat(\Sigma)$, and Σ consists of one join dependency $*[R_1,\ldots,R_n]$ and a set of equality generating dependencies, and furthermore, provided that the selection expression E involves only attributes in some R_i. If these restrictions hold, we define p-del$_\phi(\mathcal{X}, \Sigma) = \{\sigma_{\neg E}(r) : r \in \mathcal{X}\}$. Now we have the following result.

Theorem 3.9. Let p-del$_\phi(\mathcal{X}, \Sigma)$ be the result of a positive deletion under the restrictions above. Then

(i) $|\text{p-del}_\phi(\mathcal{X}, \Sigma)| <_+ |\mathcal{X}|$,

(ii) p-del$_\phi(\mathcal{X}, \Sigma) \subseteq Sat(\phi)$,

(iii) p-del$_\phi(\mathcal{X}, \Sigma) \subseteq Sat(\Sigma)$, and

(iv) for any $\mathcal{Y} \in Inc(\alpha(\phi))$, such that $|\mathcal{Y}| <_+ |\mathcal{X}|$, $\mathcal{Y} \subseteq Sat(\phi)$, and $\mathcal{Y} \subseteq Sat(\Sigma)$, it is true that $|\mathcal{Y}| <_+ |\text{p-del}_\phi(\mathcal{X},\Sigma)|$.

Proof. Requirements (i), (ii), and (iv) follow from Theorem 3.7. For requirement (iii), we note that $Comp_\Sigma(\text{p-del}_\phi(\mathcal{X}, \Sigma)) = Comp_\Sigma(\{\sigma_{\neg E}(r) : r \in \mathcal{X}\}) = \{comp_\Sigma(\sigma_{\neg E}(r)) : r \in \mathcal{X}\}$, which by Corollary 2.3 is equal to $\{(\sigma_{\neg E}(r)) : r \in \mathcal{X}\}$, which again is equal to p-del$_\phi(\mathcal{X}, \Sigma)$. Thus p-del$_\phi(\mathcal{X}, \Sigma) \subseteq Sat(\Sigma)$. *Q.E.D.*

Next we shall look at the absolute updates under a set Σ of dependencies. Let ϕ be a equation of the form $\{t\} \subseteq \pi_X(R)$. Then an *absolute insertion* by ϕ into a database $\mathcal{X} \subseteq Sat(\Sigma)$ *under* Σ, is a database $\mathcal{Y}$, such that

(i) $\mathcal{X} < \mathcal{Y}$,

(ii) $\mathcal{Y} \subseteq Sat(\phi)$,

(iii) $\mathcal{Y} \subseteq Sat(\Sigma)$, and

(iv) for any $\mathcal{Z}$ such that $\mathcal{X} < \mathcal{Z}$, $\mathcal{Z} \subseteq Sat(\phi)$, and $\mathcal{Z} \subseteq Sat(\Sigma)$, it is true that $\mathcal{Y} < \mathcal{Z}$.

We assume above that $\alpha(R) = \alpha(\Sigma) = \alpha(\mathcal{X}) = \alpha(\mathcal{Y}) = \alpha(\mathcal{Z})$. We shall denote the result by a-ins$_\phi(\mathcal{X}, \Sigma)$, and we claim that it is uniquely given by $\mathcal{X} \cap Sat(\phi)$. Requirements (i) and (ii) are obviously fulfilled. Since $\mathcal{X} \subseteq Sat(\Sigma)$, it is obvious that $\mathcal{X} \cap Sat(\phi) \subseteq Sat(\Sigma)$. Thus requirement (iii) is fulfilled. Any $\mathcal{Y}$ satisfying (i) and (ii) must be a subset of $\mathcal{X} \cap Sat(\phi)$, and hence the minimality requirement (iv) is fulfilled.

Let ϕ be an equation of the form $\sigma_E(R) \subseteq \emptyset$, let Σ be a set of dependencies on $\alpha(R) = R$, and let $\mathcal{X}$ be an incomplete database on R, such that $\mathcal{X} \subseteq Sat(\Sigma)$. Then the *absolute deletion* by ϕ from $\mathcal{X}$ *under* Σ is an incomplete database $\mathcal{Y}$ on R, such that

(i) $\mathcal{X} < \mathcal{Y}$,

(ii) $\mathcal{Y} \subseteq Sat(\phi)$,

(iii) $\mathcal{Y} \subseteq Sat(\Sigma)$, and

(iv) for any $\mathcal{Z} \in Inc(\mathrm{R})$ such that $\mathcal{X} < \mathcal{Z}$, $\mathcal{Z} \subseteq Sat(\phi)$, and $\mathcal{Z} \subseteq Sat(\Sigma)$, it is true that $\mathcal{Y} < \mathcal{Z}$.

The result of the absolute deletion is clearly $\mathcal{X} \cap Sat(\phi)$, which we denote a-del$_\phi(\mathcal{X}, \Sigma)$.

4. Syntactic and algorithmic aspects of incomplete information

So far our exposition has been on a semantic level. We shall now consider the problem of representing sets of multirelations in a way that is suitable for storing and manipulating the databases. The syntactic devices that we are going to use are called tables. The tables resemble traditional relations except that we allow variables (representing null-values) and restrictions on variables as entries. We then give algorithms for query evaluation, dependency enforcement and updates, for the case where the incomplete database is stored as a table. We shall also define syntactically restricted classes of tables. The computational complexity of the various operations on the different classes of tables is analyzed in Chapter 5.

4.1. Tables as representations of incomplete information

As relations, tables are defined on a scheme R. (We shall consider multitables later on.) First we however need the concept of a condition.

A *condition* is a Boolean expression formed using atoms of the form x=a, x=y, **true** and **false**. The Boolean connectives are denoted by $\wedge$, $\vee$, $\neg$ and $\Rightarrow$ (conjunction, disjunction, negation and implication, respectively). The expression is parenthesized when necessary. In the atoms above, x and y are *variables* taken from a countably infinite set *Var*(A) of uninterpreted symbols, and a is a constant (a domain element) in *Dom*(A). In addition to *Dom*(A) we have thus associated a set *Var*(A) with each attribute $A \in U$. We assume that a symbol cannot be both a constant and a variable, i.e. that $Dom(A) \cap Var(A) = \emptyset$, for all $A \in U$. We also assume that if $Dom(A) = Dom(B)$, then $Var(A) = Var(B)$, else $Var(A) \cap Var(B) = \emptyset$. Let V be a subset of *U*. We denote by *Var*(V) the set $\bigcup_{A \in V} Var(A)$. The set of all conditions (some *U* is understood) is denoted by $\mathcal{G}$.

The "relation" part of a table is defined on R and a special attribute called CON (for condition). Let $R = A_1,...,A_k$. Then a *conditional tuple* t on R is a mapping from $R \cup \{CON\}$ to $(Dom(A_1) \cup Var(A_1)) \cup ... \cup (Dom(A_k) \cup Var(A_k)) \cup \mathcal{G}$, such that $t(A_i) \in Dom(A_i)$ or $t(A_i) \in Var(A_i)$, $1 \le i \le k$, and $t(CON) \in \mathcal{G}$. The condition t(CON) is called a *local condition.* Conditional tuples will be called c-tuples for short. The *type* of the c-tuple t is $\alpha(t) = R$.

A *table* T on R is a finite set of c-tuples on R, together with a finite set $\lambda(T)$ of conditions from $\mathcal{G}$. The set $\lambda(T)$ is called the *global condition.* The *Type* $\alpha(T)$ of the table is R.

An example of a table is given below in tabular form. The condition x≠Mimi is a local condition. The global condition is y≠Romorantin. With tables we are able to express equalities and inequalities on the null values (in the global condition, and by using multiple occurrences of the same variable), as well as preconditions (in the local condition) for a tuple to exist. For example, in the first c-tuple in the table below, the precondition is intuitively interpreted as "if x is not Mimi, then x lives in Romorantin, and x supplies nails".

SUPPLIER	ADDRESS	PRODUCT	CON	$y \neq$ Romorantin
x	Romorantin	nails	$x \neq$ Mimi	
Toto	y	bolts	**true**	
Zaza	y	nuts	**true**	

The set of all tables on R is denoted by *Tab*(R). A *multitable* **T** on a multischeme **R** = $<R_1,\ldots, R_n>$ is a sequence $<T_1,\ldots,T_n>$, where each T_i is a finite set of c-tuples on R_i, and $\lambda(\mathbf{T})$ is a a global condition, common to all T_i:s. The set *Tab*(**R**) is the set of all multitables on **R**. The *type* of a multitable is its multischeme. The class of all multitables (on any scheme) is denoted by T.

Let **T** = $<T_1,\ldots, T_n>$ and **U** = $<U_1,\ldots, U_m>$ be multitables. Then the *concatenation* of **T** and **U** is $<\mathbf{T},\mathbf{U}> = <T_1,\ldots, T_n, U_1,\ldots, U_m,>$, and $\lambda(<\mathbf{T},\mathbf{U}>) = \lambda(\mathbf{T}) \cup \lambda(\mathbf{U})$.

The set of possible states (relations) that a table T represents is denoted by *rep*(T), and it is defined using particular mappings called valuations. Intuitively, a valuation maps a table to one possible state. Formally, for a finite subset V = $A_1,\ldots, A_k$ of U, a *valuation* v on V is a mapping from *Dom*(V) $\cup$ *Var*(V) to *Dom*(V), such that for $x \in Var(A_i)$, $v(x) \in Dom(A_i)$, and v(a) = a for all $a \in Dom(A_i)$, $1 \leq i \leq k$. The set of all valuations on V is denoted by *Val*(V). Valuations are extended to conditions $\phi \in \mathcal{G}$, by defining $v(\phi)$ = **true,** if ϕ evaluates to **true** according to Boolean semantics when each variable x in ϕ is substituted with v(x). Otherwise $v(\phi)$ is **false**.

Valuations map c-tuples on R to tuples on R by defining

$$(v(t))(A) = v(t(A)), \text{ for } A \in R.$$

For a table $T \in Tab(R)$

$$rep(T) = \{r \in Rel(R) : \text{there is a } v \in Val(R), \text{ such that } r = v(T), \text{ and } v(\lambda(T)) = \mathbf{true}\},$$

where

$$v(T) = \{v(t(R)) : t \in T \text{ and } v(t(CON)) = \mathbf{true}\}, \text{ and}$$

$$v(\lambda(T)) = \mathbf{true} \text{ if } v(\phi) = \mathbf{true}, \text{ for all } \phi \in \lambda(T).$$

For a multitable $\mathbf{T} = <T_1,..., T_n> \in Tab(\mathbf{R})$ we define analogously

$$rep(\mathbf{T}) = \{<r_1,...,r_n> \in Rel(\mathbf{R}) : \text{there is a } v \in Val(V) \text{ such that } r_i = v(T_i) \text{ and } v(\lambda(\mathbf{T})) = \mathbf{true},\ 1 \le i \le n\}$$

V in $Val(V)$ above stands for the union of all R_i in **R**.

Two relations in *rep*(T), for T as in the previous example are given below.

SUPPLIER	ADDRESS	PRODUCT
Lulu	Romorantin	nails
Toto	London	bolts
Zaza	London	nuts

SUPPLIER	ADDRESS	PRODUCT
Toto	Paris	bolts
Zaza	Paris	nuts

We note that if $v(\lambda(\mathbf{T})) = \mathbf{false}$ for all valuations v, then $rep(\mathbf{T}) = \emptyset$, i.e. **T** represents no relations at all. On the other hand, if $v(\lambda(\mathbf{T})) = \mathbf{true}$ for at least one valuation v, but all local conditions are false for any valuation, then $rep(\mathbf{T}) = \{<\emptyset, \emptyset, ..., \emptyset>\}$, i.e. the empty multirelation only.

The closed and open world assumptions

The closed world assumption [Rei78, Rei84] states that a fact represented by a tuple is true only if it is implied by the database (cf. page 46). Applied to tables the assumption means that a tuple t is false if it is not a member of any r_i in some **r** in *rep*(**T**). Thus *rep*, which is a mapping from *Tab*(**R**) to *Inc*(**R**) captures this assumption. The *open world assumption,* on the other hand, states that if a tuple (fact) is not implied by the database, then we do not know whether it is true or false. In tables we could model this property by defining a mapping $Rep : Tab(\mathbf{R}) \rightarrow Inc(\mathbf{R})$. *Rep* would be defined as *rep,* except that we replace $r_i = v(T_i)$ by $r_i \supseteq v(T_i)$. In order to keep this book within a reasonable length, we shall however consider the closed world assumption only.

Structure and normalization of tables

Let $\le$ be one of the orderings defined in Chapter 3 (i.e $<$, $<_+$, $<_+$, $<_\Omega$ or $<_\Omega$). Then we define $\mathbf{T} \le \mathbf{U}$, if $rep(\mathbf{T}) \le rep(\mathbf{U})$. In these definitions we assume that $\alpha(\mathbf{T}) = \alpha(\mathbf{U})$. In particular, two multitables **T** and **U** are *equivalent* if $rep(\mathbf{T}) = rep(\mathbf{U})$. This absolute equivalence is denoted by

T ≡ **U**. Furthermore, the multitables **T** and **U** are *Ω-equivalent*, denoted by $\mathbf{T} \equiv_{\Omega} \mathbf{U}$, if *rep*(**T**) $\equiv_{\Omega}$ *rep*(**U**).

Since there is a finite number of variables in any multitable **T**, only a finite number of members in *rep*(**T**) will be nonisomorphic. Thus the absolute equivalence will be decidable. This fact and its consequence are captured in the following two lemmas.

Lemma 4.1. Let **T** and **U** be multitables, with α(**T**) = α(**U**). Suppose that the set of constants appearing in **T** or **U** is $\mathcal{U}$, and the set of variables appearing in **T** or **U** is $\mathcal{V}$. Let $\mathcal{U}'$ be a set of constants (from the appropriate domains), such that $\mathcal{U}' \cap \mathcal{U} = \emptyset$, and such that the cardinalities of $\mathcal{U}'$ and $\mathcal{V}$ are the same. Then for each valuation v of **T** and **U**, there exists a valuation v' with values in $\mathcal{U} \cup \mathcal{U}'$, and a bijection h, such that v(**T**) = h(v'(**T**)), v(**U**) = h(v'(**U**)), v(λ(**T**)) = h(v'(λ(**T**)), and v(λ(**U**)) = h(v'(λ(**U**)).[1]

Proof. Obvious, since the cardinalities of $\mathcal{V}$ and $\mathcal{U}'$ are the same. We note that for all constants a in **T** and **U**, we have v(a) = a, and v'(a) =a. Thus h is the identity for all a∈$\mathcal{U}$. *Q.E.D.*

Lemma 4.2. Let **T** and **U** be multitables, with α(**T**) = α(**U**). Then the equivalence **T** ≡ **U** is decidable.

Proof (*by enumeration*). We shall show that it is sufficient to look at the finite set of valuations with values in $\mathcal{U} \cup \mathcal{U}'$. Suppose that for all valuations v with values in $\mathcal{U} \cup \mathcal{U}'$ there exists a valuation v' with values in $\mathcal{U} \cup \mathcal{U}'$ such that v(**T**) = v'(**U**) and v(λ(**T**)) = v'(λ(**U**)). We claim that then the same fact holds for all valuations.

Let v be an arbitrary valuation of **T**. Then, by Lemma 4.1 there is a valuation v' with values in $\mathcal{U} \cup \mathcal{U}'$, such that v(**T**) = h(v'(**T**)) and v(λ(**T**) = h(v'(λ(**T**)). By our assumption there is then a valuation v'' with values in $\mathcal{U} \cup \mathcal{U}'$, such that v'(**T**) = v''(**U**) and v'(λ(**T**)) = v''(λ(**U**)). Now h∘v'' (the composition) is a valuation of **U**. This follows from the fact that h is a bijection, and that for all a∈$\mathcal{U}$, h(a) = a, and hence h(v''(a)) = a. Thus h∘v'' fulfills the requirements for a valuation. We have v(**T**) = h(v'(**T**)) = h(v''(**U**)) and v(λ(**T**)) = h(v'(λ(**T**)) = h(v''(λ(**U**)), which implies that *rep*(**T**) ⊆ *rep*(**U**). Inclusion in the other direction can be verified in the same way. *Q.E.D.*

Next we turn our attention to the conditions. A condition φ *implies* a condition γ, denoted by φ |= γ, if for any valuation v, v(φ) = **true** implies v(γ) = **true**. The conditions φ and γ are *equivalent*, if φ |= γ and γ |= φ. This fact is denoted by φ ≈ γ. Also, φ ≈ **true** (resp. **false**), if v(φ) = **true** (resp. **false**) for all valuations v. If φ ≈ **true** (resp. **false**) the condition φ is said to

---

[1]By v(**T**) we mean <v(T_1),..., v(T_n)>.

be a *tautology* (resp. *contradiction*). If there exists at least one valuation v such that $v(\phi)$ = **true**, then the condition is said to be *satisfiable.*

It is noted in [IL84] that $\phi \approx \gamma$ if and only if ϕ can be transformed into γ by using the axioms of Boolean algebra and the axioms of equality. Now replacing conditions in multitables by equivalent ones obviously preserves the absolute equivalence of the multitable. Thus the correctness of the following equivalence preserving syntactic transformation rule should also be clear:

If for some variable x in **T**, λ(**T**) $\models$ x=a (resp. x=y), then each occurrence of x in **T** is replaced by a (resp. y). All occurrences of equalities and inequalities such as x=x, a=a or a≠b are replaced by **true**, and all occurrences of equalities such as a=b are replaced by **false**. Here x is a variable, and a and b are different constants.

For the replacement of variables we use some linear ordering on the variables appearing in **T**, and always replace the greater variable by the lesser one. Thus we avoid replacing the same elements back and forth. With this convention we say that a table **T** is *normalized*, denoted by $\mathbf{T}^{o}$, if no more replacements can be done. The normalization clearly forms a finite Church-Rosser replacement system, assuming that λ(**T**) is satisfiable. (Note that after the normalization, λ(**T**) will no longer contain any conditions that are atomic equalities, i.e. x=y has been replaced by x=x, and then by **true**.)

Restricted classes of tables

The tables have a fairly complex structure, and it will not come as a surprise that many computations on them require an intractable amount of time. We shall thus also be interested in tables with a simpler structure. There are essentially two ways of restricting tables: by restricting the syntax of the global condition, and by restricting the syntax of the local conditions.

As we saw in the definition of a table, the local conditions enable us to express quite sophisticated sets of possibilities. The local conditions will play a role in evaluating queries on tables. Thus we can restrict the local conditions to be without negation (for positive queries), and we can try to do without the local condition at all (for the certain answer). The global condition has no role in query evaluation, but it is needed in representing data dependencies. Since data dependencies are Horn clauses, we can expect a Horn-like global condition to be sufficient. We shall also study the effect of having just a **true/false** global condition.

The classification we provide separates the tables according to their ability to support queries, dependencies and updates, as well as w.r.t. the computational complexity of the various operations. Our restricted classes are the following.

Horn tables. Let δ_i be an atomic condition. A condition is said to be *Horn*, if it is in one of the following forms:

(i) δ_i,

(ii) $\neg\delta_1 \vee ... \vee \neg\delta_n$, or

(iii) $\delta_1 \wedge ... \wedge \delta_{n-1} \Rightarrow \delta_n$.

A table is a Horn table if the global condition consists of Horn conditions only, and if the local conditions are of the form $\delta_1 \wedge ... \wedge \delta_n$, i.e. they are conjunctions of atomic equalities. The class of all Horn tables is denoted by T_H.

Naive tables. If the global condition consists of just the atom **true** or the atom **false**, and if all local conditions consist of just the atom **true**, the table is a Naive table. In the definition of a Naive table and in *rep* of it we can omit all references to the local conditions. The class of all Naive tables is denoted by T_N. A c-tuple in a Naive table will sometimes simply be called a tuple.

Codd tables. If a Naive table contains only one occurrence of each variable, the table is called a Codd table. The corresponding class is denoted by T_C.

In the definitions above, the word "table" should be read "multitable". We have obviously defined increasingly stricter classes of tables, i.e. $T \supseteq T_H \supseteq T_N \supseteq T_C$.

Tables and Naive tables without a global condition were introduced in [IL84]. The Tables were generalized in [Grh84b], where the global condition was defined. Codd tables were introduced by Codd [Cod75] as one of the first attempts to model null values. Some of the properties of Codd tables were studied in [Bis83] and [IL84]. In these studies no global condition was assumed.

A different classification of tables was used by the present author together with Abiteboul and Kanellakis in [AKG87].

4.2. Querying tables

Query systems

In this section we shall consider the problem of computing the set of possible answers f(*rep*(**T**)) and the certain answer $\cap$f(*rep*(**T**)), given a multitable **T** belonging to some class **T**, and a query f from some set Ω. In the possible answer we must be able to compute a table U, such that *rep*(U) = f(*rep*(**T**)). Thus we make the following requirements.

Formally, the triple <**T**, *rep*, Ω> is a *strong query system*, if for any query f$\in\Omega$ there exists a computable function $\hat{f}$: **T** $\rightarrow$ **T**, such that for all tables **T**$\in$**T**, with α(f) = α(**T**), we have

(1) *rep*($\hat{f}$(**T**)) = f(*rep*(**T**)).

An equivalent condition would be to require the existence of a table U$\in$**T**, such that *rep*(U) = f(*rep*(**T**)). If such a U exists, it must be a combination of the finite number of values in f and **T**, and thus it can computed by an exhaustive search.

If (1) holds, then the certain answer can be computed from $\hat{f}$(**T**), since $\cap$*rep*($\hat{f}$(**T**)) in this case obviously is equal to $\cap$f(*rep*(**T**)). The certain answer is always a set of complete tuples, i.e. a relation.

As noted by [IL84], there are queries and classes of tables for which such a $\hat{f}$(**T**) does not exist. In these cases it might however be possible to obtain the certain answer. Then we could weaken the definition to the definability of a relation $\hat{f}$(**T**), for which $\hat{f}$(**T**) = $\cap$f(*rep*(**T**)). Lipski [Lip84] however argues that this would only give a system in which we could individually compute $\hat{f}$(**T**) for each f and **T**. Like in the relational algebra for complete databases, we want a uniform method for any f, based on the basic operators in Ω. The following definition is according to [Lip84]:

The triple <**T**, *rep*, Ω> is a *weak query system* if for any query f$\in\Omega$ there exists a computable function $\hat{f}$: **T** $\rightarrow$ **T**, such that for all tables **T**$\in$**T**, with α(f) = α(**T**), we have

(2) $\cap$*rep*($\hat{f}$(**T**)) = $\cap$f(*rep*(**T**)), and

(3) $(\widehat{g\circ f})$(**T**) = $\hat{g}$($\hat{f}$(**T**))

for all queries g$\in\Omega$, for which α(g)=β(f). (g$\circ$f is the composition of f and g.)

The term *representation system* is used by Imielinski and Lipski instead of our *query system.* Note that by definition the requirement (3) automatically holds in a strong query system.Thus the function f in (1) on tables can also be based on the basic operators in the relational algebra .[1]

An alternative characterization of a weak query system given in [IL84] is in [Lip84] proven to be equivalent to the one above. We shall rephrase the alternative characterization (here called representation system), since it will be useful in some proofs.

A triple <**T**, *rep*, Ω> is a *weak representation system* if for any query $f \in \Omega$ and for any $T \in \mathbf{T}$, with $\alpha(f) = \alpha(T)$, there exists a $U \in \mathbf{T}$ such that

(4) $\quad rep(U) \equiv_\Omega f(rep(T)).$

Theorem 4.1 [Lip84]. A triple <**T**, *rep*, Ω> is a weak representation system if and only if it is a weak query system.

Since $rep(\hat{f}(T)) = f(rep(T))$ obviously implies $rep(\hat{f}(T)) \equiv_\Omega f(rep(T))$ we conclude the following lemma.

Lemma 4.3. A strong query system is also a weak query system.

An interesting fact is that if Ω equals the relational algebra (as defined in Section 2.1), then the notions of weak and strong query systems coincide. This follows from Corollary 3.1, which says that for sets of multirelations, such as $rep(U)$ and $f(rep(T))$, $rep(U) = f(rep(T))$ if and only if $rep(U) \equiv_\Omega f(rep(T))$, when Ω = PSUJRD.

Lemma 4.4. The triple <**T**, *rep*, PSUJRD> is a weak query system if and only if it is a strong query system.

In the sequel we shall use the notation f, instead of $\hat{f}$, for functions on tables. It should be clear from the context whether f denotes a relational expression or a function on a class of tables.

[1] To be exact, the function f in the strong query systems is really a function on the quotient set $\mathbf{T}/_\equiv$ of equivalent tables, and on $\mathbf{T}/_{\equiv_\Omega}$ in a weak query system.

Query evaluation for the different classes of tables

The following theorem is the main result of [IL84]. Although the paper only considers weak query systems, the results (i) follows from [IL84].

Theorem 4.2. Let T' be the class of tables without a global condition. Then
(i) <T', *rep*, PSUJRD> is a strong query system.

Let T'_N be the class of Naive tables without a global condition. Then
(ii) < T'_N, *rep*, PS+UJR> is a weak query system, and
(iii) < T'_N, *rep*, PS> is <u>not</u> a weak query system.

Let T'_C be the class of Codd tables without a global condition. Then
(iv) < T'_C, *rep*, PSR> is a weak query system,
(v) < T'_C, *rep*, PSU> is <u>not</u> a weak query system, and
(vi) < T'_C, *rep*, PJ> is <u>not</u> a weak query system.

Using Lemma 4.3 or Lemma 4.4 we can conclude

Corollary 4.1. <T', *rep*, PSUJRD> is a weak query system.

We now proceed to give the definitions of f(**T**) for the different classes of tables. We shall see that the results of Theorem 4.2 easily extend to take the global condition into account.

Naive evaluation

The case for T'_N is particularly attractive. The result f(**T**) can be evaluated in the same way as on a complete multirelation (i.e. as f), if the variables are treated as constants, pairwise different, and different from all domain values, i.e for all $x,y \in Var(\alpha(\mathbf{T}))$, $x \neq y$, and for all $x \in Var(\alpha(\mathbf{T}))$ and $a \in Dom(\alpha(\mathbf{T}))$, $x \neq a$. Then $\cap rep(f(\mathbf{T}))$ is obtained by dropping all tuples in f(**T**) containing variables. In terms of complexity of query evaluation this means that there is no extra cost for the incomplete information, since the complexities will be the same as for the complete case. (We shall return to the complexity issues in Chapter 5.) When f(**T**) is evaluated according to naive tables we shall sometimes use the notation f(N). A small example will illustrate the evaluation of f(N)(**T**).

T =

A	B
a	x
y	b
a	e

U =

B	C
x	c
e	z

$$f(\boldsymbol{R}) = \sigma_{A=a}(\pi_{AC}(R * S)),\ \boldsymbol{R} = \langle R,S\rangle,\ \alpha(R) = AB,\ \alpha(S) = BC$$

$f_{(N)}(\langle T,U\rangle) =$

A	C
a	c
a	z

$\cap rep(f_{(N)}(\langle T,U\rangle)) =$

A	C
a	c

In the example we join (a, x) with (x, c) but <u>not</u> for instance with (e, z). The tuples (a, e) and (e, z) are also joined. We see that the evaluation is carried out as if we were treating ordinary relations, with the addition that in the end we drop the tuple (a, z).

Theorem 4.2 (ii) means that $rep(f(\mathbf{T})) \equiv_{PS+UJR} f(rep(\mathbf{T}))$, for the appropriate f:s and **T**:s. It should be clear that the same property holds if we extend the definition of $f_{(N)}(\mathbf{T})$ in the following way: Let **T** be a naive multitable with a global condition which is either **true** or **false**. Then $f_{(N)}(\mathbf{T})$ is obtained by the naive evaluation, and $f_{(N)}(\lambda(\mathbf{T})) = \lambda(\mathbf{T})$. Thus we have

Corollary 4.2.
(i) $\langle T_N, rep, PS{+}UJR\rangle$ is a weak query system, and
(ii) $\langle T_N, rep, PS\rangle$ is <u>not</u> a weak query system.

To complete the picture of the Naive tables we note the following quite obvious facts. For all naive tables T and U, and all valuations v, we have $v(\pi_X(T)) = \pi_X(v(T))$, $v(T \cup U) = v(T) \cup v(U)$ and $v(\theta^A_B(T)) = \theta^A_B(v(T))$. The union operator in $T \cup U$ means the union of T and U as sets of c-tuples. We assume that $X \subseteq \alpha(T)$, $\alpha(T) = \alpha(U)$ and that $A, B \in \alpha(T)$. Then it follows that for all PUR-expressions f, and naive multitables **T**, with $\alpha(f) = \alpha(\mathbf{T})$, $rep(f(\mathbf{T})) = f(rep(\mathbf{T}))$.

Furthermore, let T = {(a,x)} and U = {(y,c)}, where $\alpha(T) = AB$ and $\alpha(U) = BC$. Then $\sigma_{B=b}(rep(T)) = \{\{(a,b)\}, \emptyset\}$, and $*(rep(\langle T,U\rangle)) = \{\{(a,z,c)\} : z \in Dom(B)\} \cup \{\emptyset\}$. Let us look at the set $\{\{(a,b)\}, \emptyset\}$. If there is a naive table V, such that $rep(V) = \{\{(a,b)\}, \emptyset\}$, then for some valuation v, v(V) must be ø, and for some valuation v', v'(V) must be {(a,b)}. In the first case there can be no tuples in V, in the second case there must be at least one. Thus we conclude that there can be no naive table representing $\{\{(a,b)\}, \emptyset\}$. A similar argument holds for the set $\{\{(a,z,c)\} : z \in Dom(B)\} \cup \{\emptyset\}$.

The preceding argumentation gives us

Theorem 4.3.
(i) $< T_N, \mathit{rep}, \mathrm{PUR} >$ is a strong query system,
(ii) $< T_N, \mathit{rep}, \mathrm{S}^{+} >$ is <u>not</u> a strong query system, and
(iii) $< T_N, \mathit{rep}, \mathrm{J} >$ is <u>not</u> a strong query system.

Codd evaluation

For Codd tables the projection is evaluated exactly as in the complete case. The evaluation of a selection relies on a transformation of the selection formula into conjunctive normal form, and is quite involved. The crucial point is to recognize tautologies of the form $A=a \vee A \neq a$. The interested reader is referred to [IL84]. It should be clear that we can extend the evaluation to take into account the global condition, in the same way as for the naive tables. We conclude

Corollary 4.3.
(i) $< T_C, \mathit{rep}, \mathrm{PSR} >$ is a weak query system,
(ii) $< T_C, \mathit{rep}, \mathrm{PSU} >$ is <u>not</u> a weak query system, and
(iii) $< T_C, \mathit{rep}, \mathrm{PJ} >$ is <u>not</u> a weak query system.

In addition we have the following properties of Codd tables.

Theorem 4.4.
(i) $< T_C, \mathit{rep}, \mathrm{PR} >$ is a strong query system, and
(ii) $< T_C, \mathit{rep}, \mathrm{S}^{+} >$ is <u>not</u> a strong query system.

Proof. Similar to the argumentation of Theorem 4.3. The union operator is not included in (i), since it can require a repeated occurrence of the same variable. *Q.E.D.*

Conditional evaluation

Computing f(**T**) for a multitable in T' is a more complex task. We will give the definitions for the basic operators. For a PSUJRD-expression f, f(**T**) can be evaluated by recursively applying each operator in f, following the structure of f. The definitions are from [IL84]. We shall use the standard notation for the basic operators also when they are applied to a table.

In the following, let T and U be tables without global conditions, such that $\alpha(T) = R$ and $\alpha(U) = S$.

Projection : $\pi_X(T) = \{t(X \cup \{CON\}) : t \in T\}$, assuming $X \subseteq R$,

Selection : $\sigma_E(T) = \{\sigma_E(t) : t \in T\}$, where $\sigma_E(t)$ is a c-tuple on R with

$$\sigma_E(t)(R) = t(R),$$
$$\sigma_E(t)(CON) = t(CON) \wedge E(t)$$

(E(t) is the result of substituting t(A) for A in E, for every $A \in R$),

Union : $T \cup U = \{t : t \in T \text{ or } t \in U\}$, assuming $R = S$,

Join : $T * U = \{t * u : t \in T, u \in U\}$, where $t*u$ is a c-tuple on $R \cup S$ with

$$(t*u)(A) \quad = \quad \begin{cases} t(A) & \text{if } A \in R \\ u(A) & \text{if } A \in S\text{-}R. \end{cases}$$

$$(t*u)(CON) \quad = \quad t(CON) \wedge u(CON) \wedge \bigwedge_{A \in R \cap S} \big(t(A) = u(A)\big).$$

Renaming : Let A be an attribute in R and B an attribute in U-R, such that *Dom*(A) = *Dom*(B). Then T with A renamed to B is

$$\theta_B^A(T) \;=\; \{\theta_B^A(t) : t \in T\}, \text{ where } \theta_B^A(t) \text{ is a c-tuple on } (R\text{-}A) \cup B, \text{ with}$$

$$(\theta_B^A(t))(C) \quad = \quad \begin{cases} t(C) & \text{if } C \in R\text{-}A \\ t(A) & \text{if } C = B. \end{cases}$$

$$(\theta_B^A(t))(CON) \;=\; t(CON).$$

Difference : $T\text{-}U = \{t_u : t \in T\}$, where t_u is a c-tuple on R with

$$t_u(R) \;=\; t(R),$$
$$t_u(CON) = t(CON) \wedge \bigwedge_{u \in U} \Big(\big(\bigvee_{A \in R} (t(A) \neq u(A))\big) \vee \neg u(CON) \Big).$$

Here we assume again that R=S. (There is an error in the definition of t_u(CON) in [IL84], the part "$\vee \neg u$(CON)" is missing.)

A small example should enlighten the definitions.

Let T =

B	C	CON
x	c	

, U =

B	C	CON
y	c	(y=b)
z	w	

, W =

A	B	CON
a	y	

Then

T-U =

B	C	CON
x	c	$(x\neq y \vee c\neq c \vee y\neq b) \wedge (x\neq z \vee c\neq w)$

$U \cup T$ =

B	C	CON
y	c	(y=b)
z	w	
x	c	

W∗T =

A	B	C	CON
a	y	c	(y=x)

$\sigma_{B=b}$(W∗T) =

A	B	C	CON
a	y	c	$(y=x) \wedge (y=b)$

π_B(U) =

B	CON
y	(y=b)
z	

When f(**T**) is evaluated according to conditional evaluation, we shall sometimes use the notation f(C)(**T**).

Evaluation in Tables

Having the fundamental result of Theorem 4.2 (i) at our disposal we extend the definition of f(**T**) for a table **T** without a global condition to tables **T** in T where there is also the associated global condition λ(**T**). We do this by defining f(**T**) as for conditional tables, and by putting f(λ(**T**)) = λ(**T**). Then we obviously have

Corollary 4.4. <T, *rep*, PSUJRD> is a strong and weak query system.

The corollary (to Theorem 4.2) means that for tables **T** in T, f(**T**) is defined as for conditional tables. The global condition remains invariant. With this convention, we shall still use the notation f(C)(**T**), for the generalized evaluation method. Given f(**T**), the computation of $\cap$*rep*(f(**T**)) is a fairly complex task. The complexity analysis in the next chapter reveals that the problem of testing whether a tuple belongs to $\cap$*rep*(f(**T**)) is coNP- complete.

Evaluation in Horn tables

The last class of tables to consider is the ones with a global condition consisting of Horn conditions, and with local conditions that are conjunctive equalities, i.e. the class T_H. We apply the definition of f(C)(**T**) for these tables also. Since the global condition is not affected it remains as a set of Horn conditions. The crucial point is to assure that local conditions in f(C)(**T**) remain conjunctive equalities. If we restrict ourselves to PS$^+$UJR-expressions f it should be clear that no negations are introduced in the local conditions of f(C)(**T**). Since disjunctions can come only from selection expressions, we simply assume that the selection expressions do not contain disjunctions. There is no loss of generality, since a selection of the form $\sigma_{E_1 \vee E_2}(f(\boldsymbol{R}))$ can be transformed into the equivalent form $\sigma_{E_1}(f(\boldsymbol{R})) \cup \sigma_{E_2}(f(\boldsymbol{R}))$. These observations, and Corollary 4.4 therefore prove the next theorem.

Theorem 4.5. <T_H, *rep*, PS$^+$UJR> is a strong query system.

The interesting aspect of this theorem is that $\cap$*rep*(f(**T**)) is efficiently computable, as we shall see in Chapter 5. We will need some auxiliary results from [IL84]. Let T be a table on R, with no global condition, and with local conditions that do not contain negation (or implication). Then $T_+ = \{t(R) : t \in T \text{ and } t(CON) \approx$ **true**$\}$. For a multitable **T** = <T_1,...T_n>, with the same restrictions as above, we have $\mathbf{T}_+$ = <T_{1+},..., T_{n+}>. Then the following result is known.

Lemma 4.5 [IL84].
(i) $\cap rep(\mathbf{T}) = \cap rep(\mathbf{T}_+)$.
(ii) Let f be a PS^+UJR- expression with $\alpha(f) = \alpha(\mathbf{T})$. Then $f_{(N)}(\mathbf{T}_+) = (f_{(C)}(\mathbf{T}))_+$.

The lemma means the following. Given a suitably restricted table we can compute the certain result by two methods. In the first method we do the conditional evaluation to obtain $f_{(C)}(\mathbf{T})$, then we recognize the "tautological" tuples in $f_{(C)}(\mathbf{T})$, and from these we finally drop tuples with variables. In the second method we first drop the tuples with nontautological conditions, then we do the naive evaluation on the remaining tuples, and in the end we drop the tuples containing variables. (The proof in [IL84] of Theorem 4.2 (ii) relies on this property.)

Lemma 4.5 is extendible to Horn tables. Let **T** be a Horn table. Recall that $\mathbf{T}^o$ is the normalized version of **T**. Suppose $\mathbf{T} = <T_1,...,T_n>$. Then $\mathbf{T}_* = <T^o_{1+},..., T^o_{n+}>$, and $\lambda(\mathbf{T}_*) =$ **true** if $\lambda(\mathbf{T})$ is satisfiable, else $\lambda(\mathbf{T}_*) =$ **false**.

Lemma 4.6. Let **T** be a Horn table. Then
(i) $\cap rep(\mathbf{T}) = \cap rep(\mathbf{T}_*)$, and
(ii) for all PS^+UJR- expressions f, with $\alpha(f) = \alpha(\mathbf{T})$, we have $f_{(N)}(\mathbf{T}_*) = (f_{(C)}(\mathbf{T}))_*$.

Proof. (ii) Since f does not affect the global condition the claim follows directly from Lemma 4.5 (ii).

(i) If $\lambda(\mathbf{T})$ is not satisfiable the claim is obviously true. Suppose therefore that $\lambda(\mathbf{T})$ is satisfiable. Without loss of generality we assume that **T** is a single table T. We shall first show that $\cap rep(T_*) \subseteq \cap rep(T)$. Let t be a tuple, such that $t \notin \cap rep(T)$. Since $\cap rep(T) = \cap\{v(T) : v$ is a valuation and $v(\lambda(T)) =$ **true**$\}$, it means that there is a valuation v such that $v(\lambda(T)) =$ **true** and $t \notin v(T)$. Since T_* as a set of c-tuples is a subset of T, obviously $t \notin v(T_*)$. Thus $t \notin \cap rep(T_*)$, and consequently $\cap rep(T_*) \subseteq \cap rep(T)$.

It remains to show that $\cap rep(T) \subseteq \cap rep(T_*)$. Let t be a tuple such that $t \notin \cap rep(T_*)$. Thus there is valuation v, such that $t \notin v(T_*)$. Since the global condition is **true**, it means that $t \notin v(T_+)$. We shall construct a valuation v', such that $t \notin v'(T)$, even though $v'(\lambda(T)) =$ **true**. Then the claim follows.

Let v' be a valuation, such that $v'(x) \neq v'(y)$ for all $x \neq y$ in T, and for all x in T, v'(x) is a constant that does not appear in t or T. First we show that $t \notin v'(T)$. Now $T = T_+ \cup (T - T_+)$. Since any c-tuple t in $(T - T_+)$ has a nontautological condition, and since the condition is a conjunction of equalities, we get $v'(t(CON)) =$ **false**. On the other hand we know that $t \notin v(T_+)$. Since v' does not map any variable to a constant in t, it follows that $t \notin v'(T_+)$. It now remains to show that $v'(\lambda(T)) =$ **true**.

Let ϕ be a condition in $\lambda(T)$. Now ϕ is in one of the following forms: (i) δ_i, (ii) $\neg\delta_1 \vee ... \vee \neg\delta_n$, or (iii) $\delta_1 \wedge ... \wedge \delta_{n-1} \Rightarrow \delta_n$, where δ_i is an atomic equality. Since T is normalized, the δ_i:s of the form (i) have been replaced by **true**. Thus $v'(\phi)$ = **true.** If ϕ is of form (ii) or (iii), we clearly have $v'(\phi)$ =**true.** *Q.E.D.*

Consider now the query system <T_H, *rep*, PS+UJR>. The user submits a PS+UJR-expression f as a query to a Horn multitable **T**. We respond with f(C)(**T**) as the possible answer. The certain answer $\cap$f(*rep*(**T**)) is obtained from (f(C)(**T**))$_*$, by dropping any tuple containing variables in the "non-conditional" part. This fact is proved formally in the next lemma. In the complexity chapter we shall see that the tautology of conditions that are conjunctive equalities as well as the satisfiability of a set of Horn conditions can be tested efficiently. On the other hand, if the user wants the certain answer only, then, by Lemma 4.6, we can use the naive evaluation on **T**$_*$. In either case, we will have efficient algorithms.

Lemma 4.7. Let T be a Horn table, where $\alpha(T) = R$, and such that $\lambda(T)$ is satisfiable. Then

$$\cap rep(T) = \{t(R) : t \in T_*, \text{ and } t(A) \in Dom(A) \text{ for all } A \in R\}.$$

Proof. Let us call the latter set above r (since it is a relation). By Lemma 4.6 (i) we have $\cap rep(T) = \cap rep(T_*)$. Now a tuple t is in r if and only if for all $v \in Val(R)$, $t \in v(T_*)$. This fact holds if and only if $t \in \cap rep(T_*)$. *Q.E.D.*

Summary of the query systems

We shall now collect together the main results of this section. The abilities of the different classes of tables to support queries are summarized in the figure below.

TABLE CLASS	STRONG QUERY SYSTEM	WEAK QUERY SYSTEM
Tables	PSUJRD	PSUJRD
Horn tables	PS^+UJR	PS^+UJR
Naive tables	PUR	PS^+UJR
Codd tables	PR	PSR

Figure 4.1. The abilities of the table classes to support queries.

From the figure we see that the local conditions are necessary in order to get exact representations of queries, except for the trivial PUR and PR queries in Naive and Codd tables. If the local conditions are restricted to conjunctive equalities, then the queries cannot contain negation, i.e. they have to be PS^+UJR-expressions. Finally, Figure 4.1 also reveals that repeated occurrences of the same variable are necessary in order to be able to weakly represent queries that involve comparisons between variables, as e.g. in joins.

Least fixpoint queries with Tables

In Section 3.1 we defined the least fixpoint operation on an incomplete database as a mapping with a set of mappings $f_{\mathcal{X}}(R)$ as argument. Here f is a PSUJR-expression (the operation Y), or a PS^+UJR-expression (the operation Y^+). When the database $\mathcal{X}$ is given as a (multi)table **T**, the set of mappings is represented as $f_{\mathbf{T}}(R)$. Formally $rep(f_{\mathbf{T}}(R)) = \{f_{\mathbf{r}}(R) : \mathbf{r} \in rep(\mathbf{T})\}$. Now let $f_{\mathbf{T}}(R)$ be a representation of some particular set of mappings, with $\alpha(f_{\mathbf{T}}) = \beta(f_{\mathbf{T}}) = \alpha(R)$. Then we are interested in finding a table U, denoted by $\psi(f_{\mathbf{T}}(R))$, such that

$$(5) \qquad rep(\ \psi(f_{\mathbf{T}}(R))\ ) = \{\psi(f_{\mathbf{r}}(R)) : \mathbf{r} \in rep(\mathbf{T})\}.$$

Let us use the transitive closure as an example. The transitive closure of a relation r on AB is the least fixpoint of the mapping $f_r(R) = r \circ R \cup R$, where $\alpha(R) = \alpha(r) = AB$. Now we take a table T in Tab(AB). The "transitive closure" of T below, is $\psi(f_T(R))$. Note that formally $rep(\ \psi(f_T(R))\ ) = \{\psi(f_r(R) : r \in rep(T)\}$. The global conditions in both tables below are **true**. Local conditions with value **true** are also omitted.

T = A B	CON	$\psi(f_T(R))$ = A B	CON
a b		a b	
x c		x c	
c d		c d	
		a c	b=x
		x d	
		c c	d=x
		a d	b=x

We shall now consider the question of how to evaluate $\psi(f_T(R))$. First we define $f_T(U) = f(<T,U>)$, where $\alpha(U) = \alpha(R)$. Likewise, $f^n{}_T(U)$ is the n-fold composition of f_T. The following lemma will be needed.

Lemma 4.8. Let $f_T(R)$ be a representation for a set of mappings where $T \in T$, and let $U \in T$ be a table with $\lambda(U) = \lambda(T)$, where $\alpha(f_T) = \beta(f_T) = \alpha(R) = \alpha(U)$. Then for all $n \geq 1$, and all valuations v

$$v(f^n{}_T(U)) = f^n{}_{v(T)}(v(U)).$$

Proof. The result follows almost immediately from the definition, by an induction on n.*Q.E.D.*

The key to compute $\psi(f_T(R))$ is given in the following theorem.

Theorem 4.6. Let $f_T(R)$ be the representation of a set of mappings, where f is a PSUJR - expression, with $\alpha(f) = \beta(f) = \alpha(R) = R$, and $T \in T$. Then there is a $k \geq 1$, such that $f^k{}_T(\emptyset) \equiv \psi(f_T(R))$, and $f^k{}_T(\emptyset) \in T$. Here $\emptyset$ means an empty table of type $\alpha(R)$, with $\lambda(\emptyset) = \lambda(T)$.

Proof. By inductive use of Corollary 4.4 we know that $f^k{}_T(\emptyset)$ is a table. Let $\mathcal{U}$ be the set of constants and $\mathcal{V}$ the set of variables appearing in $f^k{}_T(\emptyset)$. Now $\mathcal{U}$ and $\mathcal{V}$ obviously do not depend on k, since no new values are introduced by folding f. Then let $\mathcal{U}'$ be a set of constants, such that $\mathcal{U} \cap \mathcal{U}' = \emptyset$, and the cardinalities of $\mathcal{U}'$ and $\mathcal{V}$ are the same.

First we claim that there is a $k \geq 1$, such that for all valuations v with values in $\mathcal{U} \cup \mathcal{U}'$, $v(f^k{}_T(\emptyset)) = v(f^{k+1}{}_T(\emptyset)) = \psi(f_{v(T)}(R))$. By Lemma 4.8 we get $v(f^k{}_T(\emptyset)) = f^k{}_{v(T)}(\emptyset)$ (note that $v(\emptyset) = \emptyset$). From Section 2.1 we know that for each $f_{v(T)}(R)$ there is an m, such that $f^m{}_{v(T)}(\emptyset) = f^{m+1}{}_{v(T)}(\emptyset) = \ldots = \psi(f_{v(T)}(R))$. Since there is a finite number of these valuations, there is a finite number of the m:s. We choose k to be the greatest of them. Then the claim follows, since the folding sequence has converged in all cases at least after the k:th folding.

The next claim is that for <u>all</u> valuations v, $v(f^k{}_T(\emptyset)) = v(f^{k+1}{}_T(\emptyset)) = \psi(f_{v(T)}(R))$. By verifying this claim we have proved the theorem. So, suppose therefore that for some particular valuation v, $v(f^k{}_T(\emptyset)) \subsetneq v(f^{k+1}{}_T(\emptyset))$. If $v(f^k{}_T(\emptyset))$ is mapped into $\mathcal{U} \cup \mathcal{U}'$ the inclusion cannot be proper.

In the remaining case we know from Lemma 4.1 there is a valuation v' with values in $\mathcal{U} \cup \mathcal{U}'$, and a bijection h, such that $v(f^k{}_T(\emptyset)) = h(v'(f^k{}_T(\emptyset)))$. But now $v'(f^k{}_T(\emptyset)) = f^k{}_{v'(T)}(\emptyset) = f^{k+1}{}_{v'(T)}(\emptyset) = v'(f^{k+1}{}_T(\emptyset))$. Thus $v(f^k{}_T(\emptyset)) = h(v'(f^k{}_T(\emptyset))) = h(v'(f^{k+1}{}_T(\emptyset))) = v(f^{k+1}{}_T(\emptyset))$; a contradiction. Thus $v(f^k{}_T(\emptyset)) = \psi(f_{v(T)}(R))$. *Q.E.D.*

Theorem 4.6 implies an algorithm to compute $\psi(f_T(R))$:

Algorithm 4.1. The least fixpoint for a set of mappings.

Input: A representation $f_T(R)$, where f is a PSUJR-expression with $\alpha(f_T) = \beta(f_T) = \alpha(R) = R$, and $T \in \mathrm{T}$.

Output: A table $U \in \mathrm{T}$, such that $rep(U) = \{\psi(f_r(R)) : r \in rep(T)\}$.

Method:

begin
  $U \leftarrow f_T(\emptyset)$;
  while $U \not\equiv f_T(U)$ **do** $U \leftarrow f_T(U)$;
end;

(* f is evaluated as f(C) *)

Theorem 4.7. Algorithm 4.1 terminates after a finite number of steps, and it correctly computes U.

Proof. By Lemma 4.2, $U \equiv f_T(U)$ is decidable. Since the algorithm is clearly a folding sequence of f_T, the finiteness and correctness follow directly from Theorem 4.6. *Q.E.D.*

Least fixpoints with Horn tables

For Horn tables we can use Algorithm 4.1, if f is restricted to be a PS+UJR-expression. The next theorem is a direct consequence of Theorem 4.5 and Theorem 4.7.

Theorem 4.8. Suppose the input to Algorithm 4.1 is a representation $f_{\mathbf{T}}(R)$, where f is a PS+UJR-expression with $\alpha(f_{\mathbf{T}}) = \beta(f_{\mathbf{T}}) = \alpha(R)$, and $\mathbf{T} \in \mathrm{T_H}$. Then the algorithm computes a table $\mathrm{U} \in \mathrm{T_H}$, such that $rep(\mathrm{U}) = \{\psi(f_{\mathbf{r}}(R)) : \mathbf{r} \in rep(\mathbf{T})\}$.

Least fixpoints with Naive tables

The next problem to consider is how to evaluate the least fixpoint queries on Naive tables. It turns out that we can use Algorithm 4.1 for this purpose, if we use the naive evaluation. We shall need a few lemmas.

Lemma 4.9. Let **T** be a Horn multitable. Then $\mathbf{T} \equiv_{\mathrm{PS^+UJR}} \mathbf{T}_*$.

Proof. We shall show that for any PS+UJR-expression f, with $\alpha(f) = \alpha(\mathbf{T})$, we have $\cap f(rep(\mathbf{T})) = \cap f(rep(\mathbf{T}_*))$. Take an arbitrary PS+UJR-expression f. Then from Theorem 4.5 it follows that $\cap f(rep(\mathbf{T}_*)) = \cap rep(f_{(C)}(\mathbf{T}_*))$. Now

$$\begin{array}{lll}
\cap rep(f_{(C)}(\mathbf{T}_*)) = \cap rep((f_{(C)}(\mathbf{T}_*))_*) & \text{by Lemma 4.6 (i)} \\
\cap rep((f_{(C)}(\mathbf{T}_*))_*) = \cap rep(f_{(N)}((\mathbf{T}_*)_*)) & \text{by Lemma 4.6 (ii)} \\
\cap rep(f_{(N)}((\mathbf{T}_*)_*)) = \cap rep(f_{(N)}(\mathbf{T}_*)) & \text{by definition} \\
\cap rep(f_{(N)}(\mathbf{T}_*)) = \cap rep((f_{(C)}(\mathbf{T}))_*) & \text{by Lemma 4.6 (ii)} \\
\cap rep((f_{(C)}(\mathbf{T}))_*) = \cap rep(f_{(C)}(\mathbf{T})) & \text{by Lemma 4.6 (i)} \\
\cap rep(f_{(C)}(\mathbf{T})) = \cap f(rep(\mathbf{T})) & \text{by Theorem 4.5.}
\end{array}$$

Q.E.D.

The next result is a generalization of Lemma 4.6 (ii). There we had $f_{(N)}(\mathbf{T}_*) = (f_{(C)}(\mathbf{T}))_*$, for appropriate f and **T**. By induction this obviously generalizes to $f_{(N)}{}^k{}_{\mathbf{T}_*}(\mathrm{U}_*) = (f_{(C)}{}^k{}_{\mathbf{T}}(\mathrm{U}))_*$, for all $k \geq 1$. Formally, we have

Lemma 4.10. Let f be a PS+UJR expression with $\alpha(f_{\mathbf{T}}) = \beta(f_{\mathbf{T}}) = \alpha(\mathrm{U})$, where **T** and U are tables in $\mathrm{T_H}$, such that $\lambda(\mathbf{T}) = \lambda(\mathrm{U})$. Then for all $k \geq 1$,

$$f_{(N)}{}^k{}_{\mathbf{T}_*}(\mathrm{U}_*) = (f_{(C)}{}^k{}_{\mathbf{T}}(\mathrm{U}))_*.$$

Theorem 4.9. Let $f_{\mathbf{T}}(R)$ be the representation of a set of mappings, where $\alpha(f_{\mathbf{T}}) = \beta(f_{\mathbf{T}}) = \alpha(R) = R$, and f is a $PS^{+}UJR$ expression, and **T** a naive multitable. Then there is a $k \geq 1$, such that $f_{(N)}{}^{k}{}_{\mathbf{T}}(\emptyset) \equiv_{PS^{+}UJR} \psi(f_{\mathbf{T}}(R))$. Here ø means an empty naive table of type $\alpha(R)$, with $\lambda(\emptyset) = \{\mathbf{true}\}$.

Proof. By Theorem 4.6, we have $\psi(f_{\mathbf{T}}(R)) = f_{(C)}{}^{k}{}_{\mathbf{T}}(\emptyset)$, for some $k \geq 1$. By Lemma 4.9, $f_{(C)}{}^{k}{}_{\mathbf{T}}(\emptyset) \equiv_{PS^{+}UJR} (f_{(C)}{}^{k}{}_{\mathbf{T}}(\emptyset))_{*}$. Since $\mathbf{T} = \mathbf{T}_{*}$ for Naive tables, it follows from Lemma 4.10, that $(f_{(C)}{}^{k}{}_{\mathbf{T}}(\emptyset))_{*} = f_{(N)}{}^{k}{}_{\mathbf{T}}(\emptyset)$. Consequently $f_{(N)}{}^{k}{}_{\mathbf{T}}(\emptyset) \equiv_{PS^{+}UJR} \psi(f_{\mathbf{T}}(R))$. *Q.E.D.*

Now Algorithm 4.1 can be modified to evaluate least fixpoints for naive tables. Algorithm 4.2 is the modification.

Algorithm 4.2. The least fixpoint for a set of mappings represented by a Naive table.

Input: A representation $f_{\mathbf{T}}(R)$, where f is a $PS^{+}UJR$-expression with $\alpha(f_{\mathbf{T}}) = \beta(f_{\mathbf{T}}) = \alpha(R)$, and $\mathbf{T} \in T_N$.

Output: A table $U \in T_N$, such that $rep(U) \equiv_{PS^{+}UJR} \{\psi(f_{\mathbf{r}}(R)) : \mathbf{r} \in rep(\mathbf{T})\}$.

Method:

```
begin
    U ← f_T(ø);
    while U ≠ f_T(U) do U ← f_T(U);
end;

(* f is evaluated as f(N) *)
```

Theorem 4.10. Algorithm 4.2 terminates after a finite number of steps, and it correctly computes U.

Proof. The correctness and finiteness is clear from Theorem 4.9. The only thing we have to be sure of is that the condition in the **while** loop is sufficient, i.e. that $U = f_T(U)$ only if $U \equiv_{PS^+UJR} f_T(U)$. But this is obvious. *Q.E.D.*

We note that a fixpoint query with a naive table can be computed exactly as the fixpoints with relations, provided that we use the naive evaluation.

The result of the study of fixpoint queries is that the menu of operations in the various query systems can be augmented with a fixpoint operator in accordance with the following theorem.

Theorem 4.11.
(i) <T, *rep*, PSUJRDY> is a strong and weak query system,
(ii) <T_H, *rep*, PS^+UJRY^+> is a strong and weak query system, and
(iii) <T_N, *rep*, PS^+UJRY^+> is a weak query system.

A final comment is that we have not considered least fixpoints with Codd tables. This is because Codd tables can weakly support only the selection, renaming and projection operators. Now, if $f(R)$ is a PSR-expression, f converges after one folding. Since this fact is quite obvious we shall spare the reader from a tedious proof. The conclusion is that the least fixpoint operator with Codd tables does not give any more power than the PSR-expressions. The same is certainly true for PUR-expressions. Thus Codd tables do not strongly or weakly support any nontrivial least fixpoint queries.

To complete the picture of the various query systems we shall augment the table in Figure 4.1 on page 71 with the results of Theorem 4.11. This gives us the table in Figure 4.2 below. From the table we see that the ability to support fixpoint queries goes hand in hand with the ability to support ordinary queries. Where we have PSUJR we also have Y, and were we have PS^+UJR we also have Y^+.

TABLE CLASS	STRONG QUERY SYSTEM	WEAK QUERY SYSTEM
Tables	PSUJRDY	PSUJRDY
Horn tables	PS+UJRY+	PS+UJRY+
Naive tables	PUR	PS+UJRY+
Codd tables	PR	PSR

Figure 4.2. The abilities of the table classes to support queries (augmented).

4.3. Dependencies and tables

Dependency systems

In Section 3.2 we saw that when the database included dependencies, the dependencies implied some additional information. This is certainly true also when the database is represented as a table. Formally, for a set of relations X, and a set of dependencies Σ, we defined the completion $Comp_{\Sigma}(X)$, another set of relations containing all the implied information. When the set of relations is represented by a table T, we are thus faced with the problem of defining a table that represents $Comp_{\Sigma}(rep(\mathrm{T}))$. If the original table belonged to a class **T** of tables, we must require that the completed table also is a member of **T**, otherwise the query evaluation algorithms do not work correctly anymore.

Let Δ be a class of dependencies. We say that a triple <**T**, *rep*, Δ> is a *strong dependency system*, if for any finite set of dependencies $\Sigma \subseteq \Delta$, and table $\mathrm{T} \in \mathbf{T}$, with $\alpha(\Sigma) = \alpha(\mathrm{T})$, there exists a table $\Sigma(\mathrm{T}) \in \mathbf{T}$, such that

(6) $$rep(\Sigma(\mathrm{T})) = Comp_{\Sigma}(rep(\mathrm{T})).$$

On the other hand, as we are going to see in the sequel, there are classes of dependencies and tables that do not form a strong dependency system. But some classes of tables rely on Ω-equivalent representations of the tables, where Ω is the allowed set of queries. Thus we can

maintain the correctness of query evaluation in the presence of dependencies, if we find a table $\Sigma(T)$ which is Ω-equivalent to $Comp_\Sigma(rep(T))$.
Formally, a quadruple $<\mathbf{T}, rep, \Delta, \Omega>$ is a *weak dependency system*, if for any finite set of dependencies $\Sigma \subseteq \Delta$, and table $T \in \mathbf{T}$, there exists a table $\Sigma(T) \in \mathbf{T}$, such that

(7) $$rep(\Sigma(T)) \equiv_\Omega Comp_\Sigma(rep(T)).$$

We shall now examine the dependency representation properties of the four classes of tables.

Dependency systems with Tables

We recall the characterization of $Comp_\Sigma(rep(T))$ from Lemma 3.3:

$$Comp_\Sigma(rep(T)) = \psi(g(\Sigma_T)_{rep(T)}) \cap Sat(\Sigma_E).$$

The set of mappings $g(\Sigma_T)_{rep(T)}$ is constructed from the subset of tuple generating dependencies Σ_T of Σ, as in Section 3.2. That is, $g(\Sigma_T)_{rep(T)} = \{g(\Sigma_T)_r : r \in rep(T)\}$, where $g(\Sigma_T)_r$ is an expression involving the projection, join and duplication operators, i.e. it is a PS^+JR-expression. Thus Algorithm 4.1 computes us a table, say U, such that

$$rep(U) = \psi(g(\Sigma_T)_{rep(T)}).$$

The remaining problem is then to compute a table V, such that $rep(V) = rep(U) \cap Sat(\Sigma_E)$. If we find V, we can put $\Sigma(T) = V$. The algorithm below performs the task. We assume that Δ is the class of all dependencies.

Algorithm 4.3. The completion of a table.

Input: A finite set $\Sigma \subseteq \Delta$ of dependencies, and a table $T \in \mathsf{T}$, where $\alpha(\Sigma) = \alpha(T)$.

Output: A table $\Sigma(T) \in \mathsf{T}$, such that $rep(\Sigma(T)) = Comp_{\Sigma}(rep(T))$.

Method:

begin
  Compute $U = \psi(\, g(\Sigma_T)_{rep(T)})$ by Algorithm 4.1.
  for each $\pi_{B_1B_2}(f(\uparrow^n(R))) \subseteq \pi_{B_1B_2}(\uparrow^n(R)) \in \Sigma_E$ **do**
  begin
    $V \leftarrow \pi_{B_1B_2}(f(\uparrow^n(U)))$;
    for each $t \in V$ **do**
    if $t(B_1) \neq t(B_2)$ **then**
      if $t(B_1)$ and $t(B_2)$ both are constants
      then $\lambda(U) \leftarrow \lambda(U) \cup \{\neg t(CON)\}$
      else $\lambda(U) \leftarrow \lambda(U) \cup \{t(CON) \Rightarrow t(B_1) = t(B_2)\}$
  end;
  $\Sigma(T) \leftarrow U$;
end;

Before we prove the correctness of the algorithm we shall give a small example of the computation of $\Sigma(T)$. Let $\Sigma = \{A \rightarrow\rightarrow B, C \rightarrow D\}$, $\alpha(\Sigma) = ABCD$. The table T is shown below (**true** conditions are omitted).

T =

A	B	C	D	CON
a	b	c	d	
x	e	y	g	

Now $g(\Sigma_T)_{rep(T)} = \{\pi_{AB}(R) * \pi_{ACD}(R) \cup r \subseteq R \ : r \in rep(T)\}$. We first compute $U = \psi(\, g(\Sigma_T)_{rep(T)})$. U is shown below (in an equivalent shorter form).

U = A B C D	CON	
a b c d		
x e y g		
a b y g		x=a
a e c d		x=a

The functional dependency C→D corresponds to the algebraic dependency

$$\pi_{DD_1}(\pi_{ABDC}(\uparrow(R)) * \pi_{A_1B_1D_1C}(\uparrow(R))) \subseteq \pi_{DD_1}(\uparrow(R)).$$

When we apply the left-hand side of the equation to U, we get (in an equivalent form)
$\pi_{DD_1}(\pi_{ABDC}(\uparrow(U)) * \pi_{A_1B_1D_1C}(\uparrow(U))) =$

D D_1	CON	
d d		
g g		
d g		y=c

Thus the final table will be

$\Sigma(T)$ = A B C D	CON	y≠c
a b c d		
x e y g		
a b y g		x=a
a e c d		x=a

We note that the algorithm can enforce some values to be equal. As an example, take T = {(a,b,c), (a,x,d)}, with λ(T) = {**true**}, and let Σ = {A→B}. Then the algorithm will add the global condition (a=a) ⇒ (x=b). Since (a=a) ≈ **true**, we have λ(T) |= x=b. Thus we can replace x by b in T. The final table Σ(T) will be equivalent to {(a,b,c), (a,b,d)}, where λ(T) = {**true**}. We see that Algorithm 4.3 in this case works as the <u>chase</u> procedure [BV84, MMS79]. In fact, Algorithm 4.3 is a generalization of this procedure.

Theorem 4.12. Algorithm 4.3 terminates after a finite number of steps, and it correctly computes the table Σ(T).

Proof. The termination is obvious. Also, by Theorem 4.7, the intermediate table U satisfies *rep*(U) = $\psi(g(\Sigma_T)_{rep(T)})$. Thus we have to show that the first **for each** loop computes a table V, such that *rep*(V) = *rep*(U) ∩ *Sat*(Σ_E). Since the first **for each** loop adds conditions to λ(U), it is clear that the set of valuations v for which v(λ(U)) = **true** does not grow. The set of c-tuples in U is not affected. Thus we have $rep(V) \subseteq rep(U)$. We shall show that $rep(V) \subseteq Sat(\Sigma_E)$.

Take a relation r in $rep(V)$, i.e. $r = v(V)$, for some valuation v, and $v(\lambda(V)) =$ **true**. Suppose that r is not in $Sat(\Sigma_E)$. Then there must be some dependency $\rho \in \Sigma_E$, such that $r \notin Sat(\rho)$. Let $\rho = \pi_{B_1B_2}(f(\uparrow^n(R))) \subseteq \pi_{B_1B_2}(\uparrow^n(R))$, and let R' be the result type of $\uparrow^n(R)$. By Lemma 2.3 there must be a tuple $t \in \pi_{B_1B_2}(f(\uparrow^n(r)))$, such that $t(B_1) \neq t(B_2)$. Since $r = v(V)$, and $\pi_{B_1B_2}(f(\uparrow^n(v(V)))) = v(\pi_{B_1B_2}(f(\uparrow^n(V))))$ this means that there is a c-tuple t' in $\pi_{B_1B_2}(f(\uparrow^n(V)))$, such that $t = v(t'(R'))$, and $v(t'(CON)) =$ **true**. In particular $v(t'(B_1)) \neq v(t'(B_2))$. But this means that $t'(B_1) \neq t'(B_2)$, and consequently the condition $\phi = (t'(CON) \Rightarrow t'(B_1) = t'(B_2))$ or $\phi = \neg t'(CON)$ is added to $\lambda(V)$. Since $v(t'(CON)) =$ **true** and $v(\lambda(V)) =$ **true**, ϕ cannot be $\neg t'(CON)$. Then ϕ must be $t'(CON) \Rightarrow t'(B_1) = t'(B_2)$. Thus $v(\phi) =$ **true** implies that $v(t'(B_1)) = v(t'(B_2))$. We had $v(\lambda(V)) =$ **true**, $v(t'(CON)) =$ **true**, and $v(t'(B_1)) \neq v(t'(B_2))$; a contradiction. Thus the assumption $r \notin Sat(\rho)$ is wrong. Since r was chosen arbitrarily, it must be the case that $rep(V) \subseteq Sat(\Sigma)$.

Note 1. We assumed that there was a valuation v, such that $v(\lambda(V)) =$ **true**. Then it followed that $\emptyset \neq rep(V) \subseteq Sat(\Sigma_E)$. Since $rep(V) \subseteq rep(U)$, we conclude that $rep(V) \neq \emptyset$ implies that $rep(U) \cap Sat(\Sigma_E) \neq \emptyset$.

It remains to show that $rep(U) \cap Sat(\Sigma_E) \subseteq rep(V)$. Let r be in $rep(U) \cap Sat(\Sigma_E)$. Then there is a valuation v, such that $r = v(U)$, $v(\lambda(U)) =$ **true**, and $r \in Sat(\Sigma_E)$. We shall show that $v(U) = v(V)$, and $v(\lambda(V)) =$ **true**. Then the claim follows.

Since the first **for each** loop only affects the global condition, we certainly have $v(U) = v(V)$. Suppose therefore that $v(\lambda(V))$ is **false**. Since $v(\lambda(U)) =$ **true**, there must be a condition ϕ added to $\lambda(V)$ in the **for each** loop, such that $v(\phi) =$ **false**. The condition ϕ is of the form $t(CON) \Rightarrow t(B_1) = t(B_2)$, or of the form $\neg t(CON)$, for some $\rho = \pi_{B_1B_2}(f(\uparrow^n(R))) \subseteq \pi_{B_1B_2}(\uparrow^n(R)) \in \Sigma_E$, and $t \in \pi_{B_1B_2}(f(\uparrow^n(U)))$. Since $v(U) = r \in Sat(p)$, Lemma 2.3 says that for <u>all</u> tuples t' in $\pi_{B_1B_2}(f(\uparrow^n(v(U)))$ we have $t'(B_1) = t'(B_2)$, i.e. for all c-tuples t'' in $\pi_{B_1B_2}(f(\uparrow^n(U)))$, it is true that $v(t''(B_1)) = v(t''(B_2))$. Thus ϕ cannot be of the form $\neg t(CON)$. Now $v(\phi) =$**false** precisely when $v(t(CON)) =$ **true** and $v(t(B_1)) \neq v(t(B_2))$. But this is impossible by Lemma 2.3. Thus it must be that $v(\lambda(V)) =$ **true**. This proves the claim.

Note 2. We assumed that $rep(U) \cap Sat(\Sigma_E) \neq \emptyset$ and showed that there was a valuation v, such that $v(\lambda(V)) =$ **true**. Thus $rep(U) \cap Sat(\Sigma_E) \neq \emptyset$ implies $rep(V) \neq \emptyset$.

We have now proved that $rep(\Sigma(T)) = Comp_\Sigma(rep(T))$. The case where $Comp_\Sigma(rep(T)) = \emptyset$ is taken care of by the two notes. *Q.E.D.*

The preceding theorem implies the following property of the class T of tables. The theorem is a generalization of a result in [Grh84b], where the property was shown for the class of join dependencies and functional dependencies.

Theorem 4.13. Let Δ be the class of all dependencies. Then
(i) <T, *rep*, Δ> is a strong dependency system,
(ii) <T, *rep*, Δ, PSUJRD> is a weak dependency system.

Dependency systems with Horn tables

Consider Algorithm 4.3, when the input is a Horn table T. By Theorem 4.8 the intermediate table U is also a Horn table. In the **for each** loop we add conditions to λ(U). The added condition is either of the form ¬t(CON) or of the form t(CON) ⇒ $t(B_1) = t(B_2)$, where t is a tuple in $\pi_{B_1B_2}(f(\uparrow^n(U)))$, for some $\pi_{B_1B_2}(f(\uparrow^n(R)))$. By Theorem 4.5, $\pi_{B_1B_2}(f(\uparrow^n(U)))$ is also a Horn table. Obviously t(CON) ⇒ $t(B_1) = t(B_2)$ is then a Horn condition. Since t(CON) is a conjunction of equalities, ¬t(CON) is a disjunction of inequalities, and thus also a Horn condition. Consequently Algorithm 4.3 outputs a Horn table Σ(T). We have the following result.

Theorem 4.14. Let Δ be the class of all dependencies. Then
(i) <T_H, *rep*, Δ> is a strong dependency system,
(ii) <T_H, *rep*, Δ, PS^+UJR> is a weak dependency system.

Dependency systems with Naive tables

Since Naive tables have a fairly simple structure, one may ask whether they can represent dependencies. It turns out that they form a weak dependency system w.r.t. to the class of all dependencies. Let the input to Algorithm 4.3 be a Naive table T. By Theorem 4.14, the resulting table Σ(T) is a Horn table (since T is also a Horn table). By Lemma 4.9, Σ(T) $\equiv_{PS^+UJR}$ $\Sigma(T)_*$. The table $\Sigma(T)_*$ is obtained by normalizing Σ(T) and then dropping all tuples with conditions that are not tautologies. Finally the global condition is set to be {**true**} (assuming that the global condition is satisfiable). We see that $\Sigma(T)_*$ is a Naive table. The normalization can be carried out by testing for all pairs (x, δ), where x is a variable and δ is a variable or a constant in the table, whether their equality is implied by the global condition. We have thus sketched an algorithm to compute Σ(T) for a Naive table T, and a set of tuple and equality generating dependencies.

Theorem 4.15. Let Δ be the class of all dependencies. Then $<T_N, rep, \Delta, PS^{+}UJR>$ is a weak dependency system.

The algorithm we sketched computes a table that is PS⁺UJR-equivalent to the desired result. There is though a simpler way to do it, by applying a "naive" dependency enforcement algorithm. In Algorithm 4.3 we apply each dependency once. Then the desired result is obtained by normalization and dropping tuples with nontautological conditions. We shall show that we obtain the same (up to PS⁺UJR-equivalence) table by "naively" applying the dependencies. The price we have to pay is that a dependency may have to be applied more than once.

The "naive" dependency enforcement is described in Algorithm 4.4 below. In Chapter 5 we shall show that Algorithm 4.4 runs in time polynomial in the size of T.

Algorithm 4.4. The completion of a Naive table.

Input: A finite set $\Sigma \subseteq \Delta$ of dependencies, and a table $T \in T_N$, where $\alpha(\Sigma) = \alpha(T)$.
Output: A table $\Sigma(T) \in T_N$, such that $rep(\Sigma(T)) \equiv_{PS+UJR} Comp_\Sigma(rep(T))$.

Method:

```
begin
    U ← T;
    while U changes and λ(U) ≠ {false} do
    begin
        for each ρ∈ Σ do
            if ρ= f(↑n(R)) ⊆ R then
                                    (* ρ is a tuple generating dependency *)
            U ← f(↑n(U))            (* use naive evaluation *)
            else                    (* ρ is an equality generating
                                       dependency
                                    π_B1B2(f(↑n(R))) ⊆ π_B1B2(↑n(R))  *)
            begin
                V ← π_B1B2(f(↑n(U)));        (* use naive evaluation *)
                for each t ∈ V do
                if t(B1) ≠ t(B2) then
                    if t(B1) and t(B2) both are constants
                    then λ(U) ← {false}
                else replace t(B1) by t(B2) or t(B2) by t(B1) in U;
            end;
    end;
    Σ(T) ← U;
end;
```

In replacing elements in U we assume that there is a linear order on the variables (for instance the lexicographic order). Then we always replace a variable by a constant, or in the case of two variables, we replace the greater by the smaller one.

Let us look at an example before we proceed to prove the correctness of Algorithm 4.4. Let the database scheme be ABCDE, and the set of dependencies $\Sigma = \{A \rightarrow\rightarrow B, E \rightarrow A, B \rightarrow D\}$. The database is the Naive table T below.

T =

A	B	C	D	E
a	b	c	d	e
x	b'	c'	y	e

When we apply Algorithm 4.3, we get the following Horn table $\Sigma(T)$:

$\Sigma(T)$ =

A	B	C	D	E	CON	x=a, x=a ⇒y=d
a	b	c	d	e	**true**	
x	b'	c'	y	e	**true**	
x	b	c'	y	e	x=a	
x	b'	c	d	e	x=a	

Now $\Sigma(T)_*$ is clearly

A	B	C	D	E	**true**
a	b	c	d	e	
a	b'	c'	d	e	
a	b	c'	d	e	
a	b'	c	d	e	

On the other hand, starting from the original table T, we can use Algorithm 4.4, and first apply the functional dependency $E \rightarrow A$. Then we get

A	B	C	D	E	**true**
a	b	c	d	e	
a	b'	c'	y	e	

If we then apply the multivalued dependency $A \rightarrow\rightarrow B$, we obtain

A	B	C	D	E	**true**
a	b	c	d	e	
a	b'	c'	y	e	
a	b	c'	y	e	
a	b'	c	d	e	

Finally we can use the functional dependency B→D to equate y and d.

A	B	C	D	E	true
a	b	c	d	e	
a	b'	c'	d	e	
a	b	c'	d	e	
a	b'	c	d	e	

We see that the result is the same as $\Sigma(T)_*$. We note that applying the dependencies in another order would have given us different intermediate tables, but that the final result would be the same. Thus the order in which the dependencies are applied is immaterial. Formally, we have

Lemma 4.11. Algorithm 4.4 is a finite Church-Rosser replacement system, i.e. it halts after a finite number of steps, and the unique outcome does not depend on the order in which the dependencies are applied.

Proof. Algorithm 4.4 is clearly a variation of the chase-process, as it is defined in [BV84]. The chase-process is a finite Church-Rosser replacement system. *Q.E.D.*

In order to prove the correctness of Algorithm 4.4 we need some auxiliary definitions. A *homomorphism* h is a mapping on $\bigcup_{A\in U}(Dom(A) \cup Var(A))$, such that for all $a\in Dom(A)$, $h(a) = a$, and for all $x\in Var(A)$, $h(x)\in (Dom(A) \cup Var(A))$. The mapping h is extended to Naive tuples and Naive tables in the same way as valuations. Let T and U be Naive tables on some R. Then T is *embedded* in U, denoted by T«U, if there is a homomorphism h, such that $h(T) \subseteq U$. The relationship « is clearly transitive. If both T«U and U«T, then we write $T \cong U$.

Lemma 4.12. If T « U, then $T <_+ U$, i.e. $rep(T) <_+ rep(U)$.

Proof. We have $h(T) \subseteq U$, for some h. Let v be a valuation of U. Now $v \circ h$ is a valuation of T, and $v(h(T)) \subseteq v(U)$. *Q.E.D.*

Corollary 4.5. If $T \cong U$, then $T \equiv_+ U$.

Let T be the input to Algorithm 4.4. We assume that the dependencies are applied in some fixed order. By Lemma 4.11, we thereby do not lose generality. Then we denote by T^i the table obtained after applying i dependencies in Σ. Let T^∞ be the outcome of the algorithm. Since the application of a dependency either equates some values, or adds some tuples, we clearly have T « T^1« T^2« ..., and since the process is finite we get T « T^1« T^2« ... « $T^n = T^{n+1} = ... = T^\infty$, for some n.

Let U be the outcome of Algorithm 4.3 when T is given as input. Then U is a Horn table, such that all global conditions are produced by the equality generating dependencies, and all non-tautological local conditions are in tuples produced by the tuple generating dependencies. Our intention is to show that $T^{\infty} \cong U_*$. Then the correctness of Algorithm 4.4 follows, since $T^{\infty} \cong U_*$ implies (by Corollary 4.5) that $T^{\infty} \equiv_+ U_*$, and thus $T^{\infty} \equiv_{PSUJR} U_*$ (by Corollary 3.3). Furthermore $U_* \equiv_{PS^+UJR} U$ (by Lemma 4.9), and $U = Comp_{\Sigma}(rep(T))$. Consequently $T^{\infty} \equiv_{PS^+UJR} Comp_{\Sigma}(rep(T))$.

We note that U_* is obtained from U by normalizing U and keeping tuples with tautological local conditions. In computing U_* from U, we thus incorporate in U equalities of the form $x=\delta$, where $\lambda(U) \models (x=\delta)$. Here x is a variable, and δ is a variable or a constant. The language of conditions is axiomatized by the axioms of Boolean algebra and the axioms of equality. Let c be a condition. If $\lambda(U) \models c$, there is then a deduction sequence $(c_1,\ldots,c_m,c)$, where each condition c_i or c is obtained from previous conditions by the application of a deduction rule. In particular, some of the c_i:s are conditions ϕ_i in $\lambda(U)$. If the shortest deduction sequence for a condition c contains k occurrences (repetitions may occur) of conditions from $\lambda(U)$, then we denote $\lambda(U) \models_k c$. Now U_k is U with x replaced by δ, for all (x, δ), such that $\lambda(U) \models_p (x=\delta)$, where $p \leq k$. Then $(U_k)_* = \{t(R) : t \in U_k \text{ and } t(CON) \approx \textbf{true}\}$.

Let U_{∞} be U with <u>all</u> replacements done, i.e. the normalized version of U. Obviously we have $(U_1)_* \ll (U_2)_* \ll \ldots \ll (U_n)_* = (U_{n+1})_* = \ldots = (U_{\infty})_* = U_*$, for some n.

Let us illustrate the new definitions by the example from page 85. We had

T =

A	B	C	D	E	**true**
a	b	c	d	e	
x	b'	c'	y	e	

The output of Algorithm 4.3, when given T, is

U =

A	B	C	D	E	CON	x=a, x=a ⇒y=d
a	b	c	d	e	**true**	
x	b'	c	y	e	**true**	
x	b	c'	y	e	x=a	
x	b'	c	d	e	x=a	

Then

$(U_0)_*$ =

A	B	C	D	E	**true**
a	b	c	d	e	
x	b'	c'	y	e	

$(U_1)_*$ =

A	B	C	D	E	true
a	b	c	d	e	
a	b'	c'	y	e	
a	b	c'	d	e	
a	b'	c	y	e	

x is replaced by a

$(U_2)_*$ = $= (U_\infty)_* = U_*$ y is replaced by d

A	B	C	D	E	true
a	b	c	d	e	
a	b'	c'	d	e	
a	b	c'	d	e	
a	b'	c	d	e	

Applying Algorithm 4.4 to T, we get the following sequence.

T^1 = From E→A.

A	B	C	D	E	true
a	b	c	d	e	
a	b'	c'	y	e	

T^2 = From A→→B.

A	B	C	D	E	true
a	b	c	d	e	
a	b'	c	y	e	
a	b	c'	y	e	
a	b'	c	d	e	

T^3 = $= T^\infty$ From B→D.

A	B	C	D	E	true
a	b	c	d	e	
a	b'	c'	d	e	
a	b	c'	d	e	
a	b'	c	d	e	

The following theorem is the key to the correctness of Algorithm 4.4.

Theorem 4.16. $T^\infty \cong U_*$.

Proof. (i) To prove that $U_* \ll T^\infty$, we shall show by an induction on n, that for all n there is a k and a homomorphism h, such that $h((U_n)_*) \subseteq T^k$, and thus $(U_n)_* \ll T^k$. Then the claim follows, since there is then an n' and a k' such that $U_* = (U_{n'})_* \ll T^{k'} \ll T^\infty$.

(*Basis*). U_0 is clearly U with no replacements done. Thus $(U_0)_*$ can be obtained by using only the tuple generating dependencies in Algorithm 4.3, i.e. by calling Algorithm 4.1 for the mapping $g(\Sigma_T)$, which is the composition of all tuple generating dependencies. Let k be the number of iterations needed in Algorithm 4.1 to obtain U_0. If we in Algorithm 4.4 apply the tuple generating dependencies in a cyclic way k times, and if the number of tuple generating dependencies is p, it follows from Lemma 4.10 that $(U_0)_* = T^{kp}$. The mapping h is in this case the identity.

(*Induction hypothesis*). Suppose that $h((U_n)_*) \subseteq T^k$, for some n, k and h.

(*Induction step*). Let t be a tuple in $(U_{n+1})_*$. Then there is a tuple t' in U_{n+1}, with t'(R) =t, and t'(CON)≈**true**. If t' is in U_n then, by the induction hypothesis, h(t') is in T^k, and the claim follows. If t' is not in U_n, there must be an equality x=δ, such that $\lambda(U) \models_{n+1} (x=\delta)$, and $\lambda(U) \not\models_n (x=\delta)$, and replacing x by δ in U either gives us t'(R) = t or t'(CON) ≈ **true**, or both.

There can be 0 or more such equalities obtained in the n+1:st step. If there are 0 equalities, then t' is in U_n. Suppose that x=δ is the m+1:th equality incorporated in the n+1:st step, and that by a second level induction hypothesis the claim for the first level induction step is true if there are only m equalities.

Let t" be t' without x replaced by δ. There are two cases to consider.

Case 1. Replacing x by δ makes t"(R) = t and does not affect t"(CON). Then t"(CON) ≈ **true** already in U_n. By the induction hypothesis there is a $k \geq 0$, and a tuple p in T^k, such that h(t") = p. Note that the n+1:st condition used in the deduction to compute U_{n+1} must be of the form $\phi \Rightarrow (x=\delta)$, such that $\lambda(U) \models_n \phi$. Since the n+1:st condition is obtained from the application of an equality generating dependency ρ to U, φ is the conjunction of local conditions of tuples $t_1,\ldots,t_m$ in U, and of equalities among the values in these tuples. Since $\lambda(U) \models_n \phi$, it follows from the induction hypothesis that there are tuples $t_1',\ldots,t_m'$ in T^k, such that $h(t_i) = t_i'$, $1 \leq i \leq m$. Consequently, the images under h of the equalities among the values in the tuples $t_1,\ldots,t_m$ making φ true are present in the tuples $t_1',\ldots,t_m'$ in T^k. Since h is a mapping, the equalities are preserved.

Thus, when we apply the dependencies to T^k a sufficient number of times, say s times, we reach the equality generating dependency ρ. When we apply ρ to T^{k+s}, we produce T^{k+s+1}, where we have a tuple p', obtained by replacing h(x) with h(δ) in p. We then have h(t'(R)) = p', and consequently $h((U_{n+1})_*) \subseteq T^{k+s+1}$. If, in the process of going from T^k to T^{k+s+1}, other replacements of x' by δ' have been done, we note that x' is always a variable, and thus the mapping h can be changed accordingly, so that h(y) = δ', where h(y) previously was equal to x'. The change is possible, since y necessarily is a variable.

Case 2. Incorporating $x=\delta$ makes $t''(CON) \approx$ **true**. As in Case 1, we apply the dependencies s+1 times to T^k, obtaining T^{k+s+1} where h(x) is replaced by h(δ), and h is possibly changed to conform to other replacements. Since $t''(CON)$ was not **true** in U_n (nor in the original table), it must be that t" is a tuple added by the application of the tuple generating dependencies. Thus t" is composed of tuples $t_1'',\ldots,t_m''$ in the original table, and $t''(CON)$ is a conjunction of equalities among the values of these tuples. By the induction hypothesis and the application of the equality generating dependency ρ (in the k+s+1:st step), these original tuples t_i'' with values making the equalities in $t''(CON)$ **true** all have a counterpart-tuple p_i in T^{k+s+1}, such that $h(t_i''(R)) = p_i$, $1 \leq i \leq m$. When we then apply the tuple generating dependencies a sufficient number of times, say q times, to T^{k+s+1}, we will produce a tuple p, in $T^{k+s+1+q}$, such that $h(t''(R)) = p$. Thus $h((U_{n+1})_*) \subseteq T^{k+s+1+q}$.

(ii) To show that $T^\infty \ll U_*$, we use an induction on n to demonstrate that for all n, there is a k, and a mapping h, such that $h(T^n) \subseteq (U_k)_*$.

(*Basis*). If t belongs to $T^0 = T$, then clearly t belongs to $(U_0)_*$. The mapping h is the identity in this case.

(*Induction hypothesis*). Suppose that $h(T^n) \subseteq (U_k)_*$, for some n, k and h.

(*Induction step*). Let t be a tuple in T^{n+1}. If t belongs to T^n, the claim follows from the induction hypothesis. If not, there are two cases to consider.

Case 1. t is obtained from a tuple t' in T^n, by the application of an equality generating dependency ρ to T^n, replacing an x by a δ. This means that there are tuples $t_1,\ldots,t_m$ in T^n, such that some equalities of values between these tuples by the application of ρ produces the equality $x = \delta$. By the induction hypothesis there are tuples $p_1,\ldots,p_m$ and p' in $(U_k)_*$, such that $h(t_i) = p_i$, and $h(t') = p'$. This means that the tuples $p_1,\ldots,p_m$, p' with local conditions **true** are all in U_k, and since the local conditions are conjunctions of equalities, he have $\lambda(U) \models_k p_i(CON)$ and $\lambda(U) \models_k p'(CON)$. Since the equality generating dependency ρ has been applied to U, it follows that we will have a condition $\phi \Rightarrow h(x)=h(\delta)$ in λ(U), where φ is the conjunction of the local conditions of the p_i:s and equalities among values in these tuples. Thus $\lambda(U) \models_k \phi$, and consequently $\lambda(U) \models_{k+1} h(x)=h(\delta)$, and when we replace h(x) by h(δ) in p', we obtain the tuple p in $(U_{k+1})_*$, where $h(t) = p$. Consequently $h(T^{n+1}) \subseteq (U_{k+1})_*$. If there are any other x' and δ', such that $\lambda(U) \models_{k+1} x'=\delta'$ and $\lambda(U) \not\models_k x'=\delta'$, then we change h to conform to these replacements.

Case 2. t is obtained from tuples $t_1,\ldots,t_m$ in T^n, by the application of a tuple generating dependency ρ to T^n. By the induction hypothesis there are tuples $p_1,\ldots,p_m$ in $(U_k)_*$, such that $h(t_i) = p_i$, $1 \leq i \leq m$. Thus the tuples $p_1,\ldots,p_m$ with local conditions **true** are in U_k. Since all tuple generating dependencies have been applied to U, it follows that a tuple p, produced by $p_1,\ldots,p_m$, is in U. Now p(CON) consists of the conjunction of the local conditions of the p_i:s, and of possible equalities among the values in $p_1,\ldots,p_m$. These equalities were present in $t_1,\ldots,t_m$, and since they are preserved by h they are also present in $p_1,\ldots,p_m$. Consequently the equalities making p(CON) **true** are already incorporated in U_k. Thus p(R) is in $(U_k)_*$, and h(t) = p(R), which means that $h(T^{n+1}) \subseteq (U_k)_*$. *Q.E.D.*

Corollary 4.6. Let the input to Algorithm 4.4. be a Naive table T and a set Σ of dependencies. Then the algorithm outputs a table Σ(T), such that $\Sigma(T) \equiv_{PS^+UJR} Comp_\Sigma(rep(T))$.

We note that a result resembling Corollary 4.6 was claimed in [IL83]. A formal proof to support it has however not appeared.

It should be clear that Naive tables cannot strongly represent tuple generating dependencies, since they cannot strongly represent joins (Theorem 4.3 (iii)). To strongly represent equality generating dependencies, it is necessary to somehow state inequalities between variables and constants. It is quite plausible that this goes beyond the capabilities of the Naive tables.

Codd tables on the other hand, cannot even weakly represent PJ-expressions (Corollary 4.3 (iii)). Thus we conclude that they cannot weakly represent tuple generating dependencies. In the discussion preceding Theorem 4.16, we saw that it might be necessary to equate some variables in order to get a weak representation of equality generating dependencies. This is not possible in Codd tables, and hence we cannot weakly represent equality generating dependencies either.

Summary of the dependency systems

The ability to represent dependencies depends on the table class, and not on the class of dependencies: our results show that whenever a class of tables has the ability to represent dependencies, it can represent both tuple and equality generating dependencies. With respect to the computational complexity, there will be a contrast between tuple and equality generation. We return to this issue in Chapter 5. The representation properties for the four classes of tables are summarized in Figure 4.3 below. The abbreviation TGD means tuple generating dependency, and EGD means equality generating dependency.

TABLE CLASS	STRONG DEP. SYSTEM	WEAK DEP. SYSTEM
Tables	TGD's and EGD's	TGD's and EGD's
Horn tables	TGD's and EGD's	TGD's and EGD's
Naive tables	no dependencies	TGD's and EGD's
Codd tables	no dependencies	no dependencies

Figure 4.3. Dependency systems.

Dependencies are in essence least fixpoint queries (they are close to Y^+, although some differences occur, mainly due to typing and equality generation). As our study shows, if we can strongly represent Y^+, then we can also strongly represent dependencies (tables and Horn tables), and if we can weakly represent Y^+, then we can also weakly represent dependencies (Naive tables). In particular, we note that nontrivial local resp. global conditions are necessary in order to strongly represent tuple generating resp. equality generating dependencies.

4.4. Updates and tables

Update systems

So far we have studied the abilities of different table classes to represent the result of queries and the additional information implied by a set of dependencies. In Section 3.3 we defined four types of updates. When we have chosen to work with a particular class **T** of tables, it is important to know what updates we can perform on the tables, and still remain in the class **T**.

Assume that ϑ is a class of update operations. Then a triple <**T**, *rep*, ϑ> is a *strong update system*, if for any update $\upsilon \in \vartheta$, and table $T \in \mathbf{T}$, there exists a table $\upsilon(T) \in \mathbf{T}$, such that

(8) $rep(\upsilon(T)) = \upsilon(rep(T))$.

As with queries and dependencies we can expect that there will be tables T and updates υ, for which such a $\upsilon(T)$ does not exist. In this case we can still hope to get an Ω-equivalent result. Then we can use $\upsilon(T)$ as a basis for querying for certain results.

Formally we state that a quadruple <**T**, *rep*, ϑ, Ω> is a *weak update system*, if for any update $\upsilon \in \vartheta$, and table T$\in$**T**, there exists a table υ(T)$\in$**T**, such that

(9) $$rep(\upsilon(T)) \equiv_{\Omega} \upsilon(rep(T)).$$

We will now study the update representation properties of the table classes.

Updating Tables

As we can expect the class T of tables is powerful enough to represent all updates. We have the following theorem.

Theorem 4.17. Let ϑ consist of the absolute and positive insertions and deletions. Then < T, *rep*, ϑ> is a strong update system.

Proof. The proof will be rather long. We shall consider one update type at a time.

(***absolute insertions***). Recall the definition of an absolute insertion. Let ϕ be an equation of the form $\{t\} \subseteq \pi_X(R)$, and T a table, where $\alpha(R) = \alpha(T) = R$ and $X \subseteq R$. Then a-ins$_\phi$(*rep*(T)) = *rep*(T) $\cap$ *Sat*(ϕ).

Let us give an example. Suppose the we have the following table T. (The table T will be used as a running example in the proof.)

EMPLOYEE	DEPARTMENT	MANAGER	CON	**true**
Jones	x	y	y≠smith	
Smith	Toys	z	z=brown	

Now we want to insert the fact that the department of Jones is cars. The equation ϕ is then $\{(\text{Jones, Cars})\} \subseteq \pi_{\text{EMPLOYEE DEPARTMENT}}(R)$. The resulting (equivalent) table will be

EMPLOYEE	DEPARTMENT	MANAGER	CON	y≠smith
Jones	Cars	y	**true**	
Smith	Toys	z	z=brown	

Note that if the insertion equation would have been

$$\{(\text{Doe, Cars})\} \subseteq \pi_{\text{EMPLOYEE DEPARTMENT}}(R),$$

then the result would be empty. In this case we would try to assert something that is not consistent with the database.

In general, the insertion algorithm is as follows. We want to compute a-ins$_\phi$(T), where ϕ is $\{t\} \subseteq \pi_X(R)$, and T is a table, with $\alpha(R) = \alpha(T) = R$ and $X \subseteq R$. Let u be a c-tuple on R and v a c-tuple on S, where S is a subset of R. Then we say that v *subsumes* u *on* S, if for all $A \in S$, such that u(A) is a constant, we have u(A) = v(A). We define the following set of c-tuples:

$$T_t = \{u : u \in T, u(CON) \text{ is satisfiable, and t subsumes u on } X\}.$$

Now

$$\text{a-ins}_\phi(T) = T,$$

$$\lambda(\text{a-ins}_\phi(T)) = \begin{cases} \lambda(T) \cup \left\{ \bigvee_{u \in T_t} \left(\left(\bigwedge_{A \in X} u(A) = t(A) \right) \wedge u(CON) \right) \right\} & \text{if } T_t \neq \emptyset \\ \{\textbf{false}\} \text{ if } T_t = \emptyset. \end{cases}$$

We have to show that *rep*(a-ins$_\phi$(T)) = *rep*(T) $\cap$ *Sat*(ϕ).

Denote a-ins$_\phi$(T) by U. Let r be a relation in *rep*(U). Then there is a valuation v, such that r = v(U), and v(λ(U)) = **true**. In particular *rep*(U) $\subseteq$ *rep*(T). Obviously v(U) = v(T). Since λ(T) is a subset of λ(U), v(λ(T)) is **true.** Since v(λ(U)) is **true**, v must make **true** at least one of the disjuncts in $\bigvee_{u \in T_t}(\ldots)$. This means that there is a c-tuple u in T and consequently in U, such that v(u(CON)) = **true**, and v(u(X)) = t. Thus $\{t\} \subseteq \pi_X(v(U))$, i.e. v(U) $\subseteq$ *Sat*(ϕ). Consequently *rep*(U) $\subseteq$ *rep*(T) $\cap$ *Sat*(ϕ).

Note 1. We assumed that *rep*(U) was nonempty, and it followed that *rep*(T) $\cap$ *Sat*(ϕ) was nonempty.

To show that *rep*(T) $\cap$ *Sat*(ϕ) $\subseteq$ *rep*(U), let r be a relation in the left hand side. Then there is a valuation v, such that r = v(T), v(λ(T)) = **true**, and $t \subseteq \pi_X$(v(T). Thus there must be a c-tuple u in T, such that v(u(X)) = t, and v(u(CON)) = **true**. It follows that v(λ(U)) = **true**. Thus r is in *rep*(U).

Note 2. We assumed that *rep*(T) $\cap$ *Sat*(ϕ) was nonempty, and we showed that *rep*(U) was nonempty.

This concludes the proof of the fact that *rep*(a-ins$_\phi$(T)) = *rep*(T) $\cap$ *Sat*(ϕ). The case where *rep*(T) $\cap$ *Sat*(ϕ) = $\emptyset$ is taken care of by the two notes.

(***positive insertions***). We recall the definition of the positive insertion. Let ϕ be $\{t\} \subseteq \pi_X(R)$, and T a table, where $\alpha(R) = \alpha(T) = R$ and $X \subseteq R$. Then $\text{p-ins}_\phi(rep(T)) = rep(T) \cup \{t' : t'$ is a tuple on R, and $\pi_X(t') = t\}$. If we take the previous example, the resulting table is

EMPLOYEE	DEPARTMENT	MANAGER	CON	**true**
Jones	x	y	y≠smith	
Smith	Toys	z	z≠brown	
Jones	Cars	w	**true**	

To compute the resulting table in general, we define a c-tuple $\pi_X^{-1}(t)$ on R:

$$(\pi_X^{-1}(t))(A) = \begin{cases} t(A) & \text{for all } A \in X \\ \text{a "new" variable in } Var(A) & \text{for all } A \in R-X. \end{cases}$$

$$(\pi_X^{-1}(t))(CON) = \mathbf{true}$$

By "new" in the definition above we mean a variable that does not occur in T. All variables in $\pi_X^{-1}(t)$ are assumed to be distinct. Now the following table, called $\text{p-ins}_\phi(T)$, accomplishes the update:

$$\text{p-ins}_\phi(T) = T \cup \{\pi_X^{-1}(t)\}, \text{ and}$$

$$\lambda(\text{p-ins}_\phi(T)) = \lambda(T).$$

The table $\text{p-ins}_\phi(T)$ is called U, for short. We claim that $rep(U) = rep(T) \cup \{t' : t'$ is a tuple on R, and $\pi_X(t') = t\}$. Call the last set X. Let r be a relation in $rep(U)$. Then there is a valuation v, such that $r = v(U)$, and $v(\lambda(U)) = \mathbf{true}$. Now $v(U) = v(T) \cup v((\pi_X^{-1}(t))(R))$. Since $v(\lambda(U)) = \mathbf{true}$, we have $v(\lambda(T)) = \mathbf{true}$. Thus v(T) is in $rep(T)$. Obviously $v((\pi_X^{-1}(t))(R))$ is in X. Thus $rep(U) \subseteq rep(T) \cup X$. Inclusion in the other direction can be shown similarly.

(***absolute deletions***). We remind the reader of the definition of the absolute deletion. Let ϕ be an equation of the form $\sigma_E(R) \subseteq \emptyset$, and T a table, where $\alpha(R) = \alpha(T) = R$. Then $\text{a-del}_\phi(rep(T)) = rep(T) \cap Sat(\phi)$. To give an example, let the T be the example table, and suppose that we want to delete the toys department with the equation $\sigma_{DEPARTMENT=Toys}(R) \subseteq \emptyset$. The resulting table is then

EMPLOYEE	DEPARTMENT	MANAGER	CON	x≠toys ∨ y=smith, z≠brown
Jones	x	y	y≠Smith	
Smith	Toys	z	z=Brown	

The second c-tuple can be dropped from the table. In general, the resulting table, called a-del$_\phi$(T) is computed as follows. The equation ϕ is $\sigma_E(R) \subseteq \emptyset$.

$$\text{a-del}_\phi(T) = T,$$

$$\lambda(\text{a-del}_\phi(T)) = \lambda(T) \cup \{\neg E(t) \vee \neg t(CON) : t \in T\}.$$

The table a-del$_\phi$(T) is called U, for short. We shall show that *rep*(U) = *rep*(T) ∩ *Sat*(ϕ).

Let r be a relation in *rep*(U). Then there is a valuation v, such that r = v(U), and v(λ(U)) = **true**. Obviously v(U)∈ *rep*(T). Since v(λ(U)) = **true**, it is the case that for all c-tuples t in U, v(E(t)) = **false** or v(t(CON)) = **false**. Thus σ_E(v(U)) = ∅. Consequently v(U) is in *Sat*(ϕ), and *rep*(U) ⊆ *rep*(T) ∩ *Sat*(ϕ).

Then, let v be a valuation, such that v(λ(T)) = **true** and v(T) is in *Sat*(ϕ).Thus σ_E(v(T)) = ∅, which means that for all c-tuples t in T, v(E(t)) = **false**, or v(t(CON)) = **false**. But this means that v(λ(U)) =**true**. Thus v(T) is in *rep*(U), and consequently *rep*(T) ∩ *Sat*(ϕ) ⊆ *rep*(U).

(positive deletions). Let ϕ be an equation of the form $\sigma_E(R) \subseteq \emptyset$, and T a table, where $\alpha(R)$ = α(T) = R. Then the result of the positive deletion, denoted by a-del$_\phi$(*rep*(T)) is $\sigma_{\neg E}$(*rep*(T)). By Corollary 4.5 this set equivalent to *rep*($\sigma_{\neg E}$(T)), where $\sigma_{\neg E}$(T) is computed using the conditional evaluation. Thus the positive deletions cause no problems. To give an example of a positive deletion we take the example table T from the absolute deletion. Applying the same deletion as a positive one, the resulting table would be equivalent to

EMPLOYEE	DEPARTMENT	MANAGER	CON	**true**
Jones	x	y	y≠smith ∧ x≠toys	

This concludes the proof of Theorem 4.17, showing that the class of tables can strongly represent the result of all four types of updates. *Q.E.D.*

As *rep*(υ(T)) = υ(*rep*(T) implies *rep*(υ(T)) $\equiv_{PSUJRD}$ υ(*rep*(T), the class of tables also form a weak update system.

Corollary 4.7. Let ϑ consist of the absolute and positive insertions and deletions. Then < T, *rep*, ϑ, PSUJRD> is a weak update system.

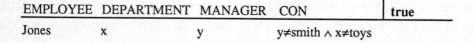

Updating Horn tables and Naive tables

Since the conditions in Horn tables and Naive tables are of a restricted form we will lose the ability to represent some updates. Let us see what happens with the absolute insertions.

Theorem 4.18. Let ϑ contain the absolute insertion. Then
(i) $< T_H$, *rep*, $\vartheta >$ is <u>not</u> a strong update system,
(ii) $< T_H$, *rep*, ϑ, $PS^+ >$ is <u>not</u> a weak update system,
(iii) $< T_N$, *rep*, $\vartheta >$ is <u>not</u> a strong update system,
(iv) $< T_N$, *rep*, ϑ, $PS^+ >$ is <u>not</u> a weak update system.

Proof. (i) Let T be the Horn table

A	B	CON	true
a	x	**true**	
a'	y	**true**	

Note that T is also a Naive table (and a Codd table). The absolute insertion is $\{(b)\} \subseteq \pi_B(R)$. Applying the algorithm of Theorem 4.17 we get the following table U:

A	B	CON	$x=b \vee y=b$
a	x	**true**	
a'	y	**true**	

Obviously U is not a Horn table. We claim that there is <u>no</u> Horn table V, such that *rep*(V) = *rep*(U), or *rep*(V) $\equiv_{PS^+}$ *rep*(U). Suppose therefore to the contrary that there <u>is</u> a Horn table V, such that *rep*(V) = *rep*(U). Then, by Lemma 4.9, V $\equiv_{PS^+} V_*$, and consequently $V_* \equiv_{PS^+}$ U. In particular, V_* is a naive table.

By inspection of U, we see that $\cap\, \pi_B(\sigma_{A=a}(rep(U))) = \emptyset$, and $\cap\, \pi_B(\sigma_{A=a'}(rep(U))) = \emptyset$, and furthermore that $\cap\, \pi_B(\sigma_{A=a \vee A=a'}(rep(U))) = \{(b)\}$. Call these expressions f_1, f_2, and f_3, respectively. We are expected to get the same result when we apply these PS^+-expressions to the Naive table V_*. From f_3 it follows that there must be a tuple t in V_* such that t(B) = b. If t(A) = a, then $\cap\, f_1(rep(V_*)) = \{(a)\}$, and if t(A) = a', then $\cap\, f_1(rep(V_*)) = \{(a')\}$; both cases contradict $V_* \equiv_{PS^+}$ U. The remaining possibilities are that either t(A) is a constant different from a and a', or t(A) is a variable. In both cases $\cap\, f_3(rep(V_*)) = \emptyset \neq \cap\, f_3(rep(U))$, again contradicting $V_* \equiv_{PS^+}$ U.

(ii), (iii), and (iv) follows directly from (i). *Q.E.D.*

In the case where there is only <u>one</u> tuple in T that is subsumed by t on X, the absolute insertion by the equation $\{t\} \subseteq \pi_X(R)$ into T yields a Horn table. This property follows directly from the definition of the absolute insertion. Formally, the restriction is that T_t contains at most one tuple. Unfortunately this restriction is state dependent, but from a practical point of view it could be used to allow (some) absolute updates to Horn tables.

The next class of updates to consider is the one of positive insertions. From the proof of Theorem 4.17 we see that the tuple $\pi_X^{-1}(t)$ is a Naive tuple. If we start with a Horn table or a Naive table the result is obviously a Horn table or a Naive table. Therefore we have

Theorem 4.19. Let ϑ consist of positive insertions. Then
(i) $< T_H, rep, \vartheta>$ is a strong update system,
(ii) $< T_H, rep, \vartheta, PS^+UJR>$ is a weak update system,
(iii) $< T_N, rep, \vartheta>$ is a strong update system,
(iv) $< T_N, rep, \vartheta, PS^+UJR>$ is a weak update system.

Then we look at the absolute deletions. The conditions added to the global condition are of the form $\neg E(t) \vee \neg t(CON)$. If we start with a Horn table, then t(CON) is a conjunction of equalities. If we in addition assume that the selection expression E is a conjunction of equalities, then $\neg E(t) \vee \neg t(CON)$ is obviously a Horn condition. The same fact holds if t(CON) is **true**, as in Naive tables. Therefore the result of the update is a Horn table. By Lemma 4.9, we can compute a Naive table PS^+UJR- equivalent to the result. We thus have the following result.

Theorem 4.20. Let ϑ consist of absolute deletions $\sigma_E(R) \subseteq \emptyset$, where E is a conjunction of equalities. Then
(i) $< T_H, rep, \vartheta>$ is a strong update system,
(ii) $< T_H, rep, \vartheta, PS^+UJR>$ is a weak update system,
(iii) $< T_N, rep, \vartheta, PS^+UJR>$ is a weak update system.

We note that the update system (iii) in the theorem is not of practical interest. If we start with a naive table, the resulting table U will have a global condition of the form $\{\neg E(t) : t \in T\}$. Thus no equalities can be implied. When the table U_* is computed, it is then obvious that U_* is U with global condition **true** or **false**. Thus the update either has no effect, or the result is empty.

To strongly represent the result of an absolute deletion requires a non-trivial global condition. Therefore the Naive tables do not form a strong update system w.r.t. absolute deletions.

Theorem 4.21. Let ϑ consist of absolute deletions $\sigma_E(R) \subseteq \emptyset$, where E is a conjunction of equalities. Then $< T_N, rep, \vartheta>$ is <u>not</u> a strong update system.

Proof. Let T be the Naive table that consists of the tuple (x,b, **true**), and with global condition **true.** The absolute deletion ϕ is $\sigma_{A=a}(R) \subseteq \emptyset$. We claim that there is <u>no</u> Naive table U, such that *rep*(U) = *rep*(T) $\cap$ *Sat*(ϕ). If U exists, it obviously must contain a tuple t with t(B) = b. If t(A) is a variable, there is a relation r in *rep*(U), such that (a,b)$\in$r, which implies that *rep*(U) $\not\subset$*Sat*(ϕ). If t(A) is a constant different from a, then *rep*(T) $\cap$ *Sat*(ϕ) $\not\subset$ *rep*(U). *Q.E.D.*

The last class of updates is finally the positive deletions. They introduce negations in the local conditions, and thus we can expect that there is no Horn table strongly or weakly representing the result. This is indeed the case. It is also the case that there are positive deletions on Naive tables, such that no Naive table is PS+-equivalent to the result of the deletion.

Theorem 4.22. Let ϑ contain positive deletions. Then
(i) $<T_H$, *rep*, $\vartheta>$ is <u>not</u> a strong update system,
(ii) $<T_H$, *rep*, ϑ, PS+> is <u>not</u> a weak update system.
(iii) $<T_N$, *rep*, ϑ, PS+> is <u>not</u> a weak update system.

Proof. (i) The proof is similar to the proof of Theorem 4.18. Let T be the Horn table

A	B	C	CON	$x \neq b \vee y \neq b$
a	x	c	**true**	
a'	y	c	**true**	

The deletion is $\sigma_{B=b}(R) \subseteq \emptyset$. The resulting table U is

A	B	C	CON	$x \neq b \vee y \neq b$
a	x	c	$x \neq b$	
a'	y	c	$y \neq b$	

We claim that there is <u>no</u> Horn table V equivalent, or PS+-equivalent to U. If such a table V would exist, then by Lemma 4.9, a Naive table V_*, with $V_* \equiv_{PS+} V$ would exist. Consequently we would have $V_* \equiv_{PS+} U$. Let us consider the PS+-expressions $\pi_A(R)$ and $\pi_C(\sigma_{A=a \vee A=a'}(R))$. We see that $\cap\, \pi_A(rep(U)) = \emptyset$, and that $\cap\, \pi_C(\sigma_{A=a \vee A=a'}(rep(U)) = \{(c)\}$. If V_* were to exist we would get the same results from V_*. Thus there would have to be a tuple t in V_*, such that t(C) =c. If t(A) was any constant, then $\cap\, \pi_A(rep(V_*))$ would not be empty. If t(A) was a variable, then $\cap\, \pi_C(\sigma_{A=a \vee A=a'}(rep(V_*))$ would be empty. Thus such a Naive table V_* cannot exist. Consequently the Horn table V cannot exist either.

(ii) follows directly from (i).

(iii). Let T be the Naive table

A	B	C	CON	true
a	x	b	true	
a'	e	x	true	

Here the deletion is $\sigma_{B=b}(R) \subseteq \emptyset$. The resulting table U is

A	B	C	CON	true
a	x	b	$x \neq b$	
a'	e	x	true	

Now we have $\cap\, \pi_C(\sigma_{A=a \vee A=a'}(rep(U)) = \{(b)\}$, $\cap\, \pi_A(rep(U)) = \{(a')\}$, and $\cap\, \pi_{AC}(rep(U)) = \emptyset$. Suppse then that there is a Naive table V, such that $V \equiv_{PS+} U$. It then follows that $\cap\, \pi_C(\sigma_{A=a \vee A=a'}(rep(V)) = \{(b)\}$. Thus there must be a tuple t in V, such that t(C) = b, and t(A) = a, or t(A) = a'. If t(A) = a, we get $(a) \in \cap\, \pi_A(rep(V))$; a contradiction to the fact that $V \equiv_{PS+} U$. If t(A) = a', we get the contradiction $(a',b) \in \cap\, \pi_{AC}(rep(V))$. Thus there exists no Naive table V, such that $V \equiv_{PS+} U$. *Q.E.D.*

Updating Codd tables

We shall end this section by studying the update properties of Codd tables. It turns out that Codd tables strongly support positive insertions and deletions, and that they do not even weakly support the absolute updates. Let us begin with the negative result. Since Codd tables form a weak query system w.r.t. PSR-expressions, the weak update system we could hope for would be w.r.t. these expressions.

Theorem 4.23. If ϑ contains either absolute insertions or absolute deletions, then $<T_C, rep, \vartheta, PS>$ is not a weak update system.

Proof. Suppose that ϑ contains the absolute insertion, and let the (general) table U be the exact result of the insertion. If there exists a Codd table V, such that $V \equiv_{PS} U$, then $V \equiv_{PS+} U$. In particular, V is also a Horn table. From the proof of Theorem 4.18, it follows that such a V cannot exist.

The proof for the absolute deletions is similar to the proof of Theorem 4.21. *Q.E.D.*

Let us then look at the positive updates. The positive insertion is accomplished by adding a tuple $\pi_X^{-1}(t)$ to the table. Obviously $\pi_X^{-1}(t)$ is a Codd tuple, and since $\pi_X^{-1}(t)$ contains only variables that do not appear in the table we are updating, the resulting table still has only one occurrence of each variable. Thus it is a Codd table.

The result of the positive deletion is $\sigma_{\neg E}(rep(T))$. By Corollary 4.3, Codd tables form a weak representation system w.r.t. PSR expressions. This means that when we use Codd evaluation, we get $rep(\sigma_{\neg E}(T)) \equiv_{PSR} \sigma_{\neg E}(rep(T))$.

To complete the picture of Codd tables, we note that Codd tables do not form a strong update system w.r.t. to positive deletions. This fact follows directly from Theorem 4.4 (ii), which states that we cannot strongly represent the result of positive selections in Codd tables.

All in all we thus have:

Theorem 4.24.
(i) $<T_C$, *rep*, $\vartheta>$ is a strong update system for ϑ consisting of positive insertions, and
(ii) $<T_C$, *rep*, $\vartheta>$ is not a strong update system if ϑ contains the positive deletion.
(iii) $<T_C$, *rep*, ϑ, PSR$>$ is a weak update system for ϑ consisting of positive deletions.

Summary of the update systems

The results of this section are collected together in the table in Figure 4.4 below. The rows show the representation properties for each table class and operation class.

TABLE CLASS	ABSOLUTE INSERTION	ABSOLUTE DELETION	POSITIVE INSERTION	POSITIVE DELETION
Tables	strong	strong	strong	strong
Horn tables	none	strong 1)	strong	none
Naive tables	none	weak 2)	strong	none
Codd tables	none	none	strong	weak

1) For deletions $\sigma_E(R) \subseteq \emptyset$, where E is a conjunction of equalities.
2) Not of practical interest.

Figure 4.4. Update representations.

As for queries and dependencies, the tables are able to strongly support all operations. The more practical class of Horn tables support strongly positive insertions and absolute deletions. From a practical point of view, it might be worthwhile to allow absolute deletions in Horn tables, and verify for each deletion that the result is a Horn table (cf. the discussion after Theorem 4.18). Since Naive tables represent positive information, it is not very surprising that this class does not allow deletions.

Updating tables in the presence of dependencies

In Chapter 3 we defined the semantics of updates. We saw that when a set of dependencies was present, it had an impact on the update operations. We assumed that the database satisfied the dependencies before the update, and we required this to be true after the update also. If we substitute $\mathcal{X}$ by *rep*(T) in the definitions we gave, the definitions of the updates will be the following:

Let ϕ be an equation of the form $\{t\} \subseteq \pi_X(R)$, and Σ a set of dependencies. Then

$$\text{a-ins}_\phi(rep(T), \Sigma) = rep(T) \cap Sat(\phi), \text{ and}$$

$$\text{p-ins}_\phi(rep(T), \Sigma) = Comp_\Sigma(rep(T) \,\dot{\cup}\, \{t' : t' \text{ is tuple on R, and } \pi_X(t') = t\}).$$

We see that $\text{a-ins}_\phi(rep(T), \Sigma) = \text{a-ins}_\phi(rep(T))$, and that $\text{p-ins}_\phi(rep(T), \Sigma) = Comp_\Sigma(\text{p-ins}_\phi(rep(T))$.

Then let ϕ be an equation of the form $\sigma_E(R) \subseteq \emptyset$, and Σ a set consisting of one join dependency $*[R_1,\ldots,R_n]$, and a set of equality generating dependencies. Furthermore, we require that the selection expression E is a conjunction of equalities, and that it involves only attributes in one R_i, $1 \leq i \leq n$. Then

$$\text{a-del}_\phi(rep(T), \Sigma) = rep(T) \cap Sat(\phi), \text{ and}$$

$$\text{p-del}_\phi(rep(T), \Sigma) = \sigma_{\neg E}(rep(T)).$$

Thus $\text{a-del}_\phi(rep(T), \Sigma) = \text{a-del}_\phi(rep(T))$, and $\text{p-del}_\phi(rep(T), \Sigma) = \text{p-del}_\phi(rep(T))$.

In conclusion, we observe that the positive insertions is the only update class where the dependencies have a computational effect, i.e. we have to compute $Comp_\Sigma(\text{p-ins}_\phi(rep(T))$. Now $\text{p-ins}_\phi(rep(T)$ is strongly representable in all table classes, and the completion is strongly representable in the class of Tables and in the class of Horn tables. In the class of Naive tables we can weakly represent the completion. Thus we will be able to weakly represent the result of a positive insertion in the presence of a set of dependencies. This is no factual loss, since the Naive tables are suitable for giving certain results. Thus a weak representation is quite sufficient.

In Codd Tables we cannot even weakly represent the completion. Thus we cannot update Codd tables taking dependencies into account.

5. Computational complexity aspects of incomplete information

In Chapter 2 we analyzed the complexity of operations on complete relations. We were interested in data complexity, i.e. in measuring the complexity as a function of the data base size. We saw that all operations had a polynomial time data complexity. In this chapter we shall study the data complexity of operations performed on tables of the various classes.

5.1. The complexity of query evaluation

Since we are going to study data complexity we need a measure of the sizes of a tables and multitables. Let T be a table. Then $|T|$ denotes the number of c-tuples in T. Since the arity of T is fixed, $|T|$ is a sufficient measure for the size of T, except for the local conditions. For a c-tuple t in T, $\|t(CON)\|$ stands for the length (in symbols) of the local condition of t. By $\|T(CON)\|$ we mean the sum of $\|t_i(CON)\|$, $1 \leq i \leq |T|$. Then the size of the entire table is

$$\|T\| = |T| + \|T(CON)\| + \|\lambda(T)\|,$$

where $\|\lambda(T)\|$ is the length of the global condition $\lambda(T)$. For a multitable $\mathbf{T} = <T_1, ..., T_m>$, we define

$$\|\mathbf{T}\| = |T_1| + \|T_1(CON)\| + ... + |T_m| + \|T_m(CON)\| + \|\lambda(\mathbf{T})\|.$$

The arities of the tables are assumed to be fixed constants $a_1,..., a_n$.

The first result is a bound on the size of $f(\mathbf{T})$ and on the time needed to evaluate it. If f is a fixed PSUJRD-expression then the bounds are polynomial, as stated in the next theorem.

Theorem 5.1. Let f be a fixed PSUJRD-expression, and $\mathbf{T} = <T_1, ...,T_m>$ a multitable, with $\alpha(f) = \alpha(\mathbf{T})$. Let n be $max(|T_1|, \|T_1(CON)\|, ... ,|T_m|, \|T_m(CON)\|)$. Then $f(\mathbf{T})$ can be evaluated in time $O(n^2)$, and $\|(f(\mathbf{T}))\| = O(n^2)$.

Proof. We know that the global condition remains invariant. Thus we have $\|f(\lambda(\mathbf{T}))\| = \|\lambda(\mathbf{T})\|$. Let us then look at each operator separately. We assume that the result is not normalized. Since the construction of each resulting tuple takes constant time, the evaluation time is directly determined by the size of the result. For the size we clearly have the following bounds:

(i) $|(\pi_X(T_i))| \leq |T_i|$ and $\| \pi_X(T_i)(CON) \| \leq \|T_i(CON)\|$,

(ii) $|(\sigma_E(T_i))| = |T_i|$ and $\| (\sigma_E(T_i))(CON) \| = \|T_i(CON)\| + |T_i| \cdot k_1$, where k_1 is the (fixed) length of the selection expression E,

(iii) $|T_i \cup T_j| \leq |T_i| + |T_j|$ and $\| (T_i \cup T_j)(CON) \| \leq \|T_i(CON)\| + \|T_j(CON)\|$,

(iv) $|(\theta_B^A(T_i))| = |T_i|$ and $\| (\theta_B^A(T_i))(CON) \| = \|T_i(CON)\|$.

Let us then recall the definition of the join. We had $T_i * T_j = \{t*u : t \in T_i \text{ and } u \in T_j\}$. Thus we get $|T_i * T_j| = |T_i| \cdot |T_j|$. The local condition of $t*u$ is $(t*u)(CON) = t(CON) \wedge u(CON) \wedge \bigwedge_{A \in \alpha(T_i) \cap \alpha(T_j)} \big(t(A) = u(A)\big)$. Thus each t(CON) is repeated $|T_j|$ times, and each u(CON) is repeated $|T_i|$ times. Since the arities are fixed, $\alpha(T_i) \cap \alpha(T_j)$ is of a fixed size, say k_2. The conjunction is repeated $|T_i| \cdot |T_j|$ times. All in all we get

(v) $|(T_i * T_j)| = |T_i| \cdot |T_j|$, and
$\| (T_i * T_j)(CON) \| = |T_j| \cdot \|T_i(CON)\| + |T_i| \cdot \|T_j(CON)\| + k_2 \cdot |T_i| \cdot |T_j|$.

The difference $T_i - T_j$ was defined as $\{t_u : t \in T_i\}$. Thus $|T_i - T_j| = |T_i|$. The local condition in t_u is $t_u(CON) = t(CON) \wedge \bigwedge_{u \in T_j} \Big(\big(\bigvee_{A \in \alpha(T_i)} ((t(A) \neq u(A))\big) \vee \neg u(CON) \Big)$. Since the arity of T_i is fixed, each conjunct is of fixed size, say k_3. Every local condition in T_j is repeated $|T_i|$ times. All in all we get

(vi) $|T_i - T_j| = |T_i|$, and
$\| (T_i - T_j)(CON) \| = \|T_i(CON)\| + |T_i| \cdot |T_j| \cdot k_3 + |T_i| \cdot \|T_j(CON)\|$.

For all operators we thus have a $O(n^2)$ bound. Since f is fixed, there is a fixed number of operators in f. The claim follows. *Q.E.D.*

A fixpoint query $f_T(R)$ does not introduce any new values, i.e. any tuple in the result must be a combination of values already in **T**. Let **T** be $\langle T_1, ..., T_m \rangle$, with arities $a_1, ..., a_m$. Then there are at most $a_1 \cdot |T_1| + ... + a_m \cdot |T_m|$ different values in **T**. If a is the arity of the result, i.e. of $\alpha(R)$ we get

(vii) $|(\psi(f_T(R)))| \leq (a_1 \cdot |T_1| + ... + a_m \cdot |T_m|)^a$.

Thus the number of tuples in $\psi(f_T(R))$ is bounded by a polynomial of the number of tuples in **T**. This also means that the number of iterations needed in Algorithm 4.1 is bounded by the same polynomial. Unfortunately, Algorithm 4.1 will not run in polynomial time, since it involves testing the equivalence of tables. The exception to this will be the case where the input is a join dependency. Then we can do just one iteration, without testing the equivalence. We will return to these issues later on.

The possibility problem

Theorem 5.1 means that PSUJDR queries can be evaluated in polynomial time. But the structure of the resulting table can be quite complex, and it can be difficult for the user to see the meaning of the table. Therefore the user might want to ask if a fact represented by a complete tuple t is possible, i.e. if there is a relation r represented by the resulting table, such that $t \in r$. The same question can be asked for a restricted or unrestricted set of complete tuples. This decision problem is called the possibility problem. The problem is formally as follows:

Let f be a fixed query, and **T** a class of tables. Then the *possibility problem* for the query f is, given a relation r and a table $T \in \mathbf{T}$, to decide if there is a relation s in f(*rep*(**T**)), such that $r \subseteq s$. When the size of r is bounded by a constant independent of **T**, the problem is called the *restricted* possibility problem, otherwise it is the *unrestricted* possibility problem. We assume that $\alpha(f) = \alpha(\mathbf{T})$, $\beta(f) = \alpha(r)$.

An instance of the possibility problem is denoted by (r, **T**). Obviously the unrestricted version is harder. We shall first give the upper bound for the problem.

Theorem 5.2. Let f be a fixed PSUJRDY-expression, and T the class of tables. Then the unrestricted possibility problem for f is in NP.

Proof. Let (r, **T**) be an instance of the problem. We are interested to know if there is a valuation v, such that $r \subseteq f(v(\mathbf{T}))$. Thus we can guess a valuation v. Then we compute f(v(**T**)) in polynomial time (by Theorem 2.6), and verify if $r \subseteq f(v(\mathbf{T}))$. *Q.E.D.*

By restricting the class of tables and the query we will get a more refined characterization of the problem. We want to keep the analysis in the borders of the various strong representation systems <**T**, *rep*, Ω>. Thus, when the table is restricted to be in **T**, f will be restricted to be an Ω-expression.

Possibility in tables

We recall that <T, *rep*, PSUJRDY> is a strong representation system, meaning that we can represent the possible answer f(T) as a table, whenever $T \in \mathcal{T}$, and f is a PRUJRDY-expression. For tables we however get an NP-hardness result already for the restricted possibility problem and identity queries.

Theorem 5.3. Let f be the identity, and $\mathcal{T}$ the class of tables. Then the restricted possibility problem for f is NP-complete.

Proof. We have to show that the problem is NP-hard. This is done by a reduction from the 3CNF satisfiability, which is known to be NP-complete [GJ79]. The 3CNF problem is stated in Appendix A1.

Let $C = \{c_1,\ldots, c_m\}$ over $Z = \{z_1,\ldots, z_n\}$ be an instance of the 3CNF problem. We construct a table T and a one-tuple relation r, which will be our instance of the possibility problem. The type of T and r is A. The relation r consists of the tuple (a). T is as follows. The set of c-tuples is $\{(a, \textbf{true})\}$. Let $x_1, \ldots, x_n$ be variables in *Var*(A). We shall put conditions formed from these variables in $\lambda(T)$. Each variable z_i will correspond to the variable x_i, $1 \leq i \leq n$. Now we have

$$\lambda(T) = \{\phi_i : c_i \text{ is in } C\}.$$

Let c_i consist of variables $z_{i(1)}$, $z_{i(2)}$ and $z_{i(3)}$. Then $\phi_i = \delta_1 \vee \delta_2 \vee \delta_3$, where $\delta_j = (x_{i(j)} = 1)$, if $z_{i(j)}$ is not negated in c_i, and $\delta_j = (x_{i(j)} \neq 1)$, if $z_{i(j)}$ is negated in c_i.

For an example, let C be the example instance of the 3CNF problem in Appendix A1. The corresponding table T is shown below.

A	CON	
		$(x_1= 1) \vee (x_2= 1) \vee (x_3= 1)$, $(x_1= 1) \vee (x_2\neq 1) \vee (x_4= 1)$, $(x_1= 1) \vee (x_4= 1) \vee (x_5= 1)$, $(x_2= 1) \vee (x_1\neq 1) \vee (x_5= 1)$, $(x_1\neq 1) \vee (x_2\neq 1) \vee (x_5\neq 1)$.
a	**true**	

Now, let τ be a truth assignment for C. We define a valuation v_τ by putting $v_\tau(x_i) = 1$, if $\tau(z_i) = 1$, and $v_\tau(x_i) = 5$, if $\tau(z_i) = 0$. Conversely, let v be a valuation. Then we define a truth assignment τ_v, by putting $\tau_v(z_i) = 1$, if $v(x_i) = 1$, and $\tau_v(z_i) = 0$, if $v(x_i) \neq 1$. It should now be clear that $v_\tau(\lambda\ (T))$ = **true** if $\tau(C) = 1$, and that $\tau_v\ (C) = 1$ if $v(\lambda\ (T))$ = **true**.

Since (a) is a possible fact of *rep*(T) if and only if there is a valuation v, such that $v(\lambda(T))$ = **true**, and since such a valuation v exists if and only if there is a truth assignment that satisfies C, it follows that (a) is a possible fact of *rep*(T) if and only if C is satisfiable. Finally we note that the reduction is indeed polynomial. *Q.E.D.*

Possibility in Horn tables

Recall that $<T_H$, *rep*, $PS^+UJRY^+ >$ is a strong representation system. We will show that the restricted possibility problem can be solved in polynomial time for PS^+UJR-expressions, and that the same problem is NP-complete for Y^+-expressions. First, we however need to consider the complexity of Horn conditions.

Theorem 5.4. Let C be a finite set of Horn conditions. Then testing whether C is satisfiable can be done in time polynomial in the size of C.

Proof. We shall reduce the problem to testing whether a set $\mathcal{H}$ of propositional Horn clauses is satisfiable. The latter problem is formulated in Appendix A3, and it can be solved in polynomial time.

Let C be $\{\phi_i : 1 \leq i \leq n\}$. Suppose w.l.o.g. that the set of constants occurring in C is $\{a_1,\ldots, a_p\}$ and that the set of variables occurring in C is $\{x_{p+1},\ldots, x_m\}$. Then $\mathcal{H}$ is formed out of the propositional variables $\{e_{ij} : 1 \leq i \leq m, 1 \leq j \leq m\}$. For each condition ϕ_i in C we put a clause c_i in $\mathcal{H}$. Depending on the structure of ϕ_i there are three cases to consider: Let δ_i stand for a constant or a variable in C.

(i) ϕ_i is of the form $\delta_i = \delta_j$. Then c_i is e_{ij}.

(ii) ϕ_i is of the form $\delta_{i(1)} \neq \delta_{i(2)} \vee \ldots \vee \delta_{i(q-1)} \neq \delta_{i(q)}$.
Then c_i is $\neg e_{i(1)i(2)} \vee \ldots \vee \neg e_{i(q-1)i(q)}$.

(iii) ϕ_i is of the form $\delta_{i(1)} = \delta_{i(2)} \wedge \ldots \wedge \delta_{i(q-1)} = \delta_{i(q)} \Rightarrow \delta_i = \delta_j$.
Then c_i is $e_{i(1)i(2)} \wedge \ldots \wedge e_{i(q-1)i(q)} \Rightarrow e_{ij}$.

In addition $\mathcal{H}$ contains the following clauses.

(iv) For each pair of constants (a_i, a_j), $i \neq j$, there is a clause $\neg e_{ij}$.

(v) For each δ_i there is a clause e_{ii}.

(vi) For each pair (δ_i, δ_j) there is a clause $e_{ij} \Rightarrow e_{ji}$.

(vii) For each triple $(\delta_i, \delta_j, \delta_k)$ there is a clause $e_{ij} \wedge e_{jk} \Rightarrow e_{ik}$.

Each clause of the form (i) - (iii) corresponds to a condition in C. The number of clauses of the form (iv) is p^2. There are m clauses of form (v), and the number of clauses of the form (vi) is m^2. Finally, we have m^3 clauses of form (vii). Thus the size of $\mathcal{H}$ is a polynomial of the size of C. Obviously every clause in $\mathcal{H}$ is a Horn clause.

We now have to show that C is satisfiable if and only if $\mathcal{H}$ is satisfiable.

Suppose that C is satisfiable. This means that there is a valuation v, such that $v(C) =$ **true**. We define a truth assignment τ_v of $\mathcal{H}$, such that $\tau_v(\mathcal{H}) = 1$.

For each proposition e_{ij}, $\tau_v(e_{ij}) = 1$ if and only if $v(\delta_i) = v(\delta_j)$, and $\tau_v(e_{ij}) = 0$ if and only if $v(\delta_i) \neq v(\delta_j)$. Now τ_v is defined for all propositions in $\mathcal{H}$. Since $v(C) =$ **true**, it means that $v(\phi) =$ **true**, for all $\phi \in C$. Thus it should be clear that all clauses c_i of the form (i) - (iii) in $\mathcal{H}$ are assigned 1 by τ_v. Let us look at the remaining cases:

(iv) Let $\neg e_{ij}$ be in $\mathcal{H}$. Then $\tau_v(\neg e_{ij}) = 0$ means that $\tau_v(e_{ij}) = 1$, which happens if $v(a_i) = v(a_j)$ for some constants $a_i \neq a_j$. But this is not possible.

(v) Since v is a valuation, we have $v(\delta_i) = v(\delta_i)$, thus $\tau_v(e_{ii}) = 1$, for all i, $1 \leq i \leq m$.

(vi) Take a $e_{ij} \Rightarrow e_{ji}$. Now $\tau_v(e_{ij} \Rightarrow e_{ji}) = 0$, only if $\tau_v(e_{ij}) = 1$ and $\tau_v(e_{ji}) = 0$. But this happens only if $v(\delta_i) = v(\delta_j)$ and $v(\delta_j) \neq v(\delta_i)$, which is impossible.

(vii) Let $e_{ij} \wedge e_{jk} \Rightarrow e_{ik}$ be an arbitrary clause in $\mathcal{H}$. Now $\tau_v(e_{ij} \wedge e_{jk} \Rightarrow e_{ik}) = 0$ if $\tau_v(e_{ij}) = 1$ and $\tau_v(e_{jk}) = 1$ and $\tau_v(e_{ik}) = 0$. But this means that we would have $v(\delta_i) = v(\delta_j)$ and $v(\delta_j) = v(\delta_k)$ and $v(\delta_i) \neq v(\delta_k)$; a contradiction.

Suppose then that $\mathcal{H}$ is satisfiable. Then ([CK73]) $\mathcal{H}$ has a maximally consistent extension, i.e. a set $\mathcal{H}'$, such that

(a) $\mathcal{H}'$ is a superset of $\mathcal{H}$,

(b) for all e_{ij}, $1 \leq i \leq m$, $1 \leq j \leq m$, either e_{ij} or $\neg e_{ij}$ is in $\mathcal{H}'$, and

(c) $\mathcal{H}'$ is satisfiable.

Let $\sim$ be a binary relation on $\{1, \ldots, m\}$, such that for all i, where $1 \leq i \leq m$, and j, where $1 \leq j \leq m$, we have $i \sim j$ if and only if $e_{ij} \in \mathcal{H}'$. Now $\sim$ is an equivalence relation on $\{1,\ldots,m\}$: for all i, e_{ii} is in $\mathcal{H}'$, i.e. we have $i \sim i$. Thus $\sim$ is reflexive. For symmetricity, suppose that $i \sim j$. Thus e_{ij} is in $\mathcal{H}'$. By the construction of $\mathcal{H}$, $e_{ij} \Rightarrow e_{ji}$ is in $\mathcal{H}'$, and since $\mathcal{H}'$ is satisfiable, it follows that e_{ji} is in $\mathcal{H}'$. Thus $j \sim i$. Then suppose that $i \sim j$ and $j \sim k$. Then e_{ij} and e_{jk} are in $\mathcal{H}'$. Now $e_{ij} \wedge e_{jk} \Rightarrow e_{ik}$ is in $\mathcal{H}$ and consequently in $\mathcal{H}'$, by construction. Since $\mathcal{H}'$ is satisfiable, e_{ik} is in $\mathcal{H}'$. Hence $i \sim k$, i.e. the relation $\sim$ is transitive.

Let $|i|$ be the equivalence class of i. Then the set $\{|i| : 1 \leq i \leq m\}$ is a partition of $\{1,\ldots,m\}$ into equivalence classes. We associate a constant from *Dom*(A), for the proper A, with each equivalence class in the partition. For all $1 \leq i \leq p$, the class $|i|$ is associated with the constant a_i. This is possible, since all these equivalence classes are distinct as a consequence of the clauses $\neg e_{ij}$ of the form (iv). Then let v be a valuation of C, such that for all δ_i in C, $v(\delta_i)$ is the constant that the class $|i|$ is associated with. Clearly v is a valuation. It remains to show that $v(C) = \textbf{true}$. Let ϕ be a condition in C. There are three cases to consider:

(i) ϕ is of the form $\delta_i = \delta_j$. Then is e_{ij} is in $\mathcal{H}$ and in $\mathcal{H}'$, and thus $i \sim j$. Consequently $|i| = |j|$, and $v(\delta_i) = v(\delta_j)$, i.e. $v(\phi)$ is **true.**

(ii) ϕ is of the form $\delta_{i(1)} \neq \delta_{i(2)} \vee \ldots \vee \delta_{i(q-1)} \neq \delta_{i(q)}$. Then is $\neg e_{i(1)i(2)} \vee \ldots \vee \neg e_{i(q-1)i(q)}$ is in $\mathcal{H}$, and by the properties of $\mathcal{H}'$, at least one of the disjuncts, say $\neg e_{i(j)i(j+1)}$, is in $\mathcal{H}'$. Thus $|i(j)| \neq |i(j+1)|$, and consequently $v(\delta_{i(j)}) \neq v(\delta_{i(j+1)})$. Hence $v(\phi)$ is **true.**

(iii) ϕ is of the form $\delta_{i(1)} = \delta_{i(2)} \wedge \ldots \wedge \delta_{i(q-1)} = \delta_{i(q)} \Rightarrow \delta_i = \delta_j$. Then $e_{i(1)i(2)} \wedge \ldots \wedge e_{i(q-1)i(q)} \Rightarrow e_{ij}$ is in $\mathcal{H}$. By the properties of $\mathcal{H}'$, either e_{ij} is in $\mathcal{H}'$, or the negation of one of the conjuncts, say $\neg e_{i(j)i(j+1)}$, is in $\mathcal{H}'$. In the first case $|i| = |j|$, and consequently $v(\delta_i) = v(\delta_j)$. In the second case $|i(j)| \neq |i(j+1)|$, implying that $v(\delta_{i(j)}) \neq v(\delta_{i(j+1)})$. In both cases $v(\phi)$ is **true.**

This concludes the proof of the theorem since we have showed that the size of $\mathcal{H}$ is polynomial in the size of C, and that C is satisfiable if and only if $\mathcal{H}$ is satisfiable. *Q.E.D.*

We can now show the following result.

Theorem 5.5. Let f be a fixed PS+UJR-expression, and T_H the class of Horn tables. Then the restricted possibility problem for f can be solved in polynomial time.

Proof. Let (r, **T**) be an instance of the problem. By Theorem 5.1, the table f(**T**) can be computed in time polynomial of the size of **T**, and the size of f(**T**) is also polynomial of the size of **T**. By Theorem 4.5, f(**T**) is also a Horn table, which we call U.

Thus we are left with the problem of deciding whether there is a valuation v, such that $r \subseteq v(U)$. This can be done by the following exhaustive search. If there is a v, such that $r \subseteq v(U)$, there must be c-tuples $t_1,...,t_k$ in U, such that $r = \{v(t_1), ..., v(t_k)\}$, and $v(\lambda(U))$ = **true**. Here k is the number of tuples in r, and hence a constant. If there are n c-tuples in U, we can form $\binom{n}{k}$ sets of k tuples. But $\binom{n}{k} \leq n^k$, which is a polynomial of n. Now, for each set $\{t_1, ...,t_k\}$ we try to enforce it to be equal to r, by finding a partial valuation v' from the variables in the c-tuples to the constants in r.

There is a maximum of k! such partial valuations. For each partial valuation v', we substitute x by v'(x) in the conditions, for all variables x that v' was determined for. Call the new conditions $v'(t_i(CON))$ and $v'(\lambda(U))$. Note that the conditions can still contain variables, since a variable in a condition does not have to occur in any tuple. Then we check if there is an extension v" of v', such that $v''(\lambda(U))$ = **true**, and $v''(t_i(CON))$ = **true**, for all i, $1 \leq i \leq k$. Such an extension exists if $v'(\lambda(U)) \cup \{v'(t_i(CON)) : 1 \leq i \leq k\}$ is satisfiable. But the global condition is a set of Horn clauses, and the local conditions are conjunctive equalities. By Theorem 5.4 satisfiability can then be tested in time polynomial of the size of the conditions. The claim of the theorem follows. *Q.E.D.*

We still have to consider least fixpoint queries on Horn tables. In the discussion after Theorem 5.1 we mentioned that Algorithm 4.1 requires testing for the equivalence of tables. This indicates that the possibility problem is intractable for fixpoint queries. The next theorem states that it is indeed so.

Theorem 5.6. Let T_H be the class of Horn tables. Then there exists a Y+-expression f, such that the restricted possibility problem for f is NP-complete.

Proof. We will show that the problem is NP-hard, by a reduction from the 3CNF satisfiability problem (see Appendix A1). Let $C = \{c_1, ..., c_m\}$ over $Z = \{z_1, ..., z_n\}$ be an instance of the 3CNF problem. The instance (r, T) of the possibility problem is constructed as follows.

The relation r and the Horn table T is over AB, with the domain of A and B being the integers. The relation r consists of the tuple (1, m+1). For each d-clause c_i with variables $z_{i(1)}$, $z_{i(2)}$ and $z_{i(3)}$ we put c-tuples $t_{i(1)}$, $t_{i(2)}$ and $t_{i(3)}$ in T. We define $t_{i(j)}(AB) = (i, i+1)$, for all j=1,2,3, and $t_{i(j)}(CON) = (x_{i(j)} = 1)$, if $z_{i(j)}$ is not negated in c_i, and $t_{i(j)}(CON) = (x_{i(j)} = 0)$, if $z_{i(j)}$ is negated in c_i. The global condition $\lambda(T)$ is {**true**}. The query f is the transitive closure of T, which is a Y^+-expression (see page 13).

The possibility instance for the example instance of the 3CNF problem in Appendix A1 would be the following ($\lambda(T)$ = **true**).

r =

A	B
1	6

T =

A	B	CON
1	2	$x_1 = 1$
1	2	$x_2 = 1$
1	2	$x_3 = 1$
2	3	$x_1 = 1$
2	3	$x_2 = 0$
2	3	$x_4 = 1$
3	4	$x_1 = 1$
3	4	$x_4 = 1$
3	4	$x_5 = 1$
4	5	$x_2 = 1$
4	5	$x_1 = 0$
4	5	$x_5 = 1$
5	6	$x_1 = 0$
5	6	$x_2 = 0$
5	6	$x_5 = 0$

Let s^* denote the transitive closure of a relation s. Now we claim that there exists an $s \in rep(T)$, such that the tuple $(1, m+1) \in s^*$ if and only if C is satisfiable. This would prove the theorem, since the reduction clearly is polynomial.

Let us therefore prove the claim. Suppose that C is satisfiable, and let τ be an assignment, such that $\tau(C) = 1$. Consider now the valuation v_τ defined by $v_\tau(x_i) = 1$, if $\tau(z_i) = 1$, and $v_\tau(x_i) = 0$, if $\tau(z_i) = 0$, $1 \leq i \leq n$. Each d-clause c_i has at least one literal assigned the value 1. The literal is $z_{i(j)}$ or $\neg z_{i(j)}$. If $\tau(z_{i(j)}) = 1$, then $v_\tau(x_{i(j)}) = 1$. Since the c-tuple $(i, i+1, x_{i(j)} = 1)$ is in

T, the tuple (i, i+1) is in $v_\tau(T)$. Similarly, if $\tau(\neg z_{i(j)}) = 1$, then $\tau(z_{i(j)}) = 0$. The c-tuple $(i, i+1, x_{ij} = 0)$ is in T, and thus the tuple (i, i+1) is in $v_\tau(T)$.

We see that for all i, s.t. $1 \leq i \leq m$, the tuple (i, i+1) is in $v_\tau(T)$. Then it follows that the tuple (1, m+1) is in $(v_\tau(T))^*$.

Suppose then that there exists a $s \in rep(T)$, such that $(1, m+1) \in s^*$. This means that there is a valuation v, such that $(1, m+1) \in (v(T))^*$, which is true only if $(i, i+1) \in v(T)$, for $1 \leq i \leq m$. We define an assignment τ_v be putting $\tau_v(z_i) = 1$, if $v(x_i) = 1$, and $\tau_v(z_i) = 0$, if $v(x_i) \neq 1$. Since $(i, i+1) \in v(T)$, there must be a c-tuple $t_{i(j)}$ in T, such that $v(t_{i(j)}(CON))$ = **true**. Now $t_{i(j)}(CON)$ is either $x_{i(j)} = 1$, or $x_{i(j)} = 0$. In the first case the literal $z_{i(j)}$ is in c_i, and in the second case the literal $\neg z_{i(j)}$ is in c_i. In the first case $\tau_v(z_{i(j)}) = 1$, and in the second case $\tau_v(\neg z_{i(j)}) = 1$. Thus every d-clause in $\mathcal{C}$ is satisfied by the assignment τ_v. *Q.E.D.*

The unrestricted possibility will turn out to be NP-complete, even for identity queries. Since the result will hold already for Naive tables, we will return to the issue later.

Possibility in Naive tables

First we recall that Naive tables can strongly represent only PUR-expressions. It seems plausible that the restricted possibility problem is solvable in polynomial time for such expressions. Formally, we have

Theorem 5.7. Let f be a fixed PUR expression, and T_N the class of Naive tables. Then the restricted possibility problem for f can be solved in polynomial time.

Proof. Let (r, **T**) be an instance of the problem. By Theorem 4.3 (i) the table f(**T**) is obtained by the naive evaluation. Obviously f(**T**) can be computed in time polynomial of $\|T\|$, and $\|f(T)\| \leq \|T\|$. Thus we can restrict our attention to the case where f is the identity, i.e. we want to know if there is a valuation v, such that $r \subseteq v(\mathbf{T})$. It should be clear from the proof of Theorem 5.5 that an exhaustive search can be done in time polynomial of $\|T\|$. *Q.E.D.*

A more intricate fact is that the unrestricted possibility problem becomes NP-complete even for identity queries.

Theorem 5.8. Let f be the identity, and T_N the class of Naive tables. Then the unrestricted possibility problem is NP-complete.

Proof. We show that the problem is NP-hard by a reduction of the 3CNF satisfiability problem stated in Appendix A1. Let $C = \{c_1, \ldots, c_m\}$ over $Z = \{z_1, \ldots, z_n\}$ be an instance of the 3CNF satisfiability problem. We construct the following instance (r, T) of the possibility problem. Our scheme is ABC, with all domains being the integers. For each variable z_i in Z, let x_i and y_i be variables in *Var*(A). We have

$$\begin{aligned} r \;=\; & \{(j, 0, 1) : 1 \le j \le n\} \cup \\ & \{(j, 1, 0) : 1 \le j \le n\} \cup \\ & \{(n+i, n+i, 1) : 1 \le i \le m\} \end{aligned}$$

$$\begin{aligned} T \;=\; & \{(j, x_j, y_j) : 1 \le j \le n\} \cup \{(j, y_j, x_j) : 1 \le j \le n\} \cup \\ & \{(n+i, n+i, x_j) : c_i \text{ contains } z_j\} \cup \\ & \{(n+i, n+i, y_j) : c_i \text{ contains } \neg z_j\} \end{aligned}$$

$$\lambda(T) = \{\textbf{true}\}$$

The possibility instance obtained from the example instance of the 3CNF problem in Appendix A1 is shown below r =

A	B	C
1	0	1
1	1	0
2	0	1
2	1	0
3	0	1
3	1	0
4	0	1
4	1	0
5	0	1
5	1	0
6	6	1
7	7	1
8	8	1
9	9	1
10	10	1

T =

A	B	C
1	y_1	x_1
1	x_1	y_1
2	y_2	x_2
2	x_2	y_2
3	y_3	x_3
3	x_3	y_3
4	y_4	x_4
4	x_4	y_4
5	y_5	x_5
5	x_5	y_5
6	6	x_1
6	6	x_2
6	6	x_3
7	7	x_1
7	7	y_2
7	7	x_4
8	8	x_1
8	8	x_4
8	8	x_5
9	9	x_2
9	9	y_1
9	9	x_5
10	10	y_1
10	10	y_2
10	10	y_5

We claim that there is a $s \in rep(T)$ such that $r \subseteq s$, if and only if C is satisfiable. Suppose that there is a valuation v, such that $r \subseteq v(T)$. Clearly we must have either $v(x_j) = 1$ and $v(y_j) = 0$, or $v(x_j) = 0$ and $v(y_j) = 1$, for every j, where $1 \leq j \leq n$. We define an assignment τ_v, by $\tau_v(z_j) = 1$ in the first case, and $\tau_v(z_j) = 0$ in the second case. Since $r \subseteq v(T)$, there must be a tuple $(n+i, n+i, 1)$ in $v(T)$. Thus there is at least one x_j, such that $v(x_j) = 1$, or y_j, such that $v(y_j) = 1$. The d-clause c_i then contains either z_j or $\neg z_j$. In either case $\tau_v(c_i) = 1$. The preceding argument holds for every i, $1 \leq i \leq m$. Thus $\tau_v(C) = 1$.

Suppose then that C is satisfiable, and let τ be an assignment, such that $\tau(C) = 1$. We define a valuation v_τ by $v_\tau(x_i) = 1$ and $v_\tau(y_i) = 0$, if $\tau(z_i) = 1$, and $v_\tau(x_i) = 0$ and $v_\tau(y_i) = 1$, if $\tau(z_i) = 0$. It is easily seen that $r \subseteq v_\tau(T)$.

The size of the possibility instance is clearly polynomial in the size of C. The theorem follows.*Q.E.D.*

Possibility in Codd tables

In Codd tables we can strongly represent the result of PR-expressions only. The possibility problem is combinatorially simpler than for naive tables, since there is only one occurrence of each variable. We have the following result.

Theorem 5.9. Let f be a fixed PR expression, and T_C the class of Codd tables. Then the unrestricted possibility problem for f can be solved in polynomial time.

Proof. By Theorem 4.4 (i) f(*rep*(T)) = *rep*(f(T)). Obviously $\|f(T)\| \leq \|T\|$, and f(T) can be computed in time linear in $|T|$. Without loss of generality we thus assume that f is the identity mapping. We then reduce the problem to finding a maximal matching in a bipartite graph (see Appendix A4). Let $r = \{u_1, ..., u_n\}$ and $T = \{v_1, ..., v_m\}$, where r and T are defined over R. W.l.o.g. we assume that $\lambda(T) =$ **true**. The bipartite graph $\mathbf{G} = (V_1 \cup V_2, E)$ is constructed as follows. $V_1 = \{u_1, ..., u_n\}$ and $V_2 = \{v_1, ..., v_m\}$. The u_i:s and v_i:s stand for different vertices. Now

$$E = \{(u_i, v_j) : u_i \text{ is in r and } v_j \text{ is in T, and } u_i \ll v_j\},$$

where for all tuples u and v, $u \ll v$ if $u(A) = v(A)$ for all $A \in R$, such that v(A) is a constant. Let E' be a maximal matching for **G**. We claim that there is an s in *rep*(T) such that $r \subseteq s$ if and only if the number of edges in E' is n. Since the size of **G** is polynomial in the size of r and T, and since E' can be computed in polynomial time, the theorem follows from that claim. Before we prove the claim, we give an example of the reduction. Let r be the relation and T the table below. The graph $\mathbf{G} = (V_1 = \{u_1, u_2, u_3\}, V_2 = \{v_1, v_2, v_3\}, E = \{(u_1, v_1), (u_1, v_3), (u_2, v_2), (u_3, v_3)\})$ is also shown below.

r =	A	B
u_1	a	b
u_2	c	d

T =	A	B
v_1	a	x
v_2	y	d
v_3	z	w

G =

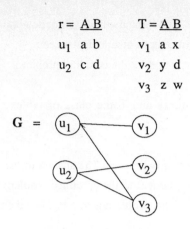

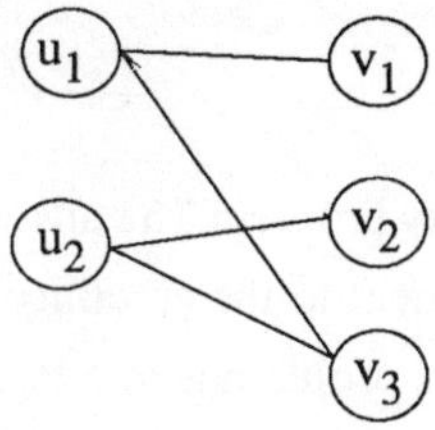

To prove the claim, suppose that there is an s in *rep*(T) such that r $\subseteq$ s. Thus there is a valuation v, such that r $\subseteq$ v(T). For each u_i in r there is thus a distinct v_j in T, such that $u_i = v(v_j)$. Then $u_i \ll v_j$, and therefore $(u_i, v_j) \in E$. This is true for all i, $1 \leq i \leq n$. Let E' = $\{(u_i,v_j) : u_i = v(v_j), 1 \leq i \leq n\}$. Clearly E' is a subset of E, and E' is a maximal matching for **G**.

Suppose then that E' is a maximal matching for **G** and that the number of edges in E' is n. Let E' = $\{(u_i, v_{j(i)}) : 1 \leq i \leq n\}$. Thus, for each u_i in r, there is a $v_{j(i)}$ in T, such that $u_i \ll v_{j(i)}$. Consequently there is a valuation v, such that $u_i = v(v_{j(i)})$, for $1 \leq i \leq n$. This means that r $\subseteq$ v(T). *Q.E.D.*

A summary of the possibility problem for queries is given at the end of this section (page 121).

The certainty problem

We have studied above the possibility problem, in order to characterize the computational complexity of evaluating the possible answer f(*rep*(**T**)). The complexity of evaluating the <u>certain</u> answer $\cap$f(*rep*(**T**)), will be characterized by the certainty problem.

Formally, let f be a fixed query and **T** a class of tables. Then the *certainty problem* for f, given a relation r and a table **T**$\in$**T**, is to decide if r $\subseteq \cap$f(*rep*(**T**)). An instance of the certainty problem is denoted by (r, **T**). We assume that $\alpha(f) = \alpha(\mathbf{T})$, $\beta(f) = \alpha(r)$.

We do not distinguish between restricted and unrestricted certainty, since the certainty problem for (r, **T**) obviously can be solved by solving (t, **T**) for each tuple t in r. Then the answer to (r, **T**) is "yes" if and only if the answer is "yes" for all (t, **T**). Thus restricted and unrestricted certainty are polynomial time equivalent. The same method cannot be applied to the possibility problem, since "yes" for each (t, **T**) might refer to distinct instances.

First we need to establish an upper bound for the certainty problem.

Theorem 5.10. Let f be the identity query and T the class of tables. Then the certainty problem for f is in coNP.

Proof. Let (r, **T**) be an instance of the certainty problem.The answer to the problem is "yes", if $r \subseteq f(v(\mathbf{T}))$ for all valuations v. The complement to the certainty problem is to verify if there exists a valuation v, such that $r \not\subseteq f(v(\mathbf{T}))$. This problem is in NP. Thus the certainty problem is in coNP. *Q.E.D.*

As in the possibility problem, the more refined characterization of the certainty problem will depend on the class of tables and on the query. However, there will be no distinction between least fixpoint queries, and "pure" relational queries.

Certainty in Tables

Theorem 5.11. Let f be the identity query and T the class of tables. Then the certainty problem is coNP-complete.

Proof. We show that the problem is coNP-hard, by a reduction from the 3DNF tautology problem, which is coNP-complete. The 3DNF tautology problem is stated in Appendix A2.

Let $\mathcal{D} = \{c_1, \ldots, c_m\}$ over $Z = \{z_1, \ldots, z_n\}$ be an instance of the 3DNF tautology problem. We construct a table T and a one-tuple relation r over A. The relation r is $\{(a)\}$. $\lambda(T)$ is $\{\mathbf{true}\}$. Let $x_1, \ldots, x_n$ be variables in *Var*(A). Each x_i will correspond to a z_i in Z. Now $T = \{t_i : 1 \leq i \leq m\}$, where $t_i(A) = a$ for all i. Let the c-clause c_i consist of variables $z_{i(1)}$, $z_{i(2)}$ and $z_{i(3)}$. Then $t_i(CON) = \delta_1 \wedge \delta_2 \wedge \delta_3$, where δ_j is $(x_{i(j)} = 1)$, if $z_{i(j)}$ is not negated in c_i, and δ_j is $(x_{i(j)} \neq 1)$, if $z_{i(j)}$ is negated in c_i.

If $\mathcal{D}$ is the example instance in Appendix A2, then T looks as follows.

A	CON	true
a	$(x_1 = 1) \wedge (x_2 = 1) \wedge (x_3 = 1)$	
a	$(x_1 = 1) \wedge (x_2 \neq 1) \wedge (x_4 = 1)$	
a	$(x_1 = 1) \wedge (x_4 = 1) \wedge (x_5 = 1)$	
a	$(x_2 = 1) \wedge (x_1 \neq 1) \wedge (x_5 = 1)$	
a	$(x_1 \neq 1) \wedge (x_2 \neq 1) \wedge (x_5 \neq 1)$	

It should now be obvious that $\{(a)\} \subseteq v(T)$, for all valuations v if and only if $\mathcal{D}$ is a tautology. Since the reduction clearly is polynomial we have proved the theorem. *Q.E.D.*

Certainty in Horn tables and in Naive tables

We saw in Section 4.2 that the certain answer in Horn tables can be obtained by using the naive evaluation. Thus we can expect to get the certain answer in polynomial time. The polynomial bound for the certainty problem is then clear.

Theorem 5.12. Let f be a fixed PS^+UJRY^+-expression and **T** a Horn multitable, such that $\alpha(f) = \alpha(\mathbf{T})$. Then $\cap f(rep(\mathbf{T}))$ can be computed in time polynomial in $\|\mathbf{T}\|$.

Proof. We have $f(rep(\mathbf{T})) = rep(f(\mathbf{T}))$ by Theorem 4.5. By Lemma 4.7 $\cap rep(f(\mathbf{T}))$ can be obtained from $(f(\mathbf{T}))_*$ by keeping only tuples without variables. By Lemma 4.6 (ii) (and 4.10 for Y^+-expressions) $(f_{(C)}(\mathbf{T}))_* = f_{(N)}(\mathbf{T}_*)$. Thus we can compute $\cap f(rep(\mathbf{T}))$ by first computing $\mathbf{T}_*$, then doing the naive evaluation, and finally dropping tuples with variables. Naive evaluation can be done in polynomial time by Theorem 2.6. Thus the last two steps can be done in polynomial time.

We can compute $\mathbf{T}_*$ by first normalizing **T**. For this we test for each pair (x, δ), where x is a variable and δ is a variable or a constant occurring in **T**, if $\lambda(\mathbf{T}) \models (x=\delta)$. Now $\lambda(\mathbf{T}) \models (x=\delta)$ if and only if $\lambda(\mathbf{T}) \cup \{x\neq\delta\}$ is not satisfiable. By Theorem 5.4 the test for the satisfiability (and thus for the nonsatisfiability) of a set of Horn conditions can be done in time polynomial in the size of the conditions. The number of pairs (x, δ) is clearly polynomial in the size of **T**.

When **T** is normalized, we obtain $\mathbf{T}_*$ from **T** by keeping only tuples with tautological local conditions. Since the local conditions are conjunctive equalities, the tautology test is clearly polynomial in the size of the condition. *Q.E.D.*

Since a Naive multitable also is a Horn multitable, we obviously have

Corollary 5.1 Let f be a fixed PS^+UJRY^+-expression and **T** a Naive multitable, such that $\alpha(f) = \alpha(\mathbf{T})$. Then $\cap f(rep(\mathbf{T}))$ can be computed in time polynomial in $\|\mathbf{T}\|$.

Certainty in Codd tables

Recall that Codd tables can weakly support only the unary PSR-expressions. Thus we can restrict ourselves to a single Codd table T. By [IL84] the evaluation of a selection expression against a tuple in a Codd table is of order linear in the length of the selection expression, assuming the selection expression is in conjunctive normal form. Since the query is fixed, the assumption can be made without loss of generality. Hence $\sigma_E(T)$ can be evaluated in time linear in T. The same bound obviously holds for the projection and renaming operators. Then $\cap$f(*rep*(T)) is obtained from f(T) by dropping all tuples containing variables. Thus we have proved the following theorem.

Theorem 5.13. Let f be a fixed PSR-expression and T a Codd table, such that $\alpha(f) = \alpha(T)$. Then $\cap$f(*rep*(T)) can be computed in time linear in the size of T.

Obviously the corresponding certainty problem can be solved in time polynomial in the size of T.

Summary of the complexity of query evaluation

We have now exhausted the restricted and unrestricted possibility problem, as well as the certainty problem for the different classes of tables and queries. The results are summarized in Figure 5.1 below. PTIME stands for polynomial time, NPC for NP-complete, and coNPC for coNP-complete. A dash entry means that the problem is not applicable.

TABLE CLASS	QUERY CLASS	UNRESTRICTED POSSIBILITY	RESTRICTED POSSIBILITY	CERTAINTY
Tables	identity	NPC	NPC	coNPC
Horn tables	Y+	NPC	NPC	PTIME
Horn tables	PS+UJR	NPC	PTIME	PTIME
Horn tables	identity	NPC	PTIME	PTIME
Naive tables	PS+UJRY+	-	-	PTIME
Naive tables	PUR	NPC	PTIME	PTIME
Naive tables	identity	NPC	PTIME	PTIME
Codd tables	PR	PTIME	PTIME	PTIME
Codd tables	PSR	-	-	PTIME

Figure 5.1. The complexity of query evaluation.

When it comes to the possible answer, the most interesting class of tables is the Horn one. In them we are able to compute f(**T**) in polynomial time, for any fixed PS+UJR-expression f. Furthermore, f(**T**) remains a Horn table of size polynomial of the size of **T.** Thus the structure of f(**T**) is quite regular, and a user who asks if a restricted set of complete facts belongs to the result can get his answer in polynomial time. One can argue that the possibility problems asked in practice are restricted ("is it possible that Jones lives in Romorantin?"). Furthermore, if f is a PS+UJR-expression, then the certain answer can be obtained in polynomial time from f(**T**). If the user wants only the certain answer, we can compute $\mathbf{T}_*$, and then do the naive evaluation. All steps can be carried out in time polynomial in the size of **T**, and in this case we can also handle positive least fixpoint queries (Y+) in polynomial time.

If the user is content with the certain answer, and never wants the possible answer, the Naive tables should be used. The answer to all positive queries and positive least fixpoint queries can be obtained in polynomial time.

We note that the proofs of Theorems 2, 8, 9 and 10 are variations of proofs in [AKG87].

5.2. The complexity of dependency enforcement

We shall consider the complexity of evaluating the table $\Sigma(T)$, given Σ and T. Here we are also interested in data complexity, that is, we regard the set of dependencies Σ as fixed. The table $\Sigma(T)$ is supposed to represent the set $Comp_\Sigma(rep(T))$ (see Section 4.3 for definitions). There are two types of dependency systems: strong ones and weak ones. In a strong dependency system we can compute a table equivalent to the desired result (as in tables and Horn tables). In a weak dependency system we get a table Ω-equivalent to the desired result, for some Ω (as in Horn and Naive tables). Thus we shall use the following decision problems to characterize the complexity of computing $\Sigma(T)$.

Suppose **T** is a strong dependency system w.r.t. a class of dependencies Δ. Let Σ be a fixed finite set of dependencies in Δ. Then the *possibility problem* for Σ is, given a relation r of restricted size and a table $T \in \mathbf{T}$, to decide if there is a relation s in $Comp_\Sigma(rep(T))$, such that $r \subseteq s$.

We shall not consider unrestricted possibility because of Theorem 5.8, which says that the problem is NP-complete already for Naive tables and identity queries. Consequently the unrestricted dependency possibility would be NP-complete for all interesting classes of tables. The restricted possibility will, on the other hand, capture the distinctions of the table and dependency classes.

In a weak dependency system we are able to compute a table Ω-equivalent to the desired result. This Ω-equivalent representation is meant to serve as a basis for evaluating certain answers. Thus we shall ask the following question:

Suppose **T** is a weak dependency system w.r.t. a class of dependencies Δ. Let Σ be a fixed finite set of dependencies in Δ. Then the *certainty problem* for Σ is, given a relation r and a table $T \in \mathbf{T}$, to decide if $r \subseteq \cap Comp_\Sigma(rep(T))$.

As for queries, the upper bounds of our problems will be NP and coNP.

Theorem 5.14. Let Σ be a fixed finite set of dependencies, and T the class of tables. Then

(i) the possibility problem for Σ is in NP, and

(ii) the certainty problem for Σ is in coNP.

Proof. (i) Let (r, T) be an instance of the problem. The answer to the problem is "yes", if there is a valuation v, such that r $\subseteq$ $comp_\Sigma$(v(T)). Thus we can guess a valuation v. By Theorem 2.7 we can verify in polynomial time if r $\subseteq comp_\Sigma$(v(T)).

(ii) The answer is "yes" to an instance (r, T) of the problem if r $\subseteq$ $comp_\Sigma$(v(T)), for all valuations v. Now the complement of the problem is to verify if there exists a valuation v, such that r $\not\subset$ $comp_\Sigma$(v(T)). This problem is in NP. Thus the certainty problem for Σ is in coNP. *Q.E.D.*

We can refine this result by considering different table classes and classes of dependencies. The crucial distinction will be between equality generating dependencies and tuple generating ones. We shall study the problems one table class at a time.

Possibility and Certainty in Tables

Since possibility and certainty problems are intractable already for the identity operation on tables, it is obvious that the same is also true for dependency enforcement. Indeed we have the following theorem.

Theorem 5.15. Let Σ be the empty set, and T the class of tables. Then

(i) the possibility problem for Σ is NP-complete, and

(ii) the certainty problem for Σ is coNP-complete.

Proof. (i) follows directly from Theorem 5.3, and (ii) from Theorem 5.11.

Possibility in Horn tables

Horn tables have the interesting property that equality generating dependencies can be enforced efficiently, while the possibility problem is intractable for tuple generating dependencies. This is an analogue to query evaluation, where least fixpoint queries were the cause of intractability. An exception to this is the class of dependencies consisting of sets of one join dependency and (possibly several) equality generating dependencies. In this case we get polynomial bounds.

Theorem 5.16. Let T_H be the class of Horn tables. Then there exists a tuple generating dependency σ, such that the possibility problem for σ is NP-complete.

Proof. The proof is a variation of the proof of Theorem 5.6, where we used the transitive closure. The transitive closure is not typed, but it can be simulated by a typed dependency. The dependency σ is

$$\pi_{XY}(\pi_{XY_1}(\uparrow(R)) * \pi_{X_1Y_1}(\uparrow(R)) * \pi_{X_1Y}(\uparrow(R))) \subseteq R, \text{ where } \alpha(R) = XY.$$

As a first order formula the dependency σ is

$$\forall x, x_1, y, y_1 \; (p(xy_1) \wedge p(x_1y_1) \wedge p(x_1y) \Rightarrow p(xy)).$$

Here p is a binary predicate referring to relations on AB.

The possibility problem is shown to be NP-hard by a reduction of the 3CNF satisfiability problem. The reduction is very similar to the one in Theorem 5.6, and thus we shall not do it formally. The reader should be convinced by the following example. Take the example instance C of the 3CNF satisfiability problem in Appendix A1. Then the instance (r, T) of the dependency possibility problem is the following (λ(T) = **true**) :

r = AB

A	B
0	6

T = AB CON

A	B	CON
0	1	**true**
1	1	$x_1 = 1$
1	1	$x_2 = 1$
1	1	$x_3 = 1$
1	2	**true**
2	2	$x_1 = 1$
2	2	$x_2 = 0$
2	2	$x_4 = 1$
2	3	**true**
3	3	$x_1 = 1$
3	3	$x_4 = 1$
3	3	$x_5 = 1$
3	4	**true**
4	4	$x_2 = 1$
4	4	$x_1 = 0$
4	4	$x_5 = 1$
4	5	**true**
5	5	$x_1 = 0$
5	5	$x_2 = 0$
5	5	$x_5 = 0$
5	6	**true**

It should be clear that there exists a relation s in $Comp_\sigma(rep(T))$, such that $r \subseteq s$, if and only if C is satisfiable. *Q.E.D.*

If we restrict ourselves to sets of dependencies consisting of one join dependency and a set of equality generating dependencies we can do the enforcement efficiently (for a definition of join dependencies, see page 20). Fagin, Mendelzon and Ullman ([FMU82]) conjecture that "every real-world application can be modeled by one join dependency and a set of functional dependencies".

Theorem 5.17. Let Σ be a set consisting of one join dependency and a set of equality generating dependencies, and let T_H be the class of Horn tables. Then a table U equivalent to $Comp_\Sigma(rep(T))$ can be computed in time polynomial in $\|T\|$.

Proof. It follows from [Sag85, Theorem 9] that a join dependency requires only one application to converge. Thus, when we compute the least fixpoint for $g(\Sigma_T)$ in Algorithm 4.3, we need to apply the mapping only once. By Theorem 5.1, the result is then polynomial in the size of the table. Call the result U.

Equality generating dependencies do not enforce any new tuples to appear in the table, only conditions to be added to the global condition. Each equality generating dependency $\pi_{B_1B_2}(f(\uparrow^n(R))) \subseteq \pi_{B_1B_2}(\uparrow^n(R))$ is treated once by applying the left hand side of the equation to the table U. By Theorem 5.1, the size of $\pi_{B_1B_2}(f(\uparrow^n(U)))$ is polynomial in the size of U. Thus only a polynomial number of conditions, of polynomial size, are added to the global condition on U. Since the set of dependencies is fixed, there is only a fixed number of dependencies to apply. Thus the resulting table $\Sigma(T)$ is a Horn table of a size polynomial of the size of T. *Q.E.D.*

Obviously, the corresponding decision problem, i.e. possibility, can also be solved in polynomial time in the size of T. (Recall that we can test for restricted possibility in polynomial time by Theorem 5.5.)

Certainty in Naive tables and in Horn tables

When we enforce a set of dependencies on a Naive table T, we use the simplified algorithm, i.e. Algorithm 4.4, to get a result PS^+UJR-equivalent to the completion. Since any new tuple produced by the algorithm is a combination of values of the tuples of the original table, we can add only a polynomial number of tuples (since the arity of the table is fixed, the number of values in the table is polynomial in the number of tuples in it). In the algorithm we also apply equality generating dependencies, resulting in the equation of some values. Since there is only a polynomial number of values, we can apply the equality generating dependencies only a polynomial number of times. Thus the whole algorithm runs in time polynomial in the size if the input table. Furthermore, the size of the resulting table is polynomial in the size of the input table. Formally we have the following result.

Theorem 5.18. Let Σ be a set of dependencies, and T a Naive table, such that $\alpha(\Sigma) = \alpha(T)$. Then a Naive table $U \equiv_{PS^+UJR} Comp_\Sigma(T)$ can be computed in time polynomial in $\|T\|$.

Since $U \equiv_{PS^+UJR} Comp_\Sigma(T)$ implies that $\cap rep(U) = \cap\, rep(Comp_\Sigma(T))$, the certainty problem can obviously be solved in time polynomial in the size of T.

Algorithm 4.4 requires the input to be a Naive table. We note however that it can be generalized to work also for Horn tables. This also generalizes the upper bound of the certainty problem.

Theorem 5.19. Let Σ be a set of dependencies, and T a Horn table, such that $\alpha(\Sigma) = \alpha(T)$. Then a Naive (and thus a Horn) table $U \equiv_{PS+UJR} Comp_{\Sigma}(T)$ can be computed in time polynomial in $\|T\|$.

Proof (*sketch*). We use Algorithm 4.4 even if the table is a Horn table. The dependencies are applied "naively", but the local conditions of the tuples are carried along, i.e. in joining two tuples, the resulting tuple will have a local condition that is the conjunction of the two local conditions. After the application of an equality generating dependency, we do not directly incorporate the equality in the table. Instead, we add the equality to the global condition, and then we normalize the table. In the end we keep only tuples with tautologically **true** local conditions. Unless the condition **false** was added, the global condition is set to **true**. An example will explain the subtleties of the process. Let $\Sigma = \{D \rightarrow E, A \rightarrow\rightarrow B\}$, and let T be the Horn table below.

T =

A	B	C	D	E	CON	$e=y \Rightarrow x=a$
a	b	c	d	e	**true**	
x	b'	c'	d	y	**true**	
f	g	h	i	k	y=e	
f	g'	h'	i	k	x=a	

If we first apply $A \rightarrow\rightarrow B$, we get

T =

A	B	C	D	E	CON	$e=y \Rightarrow x=a$
a	b	c	d	e	**true**	
x	b'	c'	d	y	**true**	
f	g	h	i	k	y=e	
f	g'	h'	i	k	x=a	
f	g'	h	i	k	$y=e \wedge x=a$	
f	g	h'	i	k	$x=a \wedge y=e$	

Then we apply D→E, to obtain

T =	A	B	C	D	E	CON	e=y⇒x=a, e=y
	a	b	c	d	e	**true**	
	x	b'	c'	d	y	**true**	
	f	g	h	i	k	y=e	
	f	g'	h'	i	k	x=a	
	f	g'	h	i	k	y=e ∧ x=a	
	f	g	h'	i	k	x=a ∧ y=e	

Normalizing this, we get the final result

T =	A	B	C	D	E	true
	a	b	c	d	e	
	x	b'	c'	d	e	
	f	g	h	i	k	
	f	g'	h'	i	k	
	f	g'	h	i	k	
	f	g	h'	i	k	

As in Algorithm 4.4, there can be only a polynomial number of iterations. In each iteration, we perform a normalization. It follows from Theorem 5.4 that the normalization can be carried out in polynomial time. $Q.E.D.$

Summary of the complexity of dependency enforcement

The complexity results of this section are shown in tabular form below. Tuple generating dependencies are abbreviated TGD's, join dependencies JD's, and equality generating dependencies EGD's.

TABLE CLASS	DEPENDENCY CLASS	POSSIBILITY	CERTAINTY
Tables	no dependencies	NPC	coNPC
Horn tables	TGD's and EGD's	NPC	PTIME
Horn tables	one TGD	NPC	PTIME
Horn tables	one JD and EGD's	PTIME	PTIME
Naive tables	TGD's and EGD's	not applicable	PTIME

Figure 5.2. The complexity of dependency enforcement.

As in query evaluation, Tables have too complex a structure to allow efficient algorithms. As far as the exact result is concerned, Horn tables can efficiently support equality generating dependencies, while tuple generating dependencies may cause an exponential growth of the local conditions. This is not surprising, since the same is true for fixpoint queries in Horn tables. A notable exception occurs if the set of tuple generating dependencies consists of a single join dependency. A join dependency is a "data independent least fixpoint query", i.e. it requires only a constant number of applications to converge, regardless of the content of the database (in this case one application is enough). Thus a join dependency together with a set of equality generating dependencies can be efficiently supported. Such a set of dependencies contains all the dependencies considered to occur in practice.

If we are content with the certain result of queries, it is enough to compute a table that weakly supports the dependencies. This can be done by the "naive" enforcement, i.e. Algorithm 4.4, which takes time polynomial in the size of the input table. We will then get a Naive table as a result, even if we started with a Horn table. Thus we conclude that for certainty, the Naive tables form an efficient basis for query evaluation and dependency enforcement.

5.3. The complexity of updates

The last class of operations that we need to analyze is the updates. Since the update operations are fairly simple, the analysis will show that the result of an update, $\upsilon(T)$, can be computed in time linear in the size of the table T. Thus we shall not consider the (restricted) possibility or certainty problems, since it follows directly from the results of Section 5.1 that these problems are solvable in polynomial time, except for the class of Tables, where the problems are intractable even for identity operations.

We recall that the class T of Tables can support all four types of updates. The following theorem shows that the updates can be carried out efficiently.

Theorem 5.20. Let υ be an absolute insertion, positive insertion, absolute deletion, or positive deletion, and let T be a table. Then $\upsilon(T)$ can be computed in time linear in $\|T\|$.

Proof. We consider one update type at a time.

(*absolute insertions*). Let the update equation ϕ be $\{t\} \subseteq \pi_X(R)$. Then T_t is the set of c-tuples in T that are subsumed on X by t. The number of tuples in T_t is less than or equal to the number of tuples in T. The resulting table a-ins$_\phi$(T) is T, with a condition of the form $\bigvee_{u \in T_t}(\ldots)$ added to the global condition. The size of each disjunct in this condition is constant. Thus we can scan through T, and for each tuple u in T that is subsumed on X by t, we add the required disjunct to $\bigvee_{u \in T_t}(\ldots)$. If no such tuples u are found, the condition **false** is added to the global condition of T. The process is clearly linear in the size of T.

(*positive insertions*). Assume that the update equation ϕ is $\{t\} \subseteq \pi_X(R)$. The resulting table is obtained by adding a tuple $\pi_X^{-1}(t)$ to the table T. In the case where X=R we have to scan through T, to see if $\pi_X^{-1}(t)$ already is in T. Thus the process is linear in the size of T.

(*absolute deletions*). Let the deletion equation ϕ be $\sigma_E(R) \subseteq \emptyset$. The resulting table is obtained by adding the set $\{\neg E(t) \vee \neg t(CON) : t \in T\}$ to the global condition of T. Thus we have to scan through T; this takes time linear in the size of T. The size of $\neg E(t)$ is constant, and thus the size of the added set is linear in the size of the local conditions of T.

(*positive deletions*). If the deletion equation is $\sigma_E(R) \subseteq \emptyset$, the resulting table is $\sigma_{\neg E}(T)$, which can be computed in time linear in the number of tuples in T. *Q.E.D.*

In Horn tables we are able to perform the absolute deletions and the positive insertions. The algorithms are the same as for tables. Thus the linear bounds apply to Horn tables also.

The class of Naive tables supports positive insertions and absolute deletions. Positive insertions are computed as for tables. Thus the same bound holds.

We argued earlier that the absolute deletion was not of practical interest in Naive tables. We note however that the result is U_*, where $U = T$, and $\lambda(U) = \{\neg(E(t) : t \in T\}$. Thus $U_* = T$, and $\lambda(U_*)$ is either **true**, if $\lambda(U)$ is satisfiable, or **false**, if $\lambda(U)$ is contradictory. Clearly we can test for these properties in time linear in the size of $\lambda(U)$.

In Codd tables we are able to do positive insertions and positive deletions. For the positive insertions we have the linear bound, as for tables. The positive deletion is computed as $\sigma_{\neg E}(T)$. In section 5.1 we saw that $\sigma_{\neg E}(T)$ could be computed in time linear in the size of T.

We have thus proved the following theorem.

Theorem 5.21. Let T be a table in **T**, where **T** is the class of Horn, Naive or Codd tables, and let υ be an update such that it is strongly or weakly supported by the class **T**. Then $\upsilon(T)$ can be computed in time linear in the size of $\|T\|$.

6. Some conclusive aspects

6.1. Relation to other work

In order to contrast the results of this thesis, we shall briefly look at two other models that explicitly or implicitly handle missing values. These models are the weak instance model, and logical databases. Especially the weak instance model is interesting, since it turns out that the decomposition of relations requires the notion of missing values in order to maintain the consistency of the approach.

The Weak Instance model

One of the fundamental paradigms in relational theory is that relations are decomposed into smaller ones. The motivation for doing this comes from the recognition of redundancies and update anomalies [Cod70, Cod72a] (see also [Ull82]).

Suppose that we have the following relation. The dependencies are EMPLOYEE → DEPARTMENT, and DEPARTMENT → MANAGER.

EMPLOYEE	DEPARTMENT	MANAGER
Jones	Toys	Smith
Brown	Cars	Doe
White	Cars	Doe

Now the fact that Doe is the manager of the Cars department is recorded for each employee in the Cars department. This is an example of a redundancy. An update anomaly arises for instance when we delete the fact that Jones works for the Toys department. Then we lose the fact that Smith is the manager of this department. Similarly we cannot record an employee for a department, unless the department has a manager. One thus wants to store partial facts. The solution offered is to decompose the relation into relations on EMPLOYEE DEPARTMENT, and on DEPARTMENT MANAGER. (Note that our solution would be to store null-values. The redundancies would of course remain.)

In general, a decomposition of a scheme R is a set $\{R_1, \ldots, R_n\}$, such that $\bigcup_{i=1,\ldots,n} R_i = R$. There are several problems with this solution. First of all there should be no loss of information [BBG78]. The information content is secured by requiring that for all relations r on R, when r is projected onto $\{R_1, \ldots, R_n\}$, yielding $<r_1, \ldots, r_n>$, the original relation r can be recovered by joining $<r_1, \ldots, r_n>$. This property is called the *lossless join* [ABU79]. But it assumes that the database is a relation on R, even if it is stored as relations on $R_1,\ldots,R_n$. Not all multirelations on $\{R_1, \ldots, R_n\}$ are projections of a relation on R.

If we for example have $r_1 = \{(\text{Jones Toys})\}$ on EMPLOYEE DEPARTMENT, and the DEPARTMENT MANAGER relation r_2 is empty, then there does not exist a relation on EMPLOYEE DEPARTMENT MANAGER, such that it can be projected to yield $<r_1, r_2>$. Thus the decomposition defeats its purpose, since we lose the ability to store partial facts ("dangling tuples") by the lossless join assumption.

The second problem is that the database remains a semantic unit, even if it is stored in decomposed form. In particular, the dependencies are formulated on R, and not on $\{R_1, \ldots, R_n\}$. Even if the dependencies are "embedded" in the schemes $\{R_1, \ldots, R_n\}$, there are still cases where it is not sufficient to check for satisfaction in the smaller relations. As an example, suppose that in the decomposition above we also want to include a scheme EMPLOYEE MANAGER. Then, consider the database below.

EMPLOYEE	DEPARTMENT	DEPARTMENT	MANAGER	EMPLOYEE	MANAGER
Jones	Toys	Toys	Smith	Jones	Brown

Now the dependency EMPLOYEE → DEPARTMENT is "embedded" in the first scheme, the dependency DEPARTMENT → MANAGER is "embedded" in the second scheme, and the (derived) dependency EMPLOYEE→ MANAGER "embedded" in the third scheme. Obviously, the individual relations satisfy the dependencies. But Jones is related to Smith, through the Toys department, and to Brown, in the third relation. Thus there must be an inconsistency somewhere.

One solution is to require that all the smaller relations come from a relation r on R, and that r satisfies the dependencies. But then, again, we lose the ability to store dangling tuples.

The solution proposed by Vassiliou [Vas80b] and Honeyman [Hon82] (independently) is to require that there is a relation r on R, such that each r_i is a subset of the projection of r onto R_i, i.e. that $r_i \subseteq \pi_{R_i}(r)$. Furthermore, r has to satisfy the dependencies in Σ. The relation r is called a *weak instance* of $<r_1, \ldots, r_n>$, w.r.t. Σ. Note that there can be several weak instances for $<r_1, \ldots, r_n>$. Thus $<r_1, \ldots, r_n>$ can be seen as an incomplete description of r. That is, in reality there is one particular r, such that $r_i = \pi_{R_i}(r)$, but because of the dangling tuples (partial facts) this r is only partially known. Thus the lossless join assumption is also rescued. (It becomes a requirement for the decomposed scheme.)

This solution is very close to our approach. The incomplete database is a set of complete relations. The difference is that we represent this set as a table with null values, while the weak instance model represents it as a vector of complete relations.

As far as dependency satisfaction is concerned, we note that the weak instance model requires that at least one of the possible relations satisfies the dependencies, while we require that every possible relation does so. Thus, there will still be some implied facts not present in

$<r_1, \ldots, r_n>$. (There is a stronger requirement for satisfaction in the weak instance model, called completeness [GMV86], but completeness is still weaker than our notion.)

There are thus some problems when querying a multirelational database in the weak instance model, since all information is not necessarily present in $<r_1, \ldots, r_n>$. This problem has been recognized in connection with the *universal relation interface* (see e.g. [MUV84]). In the universal interface the user states the query f on the scheme R, i.e. as f(*R*) (the aim is to "relieve the user of the need for logical navigation among relations" [MUV84, p. 283]). The answer to the query in a database $<r_1, \ldots, r_n>$ in the presence of a set Σ of dependencies is then $\cap\{f(r) : r \text{ is a weak instance for } <r_1, \ldots, r_n> \text{ w.r.t. } \Sigma\}$. If $<r_1, \ldots, r_n>$ corresponds to a table T, this answer then coincides with $\cap f(Comp_\Sigma(rep(T))$ in our model. Since we assume that the table is stored in its completed form, we simply evaluate f on T.

The approach taken in the weak instance model is the following [MUV84]: Suppose that the query f mentions attributes X, where $X \subseteq R$. Then it can be equivalently phrased as $f(\pi_X(R))$. There is then a variety of methods for transforming $\pi_X(R)$ to an algebraic expression g on the decomposed scheme, i.e. to $g(R_1, \ldots, R_n)$, such that

$$g(r_1, \ldots, r_n) = \cap\{ \pi_X(r) : r \text{ is a weak instance for } <r_1, \ldots, r_n> \text{ w.r.t. } \Sigma\},$$

for <u>all</u> vectors $<r_1, \ldots, r_n>$. This is called the *binding phase*. The *evaluation phase* then consists of evaluating f on $g(r_1,\ldots,r_n)$. The method has the obvious disadvantage that the answer $f(g(r_1,\ldots,r_n))$ is equal to

$$f(\cap\{ \pi_X(r) : r \text{ is a weak instance for } <r_1, \ldots, r_n> \text{ w.r.t. } \Sigma\},$$

which of course in general is <u>not</u> equal to

$$\cap\{ f(\pi_X(r)) : r \text{ is a weak instance for } <r_1, \ldots, r_n> \text{ w.r.t. } \Sigma\},$$

which again would be the correct answer (cf. the note on page 35). The answer $f(g(r_1, \ldots, r_n))$ is though a subset of the correct answer in all cases. The problem <u>is</u> recognized in the weak instance approach ("Well, perhaps asking for the 'whole truth' is too much" [MUV84, p. 305]).

An approach where the whole expression f(*R*), and not only $\pi_X(R)$, is transformed is taken in [Yan86], for the case where Σ is a single join dependency (more precisely, the join dependency for the scheme, i.e. $*[R_1, \ldots, R_n]$).

As far as updates are concerned, the research in the weak instance model has centered around the question of finding schemes $R_1, \ldots, R_n$ (w.r.t. a set Σ of dependencies), such that individual relations r_i can be updated without requiring changes to the other relations. The aim is to maintain the satisfaction in the weak instance sense of the database [CM83]. These are of course very desirable properties, but one might object to the fact that the semantics of the updates are formulated as insertions into and deletions from the individual relations. Yet the semantic meaning of a database $<r_1, \ldots, r_n>$ is formulated in terms of the weak instances r on R. Thus the update semantics should perhaps also be formulated in terms of the weak instances.

Logical databases

Another approach where incomplete information is modeled is the logical database approach. It evolved from the field of artificial intelligence, and was introduced to the database area through books as e.g. [GM78]. The area of logical databases has been largely influenced by the work of R. Reiter (e.g. [Rei78, Rei84, Rei86]), and more recently by the work of M. Vardi (summarized in [Var86b]). The main idea in the logical database approach is that a database is a theory, and that the meaning of the database is the set of models for the theory. We see that this is quite close to the approach taken in this thesis: a theory corresponds to a (multi)table T, and the set of models to *rep*(T). In this brief discourse we shall look at the area mainly through the work reported in [Var86b].

A *logical database* is a pair (L, T), where L is the relational language, and T is a finite first order theory in the vocabulary L. The theory consists of the following five components:

(i) *Atomic fact axioms.* Atomic sentences, such as TEACHES(Socrates, Plato). The axioms model the tuples in the relations. They correspond to the c-tuples in our approach.

(ii) *Uniqueness axioms.* Axioms of the form $\neg(c_i = c_j)$, where c_i and c_j are constants in the vocabulary L. In our approach these axioms can be modeled by inequalities in the global condition, and by the assumption that differently named constants stand for different elements. Note that there is no syntactic distinction between known and unknown values in the logical database approach. If one thinks of the constants in the vocabulary as of nodes in a graph, where the inequality $\neg(c_i = c_j)$ corresponds to an edge between c_i and c_j, then the known values (our constants) are the nodes of a maximal clique of the graph.

(iii) *Domain closure axioms.* An axiom $\forall x\, (x=c_1 \vee \ldots \vee x=c_n)$, where $c_1, \ldots, c_n$ are all the constant symbols in the vocabulary. This axiom formalizes partially the closed world assumption. In our approach the situation is taken care of by the valuation mappings, which force the null values to be in the domain. (Note that the domains are countably infinite in our approach, while the logical database approach assumes finite domains.)

(iv) *Completion axioms*. Let $P(c^1), \ldots, P(c^k)$ be all the atomic facts about a k-ary predicate in the vocabulary. The shorthand c^i means a k-ary vector of constants. The closed world assumption is completed by the axiom $\forall y\ (P(y) \Rightarrow y{=}c^1 \vee \ldots \vee y{=}c^k)$, meaning that no atomic facts, other that recorded, holds for P. In our approach we have the *rep* mapping, requiring that a possible relation is obtained by a valuation of the table.

If we disregard the size of the domains, we see that a logical database can be modeled by a Horn table, in the sense that the set of relations represented by the Horn table is equivalent (up to isomorphism) with the set of models for the theory. The atomic fact axioms are encoded as c-tuples (note that we do not need the local condition), the uniqueness axioms are encoded in the global condition, and the two last axiom groups are taken care of by the definition of valuations and the *rep* mapping. In fact, the class of Horn tables is a strictly stronger representation than logical databases, since every logical database can be represented as a Horn (multi)table, while the reverse is not true. Let us therefore call a logical database represented as a table an *LDB table*. The class of LDB tables lies strictly between Naive and Horn tables.

The answer to a query $x.\phi(x)$ (see page 11 for definitions) in a logical database is the set of vectors of constants (i.e. tuples) c, such that $T \models \phi(c)$. This clearly corresponds to the certain answer in our approach. (There are some slight differences due the the fact that the logical databases do not syntactically distinguish between null values and constants. Thus the null values can occur in the answer, and there is nothing that prevents one from using them in the query). We note that the logical database approach does not include the notion of a possible answer.

The research in querying logical databases is aimed at finding algorithms for the evaluation of queries, and at studying the complexity of query evaluation. As we have seen in our study, there are two parameters that influence the complexity of query evaluation: the query and the representation used. Let us therefore compare some results from logical databases with results of this thesis. We shall also take some results from a study by the present author, S. Abiteboul and P. Kanellakis [AKG87]. We consider the complexity of the certainty problem. The informal comparison is given in the table below. Values that can be directly deduced from other values are left blank in the table.

REPRESENTATION	IDENTITY	PS+UJR	PS+UJRY+	PSUJRD
Table	coNPC1)			
Horn table			PTIME1)	
LDB table			PTIME3)	coNPC3)
Naive table				
Codd table				coNPC2)

1) Result of this thesis. 2) Result of [AKG87]. 3) Result of [Var86c].

Note that the results given in the table above (and tables below) are treated as complexity results that do not assume any representation properties.

To complete the picture we make a table out of the results known of the (restricted) possibility problem.

REPRESENTATION	IDENTITY	PS+UJR	PS+UJRY+	PSUJRD
Table	NPC1)			
Horn table		PTIME1)	NPC1)	
LDB table				
Naive table				
Codd table			NPC2)	NPC2)

1) Result of this thesis. 2) Result of [AKG87].

As far as dependencies are concerned, we saw in Chapter 2 that they can be expressed as first order formulas. Thus dependencies can be uniformly treated in logical databases. The question of when a logical database (L,T) satisfies a set Σ of dependencies, is solved by requiring that theory $T \wedge \Sigma$ is satisfiable. This corresponds to the notion of satisfaction in the weak instance model, since $T \wedge \Sigma$ is satisfiable, if and only if T and Σ share at least one model, i.e. if T has at least one "completion" (model) that satisfies Σ (that is a model of Σ). Note that there can still be facts that have to be deduced when answering queries. A notion corresponding to our requirement of satisfaction is taken by Reiter [Rei84], who requires that $T \models \Sigma$ (i.e. every model of T is a model of Σ).

The complexity of testing satisfaction in Reiter's sense is not considered in the field of logical databases. The complexity of testing satisfaction in the "weak" sense is considered by Vardi in [Var86a] in the following context. Let R be a scheme, X a subset of R, and q a complete relation on X. Furthermore, let Σ be a set of dependencies on R. Then one is interested to know if there is a relation r on R, such that $q \subseteq \pi_X(r)$, and r satisfies Σ. The problem can be solved in time polynomial in the size of q [Var86a]. The relation q is taken as an incomplete relation on R. In particular, it can be modeled by a Codd table T on R, if we extend all tuples in q to tuples on R, by "padding" them with unique null values. We also see that the representation of [Var86a] is strictly weaker than Codd tables, since the null values have to appear uniformly in certain columns. We shall call such a representation a *Uniform table*. The decision problem in [Var86a] can equivalently be formulated as $Comp_\Sigma(rep(T)) \neq \emptyset$?. Thus we shall compare the result in [Var86a] with the results of this thesis. The comparison is given in the table below.

TABLE CLASS	Ø	EGD's and one JD	EGD's and TGD's
Tables	NPC1)		
Horn tables		PTIME1)	NPC*)
Naive tables			PTIME1)
Codd tables			
Uniform tables			PTIME2)

1) Follows from the results of this thesis. 2) The result of [Var86a]. *) Conjecture

The last issue in logical databases that we are going to look at is the update problem, as treated in [FKUV86]. The starting point is an arbitrary first order theory T. Note that in the query problem and the dependency problem the theories are syntactically restricted.

For brevity we consider deletions only. Let T be a theory and σ a sentence. According to [FKUV86], a theory S *accomplishes* the deletion of σ from T if $S \not\models \sigma$. (The requirement for the insertion is that $\sigma \in S$.) Since there obviously are several such theories S, one wants to minimize the changes made. The change is measured by the set inclusion $\subseteq$ of theories regarded as sets of sentences. Then T_1 has *fewer insertions* than T_2, w.r.t. T, if $T_1 - T \subseteq T_2 - T$. Similarly T_1 has *fewer deletions* than T_2, w.r.t. T, if $T - T_1 \subseteq T - T_2$. Finally, T_1 has *fever changes* than T_2, w.r.t. T, if it has fewer deletions that T_2, or T_1 and T_2 has the same deletions and T_1 has fewer insertions then T_2. Then a theory S accomplishes an insertion of σ into T *minimally* if there is no theory S' that accomplishes the insertion of σ into T with fewer changes than S. Then it is a theorem in [FKUV86] that a theory S accomplishes the deletion of σ from T minimally if and only if S is a maximal subset of T that is consistent with $\neg\sigma$.

There can be several theories S that accomplish the deletion minimally. The result is then the disjunction of these theories. An annoying fact is that if two theories are equivalent (having the same set of models), this is not necessarily true after the same update is performed on both theories. Consider the following example of propositional theories. The theories $\{A \wedge B\}$ and $\{A, B\}$ are logically equivalent. If B is deleted from both of them, the results are the empty theory Ø resp. the theory $\{A\}$.

Now this phenomenon is due to the fact that when theories are compared, they are treated as sets of sentences. The (implicit) partial order between them is then the set inclusion. We see that the meaning of the updates is defined in syntactic terms. This fact is defended by Vardi [Var86b, p. 6] who claims that "rather than being a problem, ... [it] .... is indeed a feature of the approach". As we saw in the discussion on updates in Chapter 3, there can be several ways to interpret an update. In our approach the result depends on the choice of semantics for the update (positive or absolute). In the logical database approach the result depends on the syntax of the database. In our approach the user can get the intended result by the choice of semantics, which would correspond to a conscious choice of a particular syntax of the update sentence in an update language. In the logical database approach, the user would have to change the syntax of the database in order to get the intended result.

Even if the semantic deficiencies are remedied or accepted, there is still another problem with the logical database approach to updates. If one starts with a syntactically restricted theory, the updated theory does not necessarily obey the same restrictions. The size of the updated theory can also be exponential in the size of the original theory. One would thus like to see results corresponding to our notion of update systems. What updates can one perform for instance on a theory corresponding to an LDB table, so that the result is representable as a theory also corresponding to a LDB table. Such results are necessary for any feasible implementation of updates and logical databases.

A more thorough discussion of different update semantics appears in [Win88], along with references. Update strategies are classified as either model based or formula based. Our approach (as reported in [AG85]) falls into the first category, while the [FKUV86] approach is considered as formula based.

6.2. A conclusion

We are now at the end of our "journey into the unknown". Let us see what has been achieved. The thesis has considered the problem of treating incomplete information in the context of the relational model. We have carefully defined the semantics of incomplete information, and of the most important operations on databases containing incomplete information. Then we considered various classes of tables, as means of implementing such databases. A practical implementation should be efficient, meaning that all operations should be computable in polynomial time.

The main lesson learned from the journey is thus that a database containing incomplete information should be implemented as a Horn multitable. A multitable is a sequence of tables. All dependencies are unirelational, i.e. they are defined on a single table. Since we do not use decomposition, there is no need for interrelational constraints. (An exception is perhaps the inclusion dependencies [CFP84], which would require further study.) Updates are also performed in terms of one table. When the user queries the database he is free to form expressions extracting information from several tables.

The life cycle of a database begins (and evolves) through updates. In the class of Horn tables we are able to perform positive insertions and absolute deletions. A positive insertion is an operation of the form "add this piece of information to what is already known". An absolute deletion is an operation where the set of states is decreased to those satisfying the deletion equation. Both operations can be executed in time linear in the size of the table, and the result is still a Horn table. There would perhaps be a need to do absolute insertions, i.e. operations of the form "keep only the states where this fact is true". This can be done in a Horn table in certain state dependent cases. Thus we would have to test (in linear time) if the insertion results in a Horn table, before accepting the update. As we saw in Section 4.4, there is a simple way to do this test.

When a table has been updated, we have to enforce the dependencies to assure that the states represented by the table are legal, and that all information is present in the table. If the dependencies are taken as a part of the update specification, this has to be done only after a positive insertion. The dependencies are assumed to consist of one join dependency (describing the "atomic facts" of the scheme) and a set of equality generating dependencies, e.g. functional dependencies. Then the completion of the table, a minimal extension containing all implied facts, can be computed in time polynomial in the size of the table.

The database (multitable) can now be queried. The user can get two types of answers: the possible answer and the certain answer. The possible answer is another table describing all possible facts that can be answers to the query. (It can be seen as a view on the database.) The user can also ask if some (restricted) set of facts is possible, e.g. "is it possible that Jones works in a department headed by Smith?" When the queries are monotone, i.e. when they are PS+UJR-expressions, both the possible answer and the answer to the "is it possible" question can be computed in time polynomial in the size of the database. In these cases the query is evaluated using "conditional evaluation", a bottom up method that extends the relational algebra. The method is uniformly recursive, i.e. it relies on the structure of the query, and on the basic operations in the relational algebra. It is a question of further studies how to optimize the queries. One can note that the basic equivalence preserving transformation rules (see Ull82]) can still be applied, but perhaps the optimization criteria have to be reconsidered.

Given the possible answer, i.e. a table, the user can get the certain answer, i.e. a complete relation containing tuples representing those facts that are true despite the incompleteness of the information. This certain answer can be obtained in time polynomial in the size of the possible answer. The user can also directly ask for the certain answer. For this situation we recommend that the implementation keeps track of the "naive" part of the tables, i.e. of $\mathbf{T}_*$ (see page 68). Then the certain answer can be obtained by "naive evaluation", i.e. by evaluating the query as if there were no incompleteness present (the null values are treated as constants). This evaluation can be done in time polynomial in the size of the database, and the user can also ask least fixpoint queries (e.g. "give me all the descendants of Abraham").

If the application is restricted to giving only certain answers, a Naive multitable should be used. All monotone and least fixpoint queries can be evaluated in polynomial time. The dependencies (in fact all dependencies, not only join dependencies and equality generating ones) can be enforced in time polynomial in the size of the table. The result is a Naive table sufficiently well approximating the completion, i.e. w.r.t. to the certain answers all information is present. In naive tables we can perform positive insertions, and represent the result sufficiently well (as the dependencies). These updates can be done in time linear in the size of the table.

For the future, we see two paths for continuing the work of this thesis. The first path would lead to the application of our results to the weak instance model, for instance by beginning with the question of when the bind and evaluation method produces "the whole truth" (there is one such sufficient criterium in [Yan86]). Another promising direction is the view update problem [BS81], since it seems that the null value is crucial to the solution of the problem (cf. [CP84]).

The other major path is to extend the work of this thesis. There would be several ways to do this. One could for instance study inclusion dependencies in incomplete databases. Or one could enlarge the update language to more complicated updates. Note that the classes of queries and dependencies that we have considered in this thesis are "complete", in the sense that they form what seems to be a stable closure of the respective concepts. No such closure of update classes exists to this date. On the other hand, the notions of updates and incomplete information are closely related, so arriving at such a closure would perhaps require the simultaneous consideration of incomplete information. (For a general discussion of these topics, see [Cha88] and [Abi88].) Finally, we note that we have not considered null values that are "not applicable" (e.g. the maiden name of a male employee). Incorporating them in our framework would be an interesting challenge.

References

Abi83 Abiteboul, S., Algebraic Analogues to Fundamental Notions of Query and Dependency Theory. Rapports de Recherche 201. Institut National de Recherche en Informatique et en Automatique. Rocquencourt, April 1983.

Abi85 Abiteboul, S., Coctail de Dependences. Thèse de Docteur D'état. Universite Paris-Sud, Orsay, Aug. 1985.

Abi88 Abiteboul, S., Updates, a new frontier. *Proc. 2nd Internat. Conf. on Database Theory*. Bruges, Aug. 31 - Sept. 2, 1988.

AG85 Abiteboul, S., Grahne, G., Update semantics for incomplete databases. *Proc. 11th Internat. Conf. on Very Large Data Bases*. Stockholm, Aug. 21-23, 1985, pp. 1-12.

AKG87 Abiteboul, S., Kanellakis, P., Grahne, G., On the representation and querying of sets of possible worlds. *Proc. ACM SIGMOD Internat. Conf. on Management of Data*. San Francisco, May 27-29, 1987, pp. 34-48.

AV84 Abiteboul, S., Vianu, V., Transactions in relational databases. *Proc. 10th Internat. Conf. on Very Large Data Bases*. Singapore, Aug. 27-31, 1984, pp. 46-56.

ABU79 Aho, A. V., Beeri, C., Ullman, J. D., The theory of joins in relational databases. *ACM Trans. Database Syst. 4,* 3 (Sept. 1979), 297-314.

AU79 Aho, A. V., Ullman, J. D., Universality of data retrieval languages. *Proc. 6th ACM Symp. on Principles of Programming Languages*. San Antonio, Jan. 29-31, 1979, pp. 110-120.

BR86 Bancilhon, F., Ramakrishnan, R., An amateur's introduction to recursive query processing strategies. *Proc. ACM SIGMOD Internat. Conf. on Management of Data*. Washington D. C., May 28-30, 1986, pp. 16-52.

BS81 Bancilhon, F., Spyratos, N., Update semantics of relational views. *ACM Trans. Database Syst. 6,* 4 (Dec. 1981), 557-575.

BBG78 Beeri, C., Bernstein, P. A., Goodman, N., A sophisticate's introduction to database normalization theory. *Proc. 4th Internat. Conf. on Very Large Data Bases.* Berlin, Sept. 13-15, 1978, pp. 113-124.

BV84 Beeri, C., Vardi, M., Formal systems for tuple and equality generating dependencies. *SIAM J. Comput. 13* , 1 (Feb. 1984), 76-98.

Bis81a Biskup, J., Über Datenbankrelationen mit Nullwerten und Maybe-Tupeln. Bericht 67, Schriften zur Informatik und Angewandten Mathematik. Rheinisch-Westfälische Technische Hochschule Aachen, März 1981.

Bis81b Biskup, J., A formal approach to null values in database relations. In: H. Gallaire, J. Minker and J. M. Nicolas (eds.), *Advances in Database Theory, vol. 1.* Plenum Press, New York, 1981, pp. 299-341.

Bis83 Biskup, J. A foundation of Codd's relational maybe-operations. *ACM Trans. Database Syst. 8,* 4 (Dec. 1983), 608-636.

BrVo84 Brosda, V., Vossen, G., Updating a relational database through a universal schema interface. *Proc. Fourth ACM SIGACT-SIGMOD Symp. on Principles of Database Systems.* Portland, March 25-27, 1985, pp. 66-75.

CFP84 Casanova, M. A., Fagin, R., Papadimitriou, C., Inclusion dependencies and their interaction with functional dependencies. *J. Comput. System. Sci. 28,* 1 (Feb. 1984), 29-59.

CM83 Chan, E. P. F., Mendelzon, A. O., Independent and separable database schemes. *Proc. 2nd ACM Symp. on Principles of Database Systems.* Atlanta, March 21-23, 1983, pp. 288-296.

Cha88 Chandra, A. K., Theory of database queries. *Proc. 7th ACM Symp. on Principles of Database Systems.* Austin, March 21-23, 1988, pp. 1-9.

CH82 Chandra, A. K., Harel, D., Structure and complexity of relational queries. *J. Comput. System. Sci. 25,* 1 (Aug. 1982), 99-128

CH85 Chandra, A. K., Harel, D., Horn clause programs and generalizations. *J. Logic Programming 2,* 1 (April 1985), 1-15.

CK73 Chang, C. C., Kiesler, H. J., *Model Theory*. North-Holland Publishing Co., Amsterdam, 1973.

Cod70 Codd, E. F., A relational model for large shared databanks. *Comm. Assoc. Comput. Mach. 13,* 6 (June 1970), 377-387.

Cod72a Codd, E. F., Further normalization of the data base relational model. In: R. Rustin (ed.), *Data Base Systems*. Prentic-Hall, Englewood Cliffs, New Jersey, pp. 36-64

Cod72b Codd, E. F., Relational completeness of data base sublanguages. In: R. Rustin (ed.), *Data Base Systems*. Prentic-Hall, Englewood Cliffs, New Jersey, pp. 65-98

Cod75 Codd, E.F., Understanding relations (Installment #7). *FDT Bull. of ACM SIGMOD 7,* 3-4 (March-April 1975), 23-28.

Cod79 Codd, E.F., Extending the database relational model to capture more meaning. *ACM Trans Database Syst. 4,* 4 (Dec. 1979), 379-434.

Cod82 Codd, E. F., Relational database: A practical foundation for productivity. (1981 ACM Turing Award Lecture). *Comm. Assoc. Comput. Mach. 25,* 2 (Feb. 1982), 109-117.

CP84 Cosmadakis, S., Papadimitriou, C., Updates of relational views. *J. Assoc. Comput. Mach. 31,* 4 (Oct. 1984), 742-760.

Fag82 Fagin, R., Horn clauses and database dependencies. *J. Assoc. Comput. Mach. 29,* 4 (Oct. 1982), 952-985.

FKUV86 Fagin, R., Kuper, G. M., Ullman, J. D., Vardi, M. Y., Updating logical databases. In: P. C. Kanellakis (ed.), *Advances in Computing Research, Vol. 3: The Theory of Databases*. JAI Press, London, 1986, pp. 1-18.

FMU82 Fagin, R., Mendelzon, A. O., Ullman, J. D., A simplified universal relation assumption and its properties. *ACM Trans Database Syst. 7,* 3 (Sept. 1982), 343-360.

FV86 Fagin, R., Vardi, M. Y., The theory of data dependencies - a survey. In: M. Anshel, W. Gewritz (eds.), *Mathematics of Information Processing*. American Mathematical Society, Providence, 1986, pp. 17-91.

GM78 Gallaire, H., Minker, J. (eds.), *Logic and Databases*. Plenum Press, New York, 1978.

GMN84 Gallaire, H., Minker, J., Nicolas, J.-M., Logic and databases: a deductive approach. *ACM Comp. Surveys 16,* 2 (June 1984), 153-185.

GJ79 Garey, M. R., Johnson, D. S., *Computers and Intractability: A Guide to the Theory of NP-Completeness*. W. H. Freeman and Co., San Francisco, 1979.

GMV86 Graham, M., Mendelzon, A. O., Vardi, M. Y., Notions of dependency satisfaction. *J. Assoc. Comput. Mach. 33,* 1 (Jan. 1986), 105-129,

Grh84a Grahne, G., Information incompleteness in databases. In: R. J. R. Back et al. (eds.), *Proc. Winter School on Theoretical Computer Science*. Lammi, Jan. 3-6. 1984, pp. 65-98.

Grh84b Grahne, G., Dependency satisfaction in databases with incomplete information. *Proc. 10th Internat. Conf. on Very Large Data Bases*. Singapore, Aug. 27-31, 1984, pp. 37-45.

Grt77 Grant, J., Null values in a relational data base. *Inform. Process. Lett. 6,* 5 (Oct. 1977), 156-157.

Grä71 Grätzer, G., *Lattice Theory, First Concepts and Distributive Latticies*. W. H. Freeman and Co., San Francisco, 1971.

HW74 Henschen, L., Wos, L., Unit refutation and Horn sets. *J. Assoc. Comput. Mach. 21,* 4 (Oct. 1974), 590-605.

Hon82 Honeyman, P., Testing satisfaction of functional dependencies. *J. Assoc. Comput. Mach. 29,* 3 (July 1982), 668-677.

HK73 Hopcroft, J. E., Karp, R. M., An $n^{5/2}$ algorithm for maximum matchings in bipartite graphs. *SIAM J. Comput.* 2 , 4 (Dec. 1973), 225-231.

IL81 Imielinski, T., Lipski, W., On representing incomplete information in a relational database. *Proc. 7th Internat. Conf. on Very Large Data Bases*. Cannes, Sept. 9-11, 1981, pp. 388-397.

IL83 Imielinski, T., Lipski, W., Incomplete information and dependencies in relational databases. *Proc. ACM SIGMOD Internat. Conf. on Management of Data*. San Jose, May 23-26, 1983, pp. 178-184.

IL84 Imielinski, T., Lipski, W., Incomplete information in relational databases. *J. Assoc. Comput. Mach. 31,* 4 (Oct. 1984), 761-791.

JL77 Jones, N. P., Laaser, W. T., Complete problems for polynomial time. *Theor. Comp. Sci. 3* (1977), 105-117.

Kan86 Kanellakis, P., Editor's foreword. In: P. C. Kanellakis (ed.), *Advances in Computing Research, Vol. 3: The Theory of Databases*. JAI Press, London, 1986, pp. 185-212.

Lip84 Lipski, W., On relational algebra with null values. *Proc. Third ACM SIGACT-SIGMOD Symp. on Principles of Database Systems,* Waterloo, April 2-4, 1984, pp. 201-203.

Llo84 Lloyd, J. W., *Foundations of Logic Programming*. Springer-Verlag, Berlin, 1984.

Mai83 Maier, D., *The Theory of Relational Databases*. Computer Science Press, Rockville, MD, 1983.

MMS79 Maier, D., Mendelzon, A. O., Sagiv, Y., Testing implications of data dependencies. *ACM Trans. Database Syst. 4,* 4 (Dec. 1979), 455-469.

MUV84 Maier, D., Ullman, J. D., Vardi, M.Y., On the foundations of the universal relation model. *ACM Trans. Database Syst. 9,* 2 (June 1984), 283-308.

Plo76 Plotkin, G. D., A powerdomain construction. *SIAM J. Comput 5,* 3 (Sept. 1976), 452-487.

Rei78 Reiter, R., On closed world databases. In [GM78], pp. 56-76.

Rei84 Reiter, R., Towards a logical reconstruction of relational database theory. In: M. L. Brodie, J. Mylopoulos, J. W. Schmidt (eds.), *On Conceptual Modelling*. Springer-Verlag, New York, 1984, pp. 191-233.

Rei86 Reiter, R., A sound and sometimes complete query evaluation algorithm for relational databases with null values. *J. Assoc. Comput. Mach. 33,* 2 (April 1986), 349-370.

Sag85 Sagiv, Y., On computing restricted projections of the representaive instance. *Proc. Fourth ACM SIGACT-SIGMOD Symp. on Principles of Database Systems*. Portland, March 25-27, 1985, pp. 171-180.

Sci81 Sciore, E., The universal instance and database design. Ph. D. Thesis. Princeton Univ., 1980.

Smy78 Smyth, M., Powerdomains. *J. Comput. Syst. Sci. 16,* 1 (Feb. 1978), 23-36.

Sto77 Stoy, J. E., *Denotational Semantics, The Scott-Strachey Approach to Programming Language Theory*. MIT Press, London, 1977.

Ull82 Ullman, J. D., *Principles of Database Systems, Second Edition.* Computer Science Press, Potomac, MD, 1982.

Var82 Vardi, M. Y., The complexity of relational query languages. *Proc. 14th ACM Symp. on Theory of Computing*. San Francisco, May 1982, pp. 137-146.

Var85 Vardi, M. Y., Fundamentals of dependency theory. Report RJ 4858, IBM Almaden Research Center, San Jose, Sept. 1985.

Var86a Vardi, M. Y., On the integrity of databases with incomplete information. *Proc. 5th ACM Symp. on Principles of Database Systems*. Boston, March 1986, pp. 252-266.

Var86b Vardi, M. Y., Issues in logical databases. Report RJ 5147, IBM Almaden Research Center, San Jose, July 1986.

Var86c Vardi, M. Y., Querying logical databases. *J. Comput. System. Sci. 33,* 2 (Oct. 1986), 142-160.

Vas79 Vassiliou, Y., Null values in data base management, a denotational semantics approach. *Proc. ACM SIGMOD Internat. Conf. on Management of Data.* Boston, May 30 - June 1, 1979, pp. 162-169.

Vas80a Vassiliou, Y., Functional dependencies and incomplete information. *Proc. 7th Internat. Conf. on Very Large Data Bases.* Montreal, Oct. 1-3, 1980, pp. 260-269.

Vas80b Vassiliou, Y., A formal treatment of imperfect information in database management. Ph. D. Thesis, Tech. Rep. CSRG 123, Univ. of Toronto, Nov. 1980.

Win88 Winslett, M., A framework for comparisons of update semantics. *Proc. 7th ACM Symp. on Principles of Database Systems.* Austin, March 21-23, 1988, pp. 315-324.

Yan86 Yannakakis, M., Querying Weak Instances. In: P. C. Kanellakis (ed.), *Advances in Computing Research, Vol. 3: The Theory of Databases.* JAI Press, London, 1986, pp. 185-212.

YP82 Yannakakis, M., Papadimitriou, C. H., Algebraic dependencies. *J. Comput. System. Sci. 25,* 1 (Aug. 1982), 2-41.

Index of notation

The relational algebra

$\pi_X(r)$ the projection operator 7

$\sigma_E(r)$ the selection operator 8

$r \cup s$ the union operator 8

$r * s$ the join operator 8

$\theta_B^A(r)$ the renaming operator 9

r-s the difference operator 9

$r \times s$ the cartesian product 9

$r \circ s$ the composition operator 13

$\psi(f(S))$ the least fixpoint operator 13

$\uparrow, \uparrow^n$ the duplication operator 17

Dependencies

$A \rightarrow B$ a functional dependency 17

$A \rightarrow\rightarrow B$ a multivalued dependency 17

$*[S_1,...,S_n]$ a join dependency 20

Operators

$\underline{\cup}_{i \in I} X_i$ the elementwise union 40

<T,U> the concatenation of **T** and **U** 56

Comparison

$<$ absolutely less informaive 36

$<_\Omega$ Ω-less than 37

$<_+$ +-less 39

$\ll$ embedding of tables 86

$\models$ logical entailment of conditions 58

$\models_k$ limited entailment 87

$\equiv_\Omega$ Ω-equivalent to 37

$\equiv_+$ +-equivalent to 39

$|X|_{\equiv_+}$ the quotient set of X 40

$\approx$ equivalence of conditions 58

$\cong$ table isomorphism 86

Cardinalities

$|r|$ the number of tuples in r 30

$|T|$ the number of c-tuples in T 104

$||T||$ the size of the table 104

$||t(CON)||$ the length of the condition 104

Alphabetical list

A, A_i attributes 6

a, b, c domain values (constants) 6

a-$del_\phi(X)$ absolute deletion from X by ϕ 51

a-$del_\phi(X, \Sigma)$ absolute deletion from X by ϕ under Σ 53

a-$ins_\phi(X)$ absolute insertion into X by ϕ 49

a-$ins_\phi(X, \Sigma)$ absolute insertion into X by ϕ under Σ 53

$\alpha(r)$, $\alpha(t)$ the type of the argument 7

$\alpha(f)$ the argument type of an expression 10

$\beta(f)$ the result type of an expression 10

$comp_\Sigma(r)$ the completion of r w.r.t. Σ 23

$Comp_\Sigma(X)$ the completion of X w.r.t. Σ 43

CON the condition "column" in a table 55

D generic name for the difference operator 10

$del_\phi(r)$ the deletion from r by ϕ 26

$del_\phi(r, \Sigma)$ deletion with ϕ from r under Σ 27

Dom(A) the domain of A 6

Δ a class of dependencies 77

δ a dependency 17

ε the restriction of a tuple to Ø, the empty fact 8

f(***R***) a relational expression 10

$f_{(C)}(\mathbf{T})$ conditional evaluation of f on **T** 67

$f_{(N)}(\mathbf{T})$ naive evaluation of f on **T** 63

$f^n(S)$ the n-fold composition of f with itself 13

$f_S(P)$ restricted mapping 10

$f_T(R)$ a representation for set of mappings 71

$f_X(\underline{R})$ a set of mappings 44

$\cap f(X)$ the certain answer 35

ϕ, Φ equation, set of equations 11

ϕ a condition 56

ø the empty relation 7

$\mathcal{G}$ the set of all conditions 55

glb(P) the greatest lower bound of the argument 12

$g(\Sigma)_r$ the mapping relating a set of dependencies and a relation 21

$g(\Sigma_T)_X$ the set of mappings that relate X and Σ_T 45

Inc(**R**) the powerset of *Rel*(**R**) 34

$Inc(\mathbf{R})/_{\equiv_+}$ the quotient set of $Inc(\mathbf{R})$ 40

$ins_{\phi}(r)$ the insertion into r by ϕ 25

$ins_{\phi}(r, \Sigma)$ insertion by ϕ to r under Σ 27

J generic name for the join operator 10

lfp(T) the least fixpoint of the mapping T 12

lub(P) the least upper bound of the argument 12

λ(T) the global condition of T 55

ϑ a class of update operations 92

υ an update 92

Ω set of operations, set of expressions 10

P generic name for the projection operator 10

$p\text{-}del_{\phi}(\mathcal{X})$ positive deletion from $\mathcal{X}$ by ϕ 50

$p\text{-}del_{\phi}(\mathcal{X}, \Sigma)$ positive deletion from $\mathcal{X}$ by ϕ under Σ 52

$p\text{-}ins_{\Phi}(\mathcal{X})$ positive insertion into $\mathcal{X}$ by Φ 48

$p\text{-}ins_{\Phi}(\mathcal{X}, \Sigma)$ positive insertion into $\mathcal{X}$ by Φ under Σ 52

$\pi_X^{-1}(t)$ a tuple with "new" variables 95

R generic name for the renaming operator 10

R a relational scheme 6

R a multischeme 7

r a multirelation 7

r_∞ the largest (infinite) relation 7

R , ***R*** relational and multirelational variables 9

Rel(R) the set of all relations on R 7

rep(T) the set of relations represented by T 56

ρ an algebraic dependency 18

S, S^+ generic names for the selection and positive selction operators 10

$Sat(\phi)$ the set of solutions to ϕ 11

$Sat(\Sigma)$ the set of relations satisfying Σ 17

Σ a finite set of dependencies 17

Σ(T) the completion of a table T w.r.t. to Σ 77 t a tuple 6

t(X) the restriction of t to X 6

T a table 55

T_t a subset of the c-tuples in T 94

T a multitable 56

$\mathbf{T}^o$ the normalized version of **T** 59

$\mathbf{T}_*$ an approximation of **T** 69

T the class of all tables 56

T_H the class of Horn tables 60

T_N the class of Naive tables 60

T_C the class of Codd tables 60

Tab(R) the set of all tables on R 56

U generic name for the union operator 10

U the universal set of attributes 6

v a valuation mapping 56

Var(A) the set of variables associated with A 55

X, Y sets of attributes 6

x, y, z, ... variables 55

$\mathcal{X}, \mathcal{Y}$ sets of relations, incomplete databases 34

Y, Y^+ generic names for the least fixpoint operators 13

Appendix. Problems used in reduction proofs

A1. 3CNF Satisfiability

Let $Z = \{z_1, ..., z_n\}$ be a set of Boolean *variables* . A *truth assignment* for Z is a function $\tau : Z \to \{0,1\}$. If $\tau(z_i) = 1$, we say that z_i is "true" under τ, and if $\tau(z_i) = 0$ we say that z_i is "false" under τ. If z_i is a variable in Z, then z_i and $\neg z_i$ are *literals* over Z. The literal z_i is true under τ if and only if the variable z_i is true under τ. The literal $\neg z_i$ is true under τ if and only if the variable z_i is false under τ.

A *d-clause* c over Z is a set of three literals over Z, e.g. $\{z_1, \neg z_5, z_7\}$. The clause represents the disjunction of the variables, and it is *satisfied* by a truth assignment τ, if at least one of the literals is true under τ. A *collection* C of d-clauses over Z is *satisfiable* if and only if there exists some truth assignment for Z that simultaneously satisfies all the d-clauses in C. Such a truth assignment is called a *satisfying truth assignment* for C. Now the 3CNF satisfiability problem is specified as follows.

Instance: A collection C of d-clauses over Z.

Question: Is there a satisfying truth assignment for C ?

The 3CNF satisfiability problem is NP-complete [GJ79]. The following instance will be used in the proofs as an illustration.

$Z = \{z_1, \ldots, z_5\}$ and $C = \{c_1, \ldots, c_5\}$, where

$c_1 = \{z_1, z_2, z_3\}$	i.e.	$z_1 \vee z_2 \vee z_3$
$c_2 = \{z_1, \neg z_2, z_4\}$	$\wedge$	$z_1 \vee \neg z_2 \vee z_4$
$c_3 = \{z_1, z_4, z_5\}$	$\wedge$	$z_1 \vee z_4 \vee z_5$
$c_4 = \{z_2, \neg z_1, z_5\}$	$\wedge$	$z_2 \vee \neg z_1 \vee z_5$
$c_5 = \{\neg z_1, \neg z_2, \neg z_5\}$	$\wedge$	$\neg z_1 \vee \neg z_2 \vee \neg z_5$

A2. 3DNF Tautology

A set $Z = \{z_1, \ldots, z_n\}$ of Boolean variables, truth assignments and literals are defined as in the 3CNF problem. A *c-clause* is a set of three literals over Z. It represents the conjunction of the variables, and it is *satisfied* by a truth assignment τ, if and only if all literals are true under τ. A *collection* $\mathcal{D}$ of c-clauses over Z is a *tautology* if and only if every truth assignment satisfies at least one of the c-clauses. The collection $\mathcal{D}$ thus represents the disjunction of the clauses. The 3DNF tautology problem is then formally specified as follows

Instance: A collection $\mathcal{D}$ of c-clauses over Z.

Question: Is $\mathcal{D}$ a tautology?

The 3DNF tautology problem is coNP-complete [GJ79]. An example instance is given below.

$Z = \{z_1, \ldots, z_5\}$ and $\mathcal{D} = \{c_1, \ldots, c_5\}$, where

$c_1 = \{z_1, z_2, z_3\}$ i.e. $z_1 \wedge z_2 \wedge z_3$

$c_2 = \{z_1, \neg z_2, z_4\}$ $\vee$ $z_1 \wedge \neg z_2 \wedge z_4$

$c_3 = \{z_1, z_4, z_5\}$ $\vee$ $z_1 \wedge z_4 \wedge z_5$

$c_4 = \{z_2, \neg z_1, z_5\}$ $\vee$ $z_2 \wedge \neg z_1 \wedge z_5$

$c_5 = \{\neg z_1, \neg z_2, \neg z_5\}$ $\vee$ $\neg z_1 \wedge \neg z_2 \wedge \neg z_5$

A3. HC Satisfiability

A set $Z = \{z_1, \ldots, z_n\}$, and truth assignments are defined as in the 3CNF problem. A *Horn clause* c over Z is one of the following:

(i) c is a variable z_i. Now c is *satisfied* by a truth assignment τ, if and only if $\tau(z_i) = 1$.

(ii) c is $z_{i(1)} \wedge \ldots \wedge z_{i(m)} \Rightarrow z_i$. The clause c is *satisfied* by a truth assignment τ, unless $\tau(z_i) = 0$, and $\tau(z_{i(j)}) = 1$, for $j=1,\ldots,m$.

(iii) c is $\neg z_{i(1)} \vee \ldots \vee \neg z_{i(m)}$. The clause c is *satisfied* by a truth assignment τ, if and only if $\tau(z_{i(j)}) = 0$, for at least one $j=1,\ldots,m$.

A *collection* $\mathcal{H}$ of Horn clauses over Z is *satisfiable* if and only if there exists some truth assignment for Z that simultaneously satisfies all c in $\mathcal{H}$. The HC satisfiably problem is then formally

Instance: A collection $\mathcal{H}$ of Horn clauses over Z.

Question: Is $\mathcal{H}$ satisfiable?

The problen can be solved in time polynomial of the size of $\mathcal{H}$ [HW74, JL77].

A4. Bipartite graph matching

A graph **G** = (V, E) is *bipartite* if V can be divided into two disjoint sets V_1 and V_2, such that for all $(v_i,v_j) \in E$, v_i and v_j belong to different sets. A *matching* for a graph **G** = (V, E) is a subset E' of E, such that for all (v_i,v_j) and (v_k,v_m) in E', $v_i \neq v_k$, $v_i \neq v_m$, and $v_j \neq v_k$, $v_j \neq v_m$. A *maximal matching* is a matching E', such that for all matchings E'', the number of pairs in E'' is less than or equal to the number of pairs in E'. The bipartite graph matching problem is to compute a maximal matching E'', given a bipartite graph **G** = (V, E). The problem can be solved in time polynomial in the size of **G** [HK73].

Lecture Notes in Computer Science

For information about Vols. 1–473
please contact your bookseller or Springer-Verlag

Vol. 474: D. Karagiannis (Ed.), Information Systems and Artificial Intelligence: Integration Aspects. Proceedings, 1990. X, 293 pages. 1991. (Subseries LNAI).

Vol. 475: P. Schroeder-Heister (Ed.), Extensions of Logic Programming. Proceedings, 1989. VIII, 364 pages. 1991. (Subseries LNAI).

Vol. 476: M. Filgueiras, L. Damas, N. Moreira, A.P. Tomás (Eds.), Natural Language Processing. Proceedings, 1990. VII, 253 pages. 1991. (Subseries LNAI).

Vol. 477: D. Hammer (Ed.), Compiler Compilers. Proceedings, 1990. VI, 227 pages. 1991.

Vol. 478: J. van Eijck (Ed.), Logics in AI. Proceedings, 1990. IX, 562 pages. 1991. (Subseries in LNAI).

Vol. 479: H. Schmidt, Meta-Level Control for Deductive Database Systems. VI, 155 pages. 1991.

Vol. 480: C. Choffrut, M. Jantzen (Eds.), STACS 91. Proceedings, 1991. X, 549 pages. 1991.

Vol. 481: E. Lang, K.-U. Carstensen, G. Simmons, Modelling Spatial Knowledge on a Linguistic Basis. IX, 138 pages. 1991. (Subseries LNAI).

Vol. 482: Y. Kodratoff (Ed.), Machine Learning – EWSL-91. Proceedings, 1991. XI, 537 pages. 1991. (Subseries LNAI).

Vol. 483: G. Rozenberg (Ed.), Advances in Petri Nets 1990. VI, 515 pages. 1991.

Vol. 484: R. H. Möhring (Ed.), Graph-Theoretic Concepts in Computer Science. Proceedings, 1990. IX, 360 pages. 1991.

Vol. 485: K. Furukawa, H. Tanaka, T. Fuijsaki (Eds.), Logic Programming '89. Proceedings, 1989. IX, 183 pages. 1991. (Subseries LNAI).

Vol. 486: J. van Leeuwen, N. Santoro (Eds.), Distributed Algorithms. Proceedings, 1990. VI, 433 pages. 1991.

Vol. 487: A. Bode (Ed.), Distributed Memory Computing. Proceedings, 1991. XI, 506 pages. 1991.

Vol. 488: R. V. Book (Ed.), Rewriting Techniques and Applications. Proceedings, 1991. VII, 458 pages. 1991.

Vol. 489: J. W. de Bakker, W. P. de Roever, G. Rozenberg (Eds.), Foundations of Object-Oriented Languages. Proceedings, 1990. VIII, 442 pages. 1991.

Vol. 490: J. A. Bergstra, L. M. G. Feijs (Eds.), Algebraic Methods II: Theory, Tools and Applicatlons. VI, 434 pages. 1991.

Vol. 491: A. Yonezawa, T. Ito (Eds.), Concurrency: Theory, Language, and Architecture. Proceedings, 1989. VIII, 339 pages. 1991.

Vol. 492: D. Sriram, R. Logcher, S. Fukuda (Eds.), Computer-Aided Cooperative Product Development. Proceedings, 1989 VII, 630 pages. 1991.

Vol. 493: S. Abramsky, T. S. E. Maibaum (Eds.), TAPSOFT '91. Volume 1. Proceedings, 1991. VIII, 455 pages. 1991.

Vol. 494: S. Abramsky, T. S. E. Maibaum (Eds.), TAPSOFT '91. Volume 2. Proceedings, 1991. VIII, 482 pages. 1991.

Vol. 495: 9. Thalheim, J. Demetrovics, H.-D. Gerhardt (Eds.), MFDBS '91. Proceedings, 1991. VI, 395 pages. 1991.

Vol. 496: H.-P. Schwefel, R. Männer (Eds.), Parallel Problem Solving from Nature. Proceedings, 1990. XI, 485 pages. 1991.

Vol. 497: F. Dehne, F. Fiala. W.W. Koczkodaj (Eds.), Advances in Computing and Information - ICCI '91. Proceedings, 1991. VIII, 745 pages. 1991.

Vol. 498: R. Andersen, J. A. Bubenko jr., A. Sølvberg (Eds.), Advanced Information Systems Engineering. Proceedings, 1991. VI, 579 pages. 1991.

Vol. 499: D. Christodoulakis (Ed.), Ada: The Choice for '92. Proceedings, 1991. VI, 411 pages. 1991.

Vol. 500: M. Held, On the Computational Geometry of Pocket Machining. XII, 179 pages. 1991.

Vol. 501: M. Bidoit, H.-J. Kreowski, P. Lescanne, F. Orejas, D. Sannella (Eds.), Algebraic System Specification and Development. VIII, 98 pages. 1991.

Vol. 502: J. Bārzdiņž, D. Bjørner (Eds.), Baltic Computer Science. X, 619 pages. 1991.

Vol. 503: P. America (Ed.), Parallel Database Systems. Proceedings, 1990. VIII, 433 pages. 1991.

Vol. 504: J. W. Schmidt, A. A. Stogny (Eds.), Next Generation Information System Technology. Proceedings, 1990. IX, 450 pages. 1991.

Vol. 505: E. H. L. Aarts, J. van Leeuwen, M. Rem (Eds.), PARLE '91. Parallel Architectures and Languages Europe, Volume I. Proceedings, 1991. XV, 423 pages. 1991.

Vol. 506: E. H. L. Aarts, J. van Leeuwen, M. Rem (Eds.), PARLE '91. Parallel Architectures and Languages Europe, Volume II. Proceedings, 1991. XV, 489 pages. 1991.

Vol. 507: N. A. Sherwani, E. de Doncker, J. A. Kapenga (Eds.), Computing in the 90's. Proceedings, 1989. XIII, 441 pages. 1991.

Vol. 508: S. Sakata (Ed.), Applied Algebra, Algebraic Algorithms and Error-Correcting Codes. Proceedings, 1990. IX, 390 pages. 1991.

Vol. 509: A. Endres, H. Weber (Eds.), Software Development Environments and CASE Technology. Proceedings, 1991. VIII, 286 pages. 1991.

Vol. 510: J. Leach Albert, B. Monien, M. Rodríguez (Eds.), Automata, Languages and Programming. Proceedings, 1991. XII, 763 pages. 1991.

Vol. 511: A. C. F. Colchester, D.J. Hawkes (Eds.), Information Processing in Medical Imaging. Proceedings, 1991. XI, 512 pages. 1991.

Vol. 512: P. America (Ed.), ECOOP '91. European Conference on Object-Oriented Programming. Proceedings, 1991. X, 396 pages. 1991.

Vol. 513: N. M. Mattos, An Approach to Knowledge Base Management. IX, 247 pages. 1991. (Subseries LNAI).

Vol. 514: G. Cohen, P. Charpin (Eds.), EUROCODE '90. Proceedings, 1990. XI, 392 pages. 1991.

Vol. 515: J. P. M[illegible] Reinfrank (Eds.), Truth Maintenance Systems. Procee[illegible]ings, 1990. VII, 177 pages. 1991. (Subseries LNAI).

Vol. 516: S. Kaplan, M. Okada (Eds.), Conditional and Typed Rewriting Systems. Proceedings, 1990. IX, 461 pages. 1991.

Vol. 517: K. Nökel, Temporally Distributed Symptoms in Technical Diagnosis. IX, 164 pages. 1991. (Subseries LNAI).

Vol. 518: J. G. Williams, Instantiation Theory. VIII, 133 pages. 1991. (Subseries LNAI).

Vol. 519: F. Dehne, J.-R. Sack, N. Santoro (Eds.), Algorithms and Data Structures. Proceedings, 1991. X, 496 pages. 1991.

Vol. 520: A. Tarlecki (Ed.), Mathematical Foundations of Computer Science 1991. Proceedings, 1991. XI, 435 pages. 1991.

Vol. 521: B. Bouchon-Meunier, R. R. Yager, L. A. Zadek (Eds.), Uncertainty in Knowledge-Bases. Proceedings, 1990. X, 609 pages. 1991.

Vol. 522: J. Hertzberg (Ed.), European Workshop on Planning. Proceedings, 1991. VII, 121 pages. 1991. (Subseries LNAI).

Vol. 523: J. Hughes (Ed.), Functional Programming Languages and Computer Architecture. Proceedings, 1991. VIII, 666 pages. 1991.

Vol. 524: G. Rozenberg (Ed.), Advances in Petri Nets 1991. VIII, 572 pages. 1991.

Vol. 525: O. Günther, H.-J. Schek (Eds.), Advances in Spatial Databases. Proceedings, 1991. XI, 471 pages. 1991.

Vol. 526: T. Ito, A. R. Meyer (Eds.), Theoretical Aspects of Computer Software. Proceedings, 1991. X, 772 pages. 1991.

Vol. 527: J.C.M. Baeten, J. F. Groote (Eds.), CONCUR '91. Proceedings, 1991. VIII, 541 pages. 1991.

Vol. 528: J. Maluszynski, M. Wirsing (Eds.), Programming Language Implementation and Logic Programming. Proceedings, 1991. XI, 433 pages. 1991.

Vol. 529: L. Budach (Ed.), Fundamentals of Computation Theory. Proceedings, 1991. XII, 426 pages. 1991.

Vol. 530: D. H. Pitt, P.-L. Curien, S. Abramsky, A. M. Pitts, A. Poigné, D. E. Rydeheard (Eds.), Category Theory and Computer Science. Proceedings, 1991. VII, 301 pages. 1991.

Vol. 531: E. M. Clarke, R. P. Kurshan (Eds.), Computer-Aided Verification. Proceedings, 1990. XIII, 372 pages. 1991.

Vol. 532: H. Ehrig, H.-J. Kreowski, G. Rozenberg (Eds.), Graph Grammars and Their Application to Computer Science. Proceedings, 1990. X, 703 pages. 1991.

Vol. 533: E. Börger, H. Kleine Büning, M. M. Richter, W. Schönfeld (Eds.), Computer Science Logic. Proceedings, 1990. VIII, 399 pages. 1991.

Vol. 534: H. Ehrig, K. P. Jantke, F. Orejas, H. Reichel (Eds.), Recent Trends in Data Type Specification. Proceedings, 1990. VIII, 379 pages. 1991.

Vol. 535: P. Jorrand, J. Kelemen (Eds.), Fundamentals of Artificial Intelligence Research. Proceedings, 1991. VIII, 255 pages. 1991. (Subseries LNAI).

Vol. 536: J. E. Tomayko, Software Engineering Education. Proceedings, 1991. VIII, 296 pages. 1991.

Vol. 537: A. J. Menezes, S. A. Vanstone (Eds.), Advances in Cryptology – CRYPTO '90. Proceedings. XIII, 644 pages. 1991.

Vol. 538: M. Kojima, N. Megiddo, T. Noma, A. Yoshise, A Unified Approach to Interior Point Algorithms for Linear Complementarity Problems. VIII, 108 pages. 1991.

Vol. 539: H. F. Mattson, T. Mora, T. R. N. Rao (Eds.), Applied Algebra, Algebraic Algorithms and Error-Correcting Codes. Proceedings, 1991. XI, 489 pages. 1991.

Vol. 540: A. Prieto (Ed.), Artificial Neural Networks. Proceedings, 1991. XIII, 476 pages. 1991.

Vol. 541: P. Barahona, L. Moniz Pereira, A. Porto (Eds.), EPIA '91. Proceedings, 1991. VIII, 292 pages. 1991. (Subseries LNAI).

Vol. 543: J. Dix, K. P. Jantke, P. H. Schmitt (Eds.), Nonmonotonic and Inductive Logic. Proceedings, 1990. X, 243 pages. 1991. (Subseries LNAI).

Vol. 544: M. Broy, M. Wirsing (Eds.), Methods of Programming. XII, 268 pages. 1991.

Vol. 545: H. Alblas, B. Melichar (Eds.), Attribute Grammars, Applications and Systems. Proceedings, 1991. IX, 513 pages. 1991.

Vol. 547: D. W. Davies (Ed.), Advances in Cryptology – EUROCRYPT '91. Proceedings, 1991. XII, 556 pages. 1991.

Vol. 548: R. Kruse, P. Siegel (Eds.), Symbolic and Quantitative Approaches to Uncertainty. Proceedings, 1991. XI, 362 pages. 1991.

Vol. 550: A. van Lamsweerde, A. Fugetta (Eds.), ESEC '91. Proceedings, 1991. XII, 515 pages. 1991.

Vol. 551:S. Prehn, W. J. Toetenel (Eds.), VDM '91. Formal Software Development Methods. Volume 1. Proceedings, 1991. XIII, 699 pages. 1991.

Vol. 552: S. Prehn, W. J. Toetenel (Eds.), VDM '91. Formal Software Development Methods. Volume 2. Proceedings, 1991. XIV, 430 pages. 1991.

Vol. 553: H. Bieri, H. Noltemeier (Eds.), Computational Geometry - Methods, Algorithms and Applications '91. Proceedings, 1991. VIII, 320 pages. 1991.

Vol. 554: G. Grahne, The Problem of Incomplete Information in Relational Databases. VIII, 156 pages. 1991.